There is no town quite like Liverpool. No people quite like the Liverpudlians.

The town is a mass of contradictions of riches and poverty; of massive brutal Victorian commercial architecture and gleaming new office blocks, of trim, modern housing estates and huddles of slum streets; of people who are as tough as their environment, yet who can be extraordinarily gentle and poetic. It is a town rich in larger-than-life characters like the late and much-loved Bessie Braddock; a town which has seen much misery and much violence, yet one which has produced countless comedians to laugh at the scene.

My Liverpool could have been written only by one who knew the town over many years and who had looked and listened with compassion, insight and humour.

Frank Shaw worked on the manuscript for three years after his retirement as a Customs officer in 1968. He died just as the book was going to press. It remains as his tribute to a great city – and the epitaph to a great Liverpudlian.

ISBN 0 900389 31 1

© Frank Shaw 1971.

© Wolfe Publishing Ltd. 1971.

Reprinted by Gallery Press 1987

Reprinted in this Edition 1988

Printed by Scotprint (North-West) Limited, Liverpool L3 8HA

The verses from In My Liverpool Home *on*
page 11 are reprinted by kind permission of
Pete McGovern and Spin Publications.

My Liverpool

by
FRANK SHAW

GALLERY PRESS

LEIGHTON BANASTRE, PARKGATE, SOUTH WIRRAL L64 6RW

Contents

*The photographs of Liverpool scenes and Liverpudlians
were taken by Karl Hughes, A.R.P.S.*

EDITOR'S FOREWORD

A Tribute to
Frank Shaw

I had made a date with Frank Shaw. When the first proofs of this book arrived from the printers I was to meet him in the 'Pool for a conference, a few jars of Guinness, and perhaps one or two drops of the hard stuff to top it off.

The date was not kept. Frank died just before the proofs arrived.

It seems strange to be missing a man I never met, but, through the manuscript, through our correspondence and telephone conversations, I got to know Frank very well.

The manuscript*, when all the batches of it were piled together, was mountainous. Some of it was typed, some handwritten, some on foolscap paper, some on quarto, some on the backs of old notepaper . . . all of it rich in incident, phrase and imagery.

The correspondence, on my side, was jocular, hearty, sometimes just plain goonish, in attempts to reassure Frank about the quality and progress of the manuscript and to help him forget the pain of his last, long illness. On Frank's side it was sporadic – sometimes four letters in a week, sometimes nothing for a couple of months – written as ideas came to him, words spilling all over the paper, round the back and up and down the margins, with magic phrases gleaming like leaping salmon out of the jumble of irregular typing or painfully-written longhand.

Frank spoke as richly as he wrote. Two hundred miles away, over the telephone, he could have been sitting opposite me in Mooney's, taking the top off his Guinness before opening another rich seam of Scouse anecdotes.

---

*Here credit must be given to Pat Daly, the man who did all the *real* work on the manuscript: organising the batches, shaping, trimming, deciphering with infinite patience and care.

Mainly, however, I knew Frank because of the similarities of our backgrounds. There were lots of *dis*similarities: I was a generation younger than Frank; he was a Roman Catholic with all the strength of his faith, I used the label 'Church of England' only when I was called up; he was a deeply committed Liverpudlian, I an expatriate Mancunian gone soft with southern living.

Yet the images of our early environment – the chill, damp, grey, gritty, smoky and brutal world of the pre-Welfare State industrial and commercial North – were almost identical. It was a world in which a phrase like 'the quality of life', if it had been understood at all, would have been an obscene joke. Environmentally, economically, socially, the quality was sub-zero.

Children bore a uniform pallor, wore boots a size too big or too small, depending on whether or not they were hand-me-downs, and had either snotty noses or silver sleeves, depending on the time of the last wipe. Men and women grew old years before their time and coughed themselves to death.

Work, in terms of conditions, hours and the effort demanded was of a back-breaking ferocity not far removed from the descriptions of Dickens or Zola. The only consolation was that not to have work was infinitely worse.

What quality of life there was in the North came from the people. After almost two centuries of industrialisation, with all its direct and side effects, they should have become little more than animals. They did not. God knows how, but they did not. They developed their own strengths – among the greatest of which was the ability to joke about the whole muddle of dirt, poverty and oppression – their own stern codes of conduct and their own simple, terrible beauties.

Much of the old Liverpool has gone. The quality of what has replaced it has still to be proven. But things can never again be as bad as they were – or, in a perverse way, as good. There was a gargantuan quality about life in the back streets. There were heroes, there were saints, there were giants and ogres. This larger-than-life quality Frank Shaw has captured superbly. And if the heroes, saints, giants and ogres never come again, we at least have the consolation of knowing that they do not need to, that the conditions which bred them have disappeared.

Frank was sometimes saddened about the lack of colour, the lack of gutsiness, on the new housing estates in Liverpool. But, after a lifetime of fighting for a better environment, a better social deal, he would have been the last to wish the bad old days back again.

If the old Liverpool has gone for good, Frank has made sure it will not be forgotten. He set himself the task of writing *the* book on Liverpool after his retirement three years ago. He succeeded – only just in time, God bless him – but succeeded superbly. This is his tribute to a great city. We are proud to publish it as our tribute to a great Liverpudlian.

CLIFF PARKER
September 1971.

PART ONE In My
Liverpool
Home

In My Liverpool Home

My Liverpool

In my Liverpool Home, In my Liverpool Home,
We speak with an accent exceedingly rare,
Meet under a statue exceedingly bare,
If you want a cathedral we got one to spare,
In my Liverpool Home.   *– Pete McGovern*

They were these men putting up flats in Toxteth – and that's really one of the tough areas of Liverpool. They'd got a big 'dog and they put up a notice 'Guard Dog – Beware' inside a wire fence. Well, a gang of 10 year olds just come and stole the dog!
    – Woman quoted in 'The North Country' by Graham Turner

I was born in Liverpool Down at the docks,
My religion was Cath'lic, Occupation hard knocks,
At stealing off lorries I soon was adept
And under old overcoats I often slept
In my Liverpool Home.   *– Pete McGovern*

They say, what say they

You get finer talk in Liverpool than anywhere else in the world
                                            – C. E. M. Joad

A second Venice upon the waters – *Erskine*

My spirits rise on seeing the Mersey – *C. E. Montague*

Lovely in all seasons . . . – *John Masefield*

Liverpool librarians have asked to be supplied with Airedale dogs for protection – *News item*

That rich and beautiful port – *Charles Dickens*

It might have happened in any civilised place, or in Liverpool
– *P. G. Wodehouse*

It is indeed a most unhappy place . . . – *G. Manley Hopkins*

Liverpool, what a place to commit adultery! – *Edgar Wallace*

Liverpool is one of the wonders of the world. What it may grow to in time I know not – *Defoe*

Good haven and good marchandise – *Leland*

. . . dismal grey city and a muddy river – *Sophie Peabody, of Salem, in 1835*

Dark and foul, dark and foul, by the smoky town with its dismal cowl – *Kingsley*

I have been impressed by three factors in Liverpool: they are the making of Liverpool and still a great basis for the continued prominence of Liverpool as a port. They are that Liverpool has the finest dockers in the world; that Liverpool has the finest sense of humour in the world; that Liverpool has the prettiest girls in the world – *Sydney MacKechnie, a newcomer to Liverpool, succeeding James Leggate as chairman of Liverpool Port Employers in 1971*

Except utter ruin elsewhere, what decay of sensibility would induce me to live in Liverpool? – *J. C. Squire*, when offered a post at Liverpool University; in a letter to A. Y. Campbell. He criticised our buildings but later praised our boulevards, comparing them with Nice.

. . . Liverpool is too well known for its maritime enterprise . . . and extensive commerce, to require much description. The old part of the town is ill-built and the streets are narrow; but great additions are continually making to it, and many excellent houses

are erected in the environs. Here are fourteen building yards, and three very complete and commodious basons for receiving ships. The corporation is very rich, and it has laid out its superfluous wealth in works of real utility and advantage. Liverpool contains five churches, and at least seventy-thousand inhabitants. On the east side of the town is a terrace, commanding a delightful view of the houses, the river and the circumjacent country.
  – *William Mayor:* The British Tourists, Vol. IV, London, 1798.

Mayor had come from Manchester, where he had seen miners do eight hours' piece work in the mine to earn twenty pennies a day, 'on the Duke of Bridgwater Canal through Warrington and through the agreeable little town of Prescot', then north by canal to Kendal where were made the woollen and cotton goods for Liverpool's Guinea trade. My copy of the book bears the inscription in only slightly-faded ink, the writing being exquisite copperplate, 'The Gift of Elizabeth Taylor to her Son, John Noble Taylor, July 2nd 1799.'

Henry III's lease

Henry by the Grace of God, King of England, Lord of Ireland, Duke of Normandy and Aquitaine etc. To the Sheriffs and all our Bailiffs of the County of Lancaster.
  Know ye that we have granted to our honest men of Leverpul – our vill of Leverpul to be held at farm from the feast of St Michael in the thirteenth year of our reign unto the end of four complete years: rendering therefor unto us in each of the aforesaid years, at our Exchequer, by the hand of the Sheriff of Lancaster at two terms, TEN POUNDS ...   – 1229.

Prologue

In a place like Liverpool, without any upper class as far as one can see, and now that the working class has been abolished everywhere, one would not expect to find class distinctions. One would be wrong.
  Distinction by money not applying, duality is attained by a rough division into those who like scouse and those who do not.

Actually everybody (almost) likes scouse. Some admit it. Some do not.

Scouse, by the way, is a seaman's stew (i.e. the Scandinavian lobscouse, Midland lobby, Smollett's Lobs-course) which, especially in its 'blind' or meatless form, has old associations with poverty. Like other poor man's dishes, such as spare-ribs and salt-fish, it is now as dear as any other.

At one time, working for the Pools formed the dividing line. But now almost everyone works for the Pools.

Another method of division has died in Liverpool as elsewhere – the use of the dearer part of the pub. Since the war it is not surprising to find convent-bred popsies in maxis, minis, beads or kaftans in bars where the veriest drabs would formerly not have ventured; and contrariwise, the Pools clerk or foreman from the docks sipping his penny-a-pint dearer ale is quite likely to have his bowler hat knocked sideways by a coalheaver's shovel or his elbow jogged by a tram conductor.

It is possible to step out of the scouse class by marriage. As when the Co-op manager marries a bookmaker's daughter. Or by giving birth to young who, through some such environmental influence as employment by the Pools, will drag you out of your lower class, so that before you know where you are, you are eating shepherd's pie, having your 'carrying out' wrapped in a serviette and doing the gardening while Mam (now Mum) is forced to discard her comfortable shawl and linsey petticoats.

The outsider may be interested in a brief list of speech habits and other mores which, if he visits Liverpool, will give him clues as to the class of people he may meet – Scouse (s) or non-Scouse.

It is s when you push your mouth containing an unlit cigarette into the face of a passer-by whose cigarette is lit and he obliges, to say 'Ta'. Non-s people simply wag the head.

It is s either to apologise when giving a large coin for a small fare to a bus conductor or to say, if given by him a large number of coppers: 'They'll do for church.'

It is s to eat your chips from their paper on the main road. Non-s folk use side streets.

It is non-s to clean your own windows. (The visitor might expect it to be the other way about. That's just where he's caught.)

Definitely (pronounced by s fellows 'defanely') non-s locutions are 'Long time no see', 'Pleased to meet you' (s is 'How do, whack'), 'Who d'you think you're pushing?' (usually said to s individuals), 'Here's looking at you' (s 'I paid for the last, whack') 'Age before

14

beauty' when opening the door for a lady.

Best clothes on Sunday is, above all, the clearest s indicator.

There is, however, always something kept back. It is very hard to cross over. Myself, my whole temperament shrieks out to be declassed. I am the son of unquestionably non-s parents. And I find scouse completely indigestible.

But I love Scousetown and many of its inhabitants – the Scousers. (They call themselves whackers: a 'whacker', from the Army slang 'whack', to share, being a friend, one with whom one shares. So we are a sort of profane Society of Friends.)

'Manchester men, Liverpool gentlemen'. And there is still a deal of genteel – and unjustified, since if we did not ourselves come straight from the bog or its equivalent our forefathers did – snobbery centred on our Rep. (vastly inferior these days to the average amateur theatre) and the Phil. (good music, I suppose, but nothing really to do with Liverpool – it could be any city). The whole of this group, who see themselves as descendants from the slave-trading merchants of the 18th century, I have called Pols. They affect the Latinate Liverpolitan.

The Scousers, whackers, Frisby Dykes, Dicky Sams, even with their vile catarrhal accent (in which they can be truly witty; it's the Irish in them), are my sort.

From those vile slum houses stretched along the waterfront, ugly warrens facing our lovely Mersey, comes a strange and lovely quality, of courage and humour and friendliness, which I find ever-refreshing. I hate our soul-killing garden suburbs.

They are greater folk than the Cockneys, just as our city is not just a provincial seaport but a second metropolis.

The Pols, the people of our great parks and fine houses, the Tunnel, the Cathedral, the airports and the big new trading estates and wide roads, are such as you could meet everywhere; they say, through their noses, just what you would hear in Southampton or New York. Their minds keep in the ready-made rut, their customs are copies, their life a mimicry. They take out insurance policies, wear nice clothes, take afternoon tea, wear dressing gowns, play golf and holiday in Ostend or some other English colony in Europe. They support the clergy, join secret societies, have a dinner-suit in the wardrobe, have gardens, cars, ulcers, ambition and a forget-fulness of death like anyone anyplace. You can keep them.

There is a living, lusting, shouting-with-laughter, society of real people living alongside the Mersey. 'Of these shall my songs be sung.'

15

Their lives, of course, are tragedies at bottom – aren't all lives? – but they live them in terms of comedy. They live.

When the mother of the poor came to my father's butcher shop in the Irish ghetto she asked for a 'penn'orth uv bits for the dog'. My kind father, as she left, caustically whispered; 'Anough to make scouse for six uv them!'

Praise indeed

Liverpool in 1870 as described in a letter from Samuel Derrick, Master of Ceremonies at Bath:

The assembly room . . . is grand, spacious, and finely illuminated; here is a meeting once a fortnight to dance and play cards; where you will find some women elegantly dressed and perfectly well dressed. The proceedings are regulated by a lady styled 'the Queen' and she rules with very absolute power.

There follows a passage which, says the Liverpool historian Picton drily, is worth extracting 'for its raciness if not for its truth':

The great increase of commerce is owing to the spirit and indefatigable industry of its inhabitants, the majority of whom are either Irish or of Irish descent; a fresh proof my lord, that the Hibernians thrive best when transplanted, engage in trade as in battle, with little or no spirit at home, but with unparalleled galantry abroad.

Having taken that with a pinch of snuff we may squirm before his quiz-glass as he proceeds:

Though few of the merchants have had more education than befits a counting-house, they are genteel in their address. They are hospitable, nay friendly, even to those of whom they have the least knowledge. Their tables are plenteously furnished, and their viands well served up; their rum is excellent, of which they consume large quantities, made when the West India fleet comes in with limes, which are most cooling, and afford a delicious flavour. But they pique themselves greatly upon their ale, of which almost every house brews a sufficiency for its own use; and, such is the unanimity prevailing among them, that if by accident one man's stock runs short he sends his pitcher to his neighbour to be filled.

Alwis on the borry dat feller. Watsee tink I'm ere for—t' slug me guts out makin ale to give him to show off wid his posh mate fum Bath – looks as if he cud do with a bath an all, ho, ho. He'd get round widout crutches dat feller.

A likkle monologue

There's a little yellow idler
   To the North of Scotty Road,
There's a little cap
   That cost him half-a-crown.
There's a broken hearted barmaid
   In the pub called *The Abode*,
Thinking of the many times
   He done her down.

He was known as Idle Jack
   For his habits were so slack;
In convulsions he'd not work
   Was what he said.
He hadn't worked for years;
   He drove six dole clurks to tears
And when the pubs was closed
   Just stayed in bed.

When a bevvy he felt like,
   He would go on a long hike,
Every inch of twenty yards
   To *The Abode*;
And having tottered there
   He'd slump into a chair;
Puffing piteously
   Just like a dying toad.

To the counter he'd advance,
   Ask the barmaid if by chance
She could give him something
   For his awful drought.
'When the stout is opened, lass,
   'Will you pour it in the glass
'And then Maggie dear
   'Just hold it to me mouth.'

Then he'd say he hadn't strength
   To stretch down the pocket length
Of his trousers
   To produce the bob or so.

17

When she offered to do this,
   He said: 'That would be remiss.'
'Then I'll take yer half-crown cap
   If that is so.'

Tricks like that could not stop Jack;
   He didn't try to snatch it back.
To the crowded pub
   He gave a mighty shout:
'Maggie's gorra heart of gold;
   She's collecting for some old
And thirsty sailor's
   Had his tonsils out.'

The dockers had just drawn their pay.
   It's well known that on that day
You may collect
   For anything you choose.
They filled the cap up to the brim.
   Only one chap, Moanin' Jim,
Said: 'He'll only spend the lot
   On flippin booze.'

Seeing Jack flopped in his chair
   They led Maggie over there.
Into his waiting hands
   They poured the pelf.
He thanked them, Maggie too,
   Ordered up a Mountain Dew,
And kindly said:
   'My dear, have one yourself.'

When the noise was at its height
   He went out into the night
And took a taxi
   To the Lime Street Lodge.
He drank plonk and puffed cheroots
   Till it oozed out of his boots,
Then took a taxi home
   The cops to dodge.

18

There's a little yellow idler
  Lying out in Scotty Road.
Thirsty, capless,
  And he hasn't got a brown.
In the empty pub sits Mag,
  And someone has whipped her bag,
And the yellow fog
  Forever gazes down.

(After Milton Hayes. From Radio Merseyside revue *Ullo Durr Scouse.*)

Why I love Liverpool

When two men from Liverpool meet in other parts – as they are likely to, for we are a much-travelled community – one does not ask the other what school he went to or whether he is from Rose Hill or Mossley Hill. They are as one against the 'enemy'.

When Liverpool played Arsenal in the final some years ago I was in Harwich, then the Second Fleet base. The landlord of my hotel, a Cockney, asked me to stay in the lounge for the afternoon to hear the broadcast of the game. Now, when I support a team I am entirely partisan; I am, short of fisticuffs, violent, as much against the opposition as for the team I support. Therefore, I replied sadly: 'What's the good? All your friends will be shouting for Arsenal like yourself!'

The lounge was full of sailors and the predominant accent was South Country. But, miraculously, from over the serried heads, there came to me a still, small voice: 'No they won't, whack, I'm wit' yer. I'll join yer' an' we'll tackle the lot uv um!'

Liverpool, though unsuccessful, never had heartier supporters. Later, over a 'bevvy', it transpired that back in Scousetown, we were both followers of Everton!

This standing-up for our city, wherever we may be, tends, I fear, to make us disliked. When strangers live among us long enough – I've spent over half my life here – they get to like us. When they have learnt the language. Soon enough their own noses will be stuffed up. 'Coming from Liverpool', said actor Norman Rossington, 'is like belonging to a worldwide club, an exclusive clan.'

What I like about Liverpool is the Liverpudlian. I like the Liverpolitan, too!

There is no point in denying the division between Pol and Pud, or Scouse and non-Scouse[1], but it is much narrower than you might expect. Mixing with both, and not being entirely a Pol or a Pud, I can affirm this with assurance.

The Scouser loves our majestic river and our fine buildings, our repute in the cultural fields, our municipal enterprise in housing and industrial estates and our academic fame quite as much as the 'toney', 'bay-window' type.

The most educated and urbane citizen must appreciate the rich life which floats about the market – the caged dogs, the piled vegetables in enchanting still life arrangements, the cheapjacks and 'sage a mint a parsley'.

He must feel some affection for the matey little pubs and eating houses tucked away in back cracks, the cheerful flower girls in Clayton Square, the kids paddling in the fountain by the Wellington Monument and the casual, blunt humour of bobbies and bus drivers, barmaids and binmen.

Pol may even, on the sly, eschew caviare and truffles and 'get stuck into' a large (or 'dirty big') plateful of scouse itself. Both sectors agree that Everton (or Liverpool)[2] is the best football team in the world. And both, nightly, at the various bus termini, are in accord, though their terms may vary, about our public transport!

At first, the stranger finds, besides a natural North Country brusqueness, a certain Celtic truculence – no wonder we are so fond of Punch and his Judy – and, from long association with North America maybe, a non-English loud-spoken pride in our bigness and our firsts.[3]

---

1. See Prologue, pages 13-15. The attempt by some to have the citizen known as a Liverpolitan had its period but failed. Few in Liverpool would use it – I christened them Pols and identified them, maybe unfairly, with posh or snotty types living in the better suburbs (say, Mossley Hill instead of the inaptly named Rose Hill), more pretentious in their social habits, professing higher cultural aspirations than their own humble origins usually justified. (It is long since the 'Pool had any real 'gentry'.) Liverpudlian as a word, with the North Country vowelled Pud like an exploding black-pudden, suggests the real Scouser. (A name not used in my youth, by the way, when Dicky Sam was the nickname.)

2. A keen Everton supporter once admitted that Liverpool had the two best football teams in the country – Everton and Everton Reserves. Actually there is a deal of leg-pulling and good-humoured banter about the loudly-expressed partisanship – unlike Glasgow's – and there is no truth that, in the bad winter of January 1971, a supporter of Liverpool, the Reds, cut off his pal's ears because they had turned blue. Everton supporters, however, in a city corporation estate complained bitterly when their doors were painted red and one extremist abandoned his tenancy. There is a deal of ecumenism about these days among soccer supporters.

3. Suspicious of all conjectural etymology and though I can find no other reason

Our list of firsts is indeed formidable. We even had a Charter from King John nine years before the rest of England. It takes a deal of self-denial not to point out to the stranger that we had the first public health schemes, with Dr Duncan as the first Medical Officer, the first public libraries, the first municipal baths, the first society for the prevention of cruelty to children and the first for animals, the first passenger railway and, under Stoll, the first twice-nightly theatre.

We can add that we had a 'macadamised' road – to Warrington – before Macadam was heard of, a Liverpool man invented – Lord forgive him! – flag days and (I have been told) a Liverpudlian invented crosswords. The first man to kill a Prime Minister was a Liverpudlian.[4] As for the biggest, there is a clock bigger than Big Ben, the world's biggest grain silo and many more.

Some years ago I was showing the sights to a number of students from all parts of the country, starting from the university, with a halt for fish-and-chips in Brownlow Hill. Naturally I took them to the Cathedral, where I handed over to a more knowledgeable guide. The visitors, I observed, found it difficult to conceal irreverent mirth when this guide loudly declared that 'dis is the biggest bell in the world!'

The Cathedral[5] itself typifies the strange and exciting mixture the citizens are as it gazes benignly down on the grand houses built by the great merchants, many of them slave-traders, and their many coloured inhabitants, some the descendants of slaves, and for the most part as good citizens as any; nearby a garish

---

for the name Dicky Sam (at least some hundred years old) I just won't accept that it means a Little Yank (citizen of US), 'dicky' being an old slang, indeed dialect, word for 'small' – i.e. dicky seat on a car, now the boot. But indeed whackers are often taken for 'Yanks' abroad (except in USA where, however, many could be quite at home in the Bowery, among the Chimmy Faddens).

4. Bellingham was a poor mad fellow – he had worked for the Customs – with a grievance which however was not the concern of that unimportant PM Perceval whom he shot outside the House. He was held at once by an MP from Liverpool, Bamber Gascoigne, whose descendant of the same name will be recalled by those who watched *University Challenge* on TV as a polished and sophisticated Standard-speaking Pol.

5. We did not, when this essay was first written, have two cathedrals. The second, the RC Cathedral of Christ the King, sometimes with affectionate irreverence The Mersey Funnel or Paddy's Wigwam, so very much in contrast to its neo-Gothic precursor, seems to suit the Pud, and I fancy many Pols, better. But both are a credit to their home and the citizens, admired even by those lacking religion of any kind who could not agree with Pete McGovern (educated in a Catholic school in Scotland Road, now our best-beloved folk club artiste and a possessor of extreme political views) that we have a cathedral to spare. Actually I shouldn't be surprised if one day Liverpool has the biggest Hebrew temple in the world.

dance-hall elbows one of the oldest Nonconformist chapels in the land, the smell of Eastern food curls over a centuries-old mill forgotten in a back yard, back streets run alongside rolling parkland where deer once roamed.

Many cities are lovelier, many have an even more ancient history, many are, at present, at least equal to Liverpool in the country's economy. But none invokes more love from its children, so many of whom are not native born.

Last summer I was in Copenhagen. After dinner I was sitting in the hall of the hotel when the porter told me there were two Englishmen in the bar from a ship in the harbour. I went through. They were not only English but from Liverpool – be fair, one was from Huyton – and we had a most pleasant chat over a schnapps.

'Do you like it?' I asked.

'Sooner have a good lush-up in . . .' (He named a Liverpool hostelry which, like most of them, has a good nickname.)

'Like the town? Beautiful, beautiful Copen – the Tivoli Gardens in the moonlight, the little Mermaid, the . . .'

'Lissen,' said one, 'give me Parky Lane Street on a Saturday night!'

'But the food . . .' I said, thinking of the succulent smorrabrod on delicious rye bread.

'D'you like all dat stuff on black chuck? Give me a good plate a scouse any time!'

No wonder the exile in *The Liverpool Blues* sang:

'Pork and beans is a lovely dish,
But give me Sundy mornin' an' the ould sal' fish.'

I might have told the sailors that our local dish came from these very parts. In fact, I had seen 'Skas' advertised in Odense and, in Germany, had some labscas which had most of the ingredients – though, I must say, it wasn't like 'Me Mam' used to make it.

Pride and loyalty, with humour, go with an aggressiveness, which is largely a pose, and self-reliance which made the old Scruffy Kings (a nickname given in derisive affection) a regiment of NCO's and Scousers, from the earliest sailing ships, respected – when they were not feared! – by every ships' officer afloat.

You know, the city presents a handsome face to the world. The waterfront, approached from the Mersey, never ceases to thrill the newcomer. Among the crews, from first-timer to old shellback, the slowly unfolding stretch from Crosby Channel always grips the heart. 'Lovely in all seasons, in all weathers', as locally-educated John Masefield said.

A closer study of her lineaments does not disappoint the visitor. We have grand buildings from the Bluecoat Chambers to St George's Hall, fine shops, good theatres, noble vistas, miles of parks, well-planned housing estates, modern factories and historical places like Speke Hall; markets, the Tunnel and airport, the Philharmonic. Yet it must be said that, for those seamen and others who made the wealth and the greatness, for those who laid the bricks and dug the Tunnel, the city at times proved a harsh and scabby mother.

To go down some of the dirty, smelly, crumbling ill-lit streets – surely there could be more street lamps, as many as in Aigburth say - is a shattering experience for the homecomer who has seen how much better the ordinary person is treated in other parts of the world. That he can see worse is beside the point. In many ways Dicky Sam gets a raw deal. And his wife. Lord knows, she works hard enough to keep the house clean, doorstep red-raddled, paint washed, 'flags' in front of the steps cleaned down to the sidewalk.

Their children go to insanitary grim school-buildings, with concrete playgrounds if any, while extensive and expensive schools spring up all round the suburbs. Yet they look well-fed and well-clothed, an answer to those who think dockers and such spend all their money on booze and betting and that the family allowances are abused.

I have seen, walking around those cobbled streets which tumble down to the dock road both north and south of the Pier Head, groups of schoolchildren, going to the baths or football-field with their teachers. The teachers look very young; they were surely much older, more dignified, certainly better-dressed when we were lads? The boys, in appearance and conduct, and possibly in speech, compared very favourably with grammar school boys in more salubrious areas.

Children love their mother however badly she treats them. Our love of Liverpool is often expressed on a wry note of humour.

Arthur Askey was once asked why the city had produced so many comedians like Tommy Handley, Billy Bennett, Robb Wilton, Billy Matchett, Ken Dodd, Beryl Orde. He could have referred to our long list of 'straight' actors. What he did reply was, 'You've got to be a comic to live in Liverpool!'[6]

One can encounter the humour in all parts of Liverpool. It is,

---

6. Among our straight actors could be named Rex Harrison, Rita Tushingham, Andrée Melly, Tom Bell, the late beloved Leonard Williams (Sergeant Twentyman in original *Z Cars*), John Gregson, the Oscar-winning Glenda Jackson and many, many more.

I find, in the poorer districts, from the men in the cosy dock-side pubs (much more pleasing than the giant gin palaces of the suburbs), the women with a few minutes to 'jangle'[7] on the way to the fish-shop, the children making the best of a brickfield playing-ground, that one encounters the real juicy, racy stuff, sometimes not easy to transmit, for tone and even gesture plays so much a part; and some is not printable.

I append a few remarks recently culled, but I could include a hundred –

Schoolboy: Why is he called Atlas? 'Cos he doesn't wear a 'at.

Shawlie (after a long survey of overdressed friend): You've done well since yer ould one sold the rags.

Ironic wife (to malingering husband): Ay, yer proper bad, I'll after dust the policies. – G'wan wid yew, it's 'ard to kill a bad t'ing.

Sarcastic bus-conductor (having received an 8d fare in ha'pennies): 'Aven't yew got no jam jars?

A young girl after a vigorous dance with a clumsy partner: Take yer football-boots off next time, will yer.

Sometimes the humour is unconscious, as when the slum dweller told the sanitary inspector that his house was 'alive with dead rats'.

There is, due to Celtic exuberance of speech no doubt, a delicious tendency towards the malapropism. I heard someone speak re-

---

7. Jangle for gossip, chatter (an echoic word suggesting the clatter of tongues?) was used much in its Liverpol-uh, pudlian sense by Shakespeare (*Love's Labour's Lost, A Midsummer-Night's Dream*).

Much said in this essay about the bad old houses, schools and the likes by 1971 could not always apply, but it is astonishing how much still applies. Town Improvement is often a misnomer. After all the bulldozing and destruction of old shops and houses (and some very recent ones), and my studio in St Anne St and much of the centre of the city, which was scruffy but typical and individual, we don't get better houses or civic buildings but huge and mystifying flyovers and blocks of identical offices all empty.

Schools are at last being built. When I did a New Year show for TV on January 1, 1971 in a vile tin and brick school near Scotty Road, almost down to its last brick, which should have been condemned fifty years ago – but with lovely kids playing the old games to the old tunes – I noticed that the houses near the school were being demolished. Some of the inhabitants are to be housed in new ones (cold and heartless and inconvenient) nearby but most will be bunged miles away to chilly and unfriendly new towns and the schools will stand empty while the children no longer sing the songs or play the games.

The dear old market mentioned early in the essay has quite gone and is replaced by a severe unmatey clinical new development. And now they are trying to chase our dear old flower-girls and the hard-working barrow-women. Liverpool with all thy faults I love you still! But be natural, old girl, don't Put It On.

cently of 'paralysed' lines and of a counsel in a court case who gave 'an impassive speech'.

No wonder one Pud, seeing me smile, said: 'Well, if we don't hit it we stagger it!' And for that reason, and for many another, I like Liverpudlians. Sometimes though, I wonder – why do *they* love Liverpool?

A statue exceedingly bare

The statue is the thing. It symbolises Liverpool's future, this unmistakably male nude, Liverpool Resurgent, nay Tumescent. It stands for our virility. It is larger than life, I'll say, by Epstein, quite classical high above the big department store in the city centre, opposite the expensive-looking hotel.

Stranger in Liverpool to bus driver: 'Do you stop at the Adelphi?'

Driver (anxious to maintain our reputation for spontaneous wit): 'Blimey, mate, on my flippin' wages?'

From the hotel, with only the slightest crick in the neck, you can see to the South our two cathedrals, ahead shops of all kinds, theatreland, all backing on our dear and dirty Mersey, to the North the noble George's Hall which Betjeman said he would die for ('It's behind the Punch and Judy Show', says the native). You could see the Welsh mountains on a clear day. That was June 6 last year.

You can't see the miles and miles of docks either. Since the overhead railway was scrapped, few besides dockers or seamen ever do see our docks. But for the Landing Stage, Liverpool, as a former city planning officer said, turns its back on the sea.

And opposite is the forgotten man of bronze who gave a new meaning to the local saying 'Standing there like one of Lewis's', which used to refer to standing like a shop-window dummy. Nowadays few citizens notice it.

It was, uh, erected in 1957 probably in emulation of Zadekind's Destroyed City in the centre of Rotterdam, another resurgent seaport, which had a hiding in the war. It caused a sensation when it was unveiled. It is said Lewis's shop-girls threatened to walk out – they weren't going to work under a . . . like that! From many quarters came fierce protest; the council was severely criticised. A councillor friend said to me: 'Why cudden they put it in the Art Gallery whur nobody would see ut?'

A couple of rather skinny female nudes in relief on the walls of the George's Hall caused similar trouble in the last century; how many of the thousands who daily pass the building have ever seen them? A male nude, skinny too ('like a couple a pared match-sticks'), with no arms and none of the Lewis's fellow's endowments was erected in the classy shopping street, Bold Street. He had to be taken down after organised complaints from shoppers and shopkeepers. There is a latent Puritanism, notable in the town's history, not least among the poor and the Irish. Though in the latter two classes, which often are one, ribaldry seasons the squeamishness.

Except for Dublin, if O'Connell was debagged, I know of no city where so much indignation mixed with mock modesty, low jest and pruriency could be aroused as was in my native city when Epstein depicted the new, vital 'Pool.

Nobody, well hardly anybody, but a visitor, notices him now. (Nobody ever noticed the three more interesting panels over the shop's entrance.) Without its being removed my Philistine councillor friend has had his wish realised.

Other great cities, even in England, have their male nudes without threatened riots. In Oslo you see so many that you rather long for those Victorian philanthropists in stovepipe hats and clawhammer coats of which Liverpool has more than its share.

No longer does the matron, looking upwards towards Lewis's to see if it looks like rain, furiously drag an inadequate husband past the store, nor passing males take a sly and wistful gander. No hobbledehoys stare up and hide their admiration in guffaws any more. Nor gym-slipped schoolgirls peer that way with modern frankness, storing up for themselves years of disappointment.

But there is one faithful heart. Symbol of our city's great future, as I arrange a pot pourri from its past and present, and my own, with firm belief in my city's greatness at all times, I, not without envy, in spirit, return your salute.

The old Scouse tie
Souvenir of the 'Pool

Liverpool's on the map, in the public eye, but it is not on the shelves of the souvenir shop, in the bottle. Why not? When the Cavern was re-opened, with the Prime Minister presiding, portions of the platform from which the famous Sound set off to echo round the world were sold like relics of the True Cross – and seemed almost as miraculously plentiful.

But who will bottle Mersey water?

The Irish exile says 'Sure and you can't have stout widout t' Liffey water, begorrah and faith, macushla' (if he's been in exile long enough) and the Scot similarly situated says 'Och, it's no Scotch whisky without the smell of the peat.'

Why doesn't some exile from Liverpool say: 'Lissen, youse, when you gerra cup a tea you wanna have the sphoon sthickin up in ut an youse'll not get dat widout real Mersey water, la.'

Mother would be clamouring to send bottles of Mersey water wrapped in the Liverpool Football Exile to the poor lad. Visitors would feel they couldn't go home without a bottle of the real Mersey water. Then why not bottle Liverpool air? Other places have done it.

You Too (the ad may read) *Can Sing Through Your Nose. After One Bottle of Liverpool Lanny I Went Right Through 'Maggie May' Without One Correct Vowel Sound.*

What Coty will make his fortune with a bottled and nostalgic pot pourri Eau de Moloney – the very essence of scouse, salt fish, Mersey fog and dockers' raincoats?

I met an American lady in a TV studio who is here working for an international organisation. She spends much of her time sending Liverpool street lamp posts to friends on the other side.

There must be rather a shortage of lamp posts by now.

And whatever happened to those bright-coloured glass barrels which used to dangle outside pubs? This city must have had some of the finest in the world. As it has of manhole covers, especially in the Everton area. Up to now, collectors of these circular metal things with the varied patterns of designs are making rubbings of them with the enthusiasm of Edwardian students on vacation rubbing brasses in old churches. (The manhole cover types call themselves orcupephiles, for God's sake.) But how the real thing would go on top of an oilman's fallout shelter! Pry the covers out of the ground and increase the dollar flow.

Bit awkward to get to the USA? Not as hard as wrapping up a lamp post. But nothing is impossible when you have a friend in an international organisation.

Since the obscure suburban street Penny Lane was immortalised in song by the Beatles police have to mount a round-the-clock guard to thwart daring tourists – as they have, I am told, to do the same for the little boy, or part of the little boy, in Brussels.

But they can't be everywhere. Personally I've got my eye on a mangle I saw in a back yard in Pitt Street.

It needn't be a bulky object. The exile or the tourist recalls the characteristic foodstuffs more than anything. I have never – serious now (and you are listening to a guy who has tried and failed for years to get a Liverpool restauranteur to open a Scouse Joint which could become as world-known as Dirty Dick's in London) – stopped wondering why an enterprising Liverpool merchant has never produced tinned scouse. He must not, however, call himself the Gear Meat Company as there actually is a company in New Zealand using that excellent label.

Some of our foodstuffs would, I suppose, be hard to transmit. Not all would suit tinning. I am reminded of the visitor to Liverpool who delighted in our spicy meat balls, often called savoury ducks. He bought some and put them in a box and posted them to his brother back home on a farm in Ireland with a note: 'Dear Mike, I am sending you some savoury ducks.' Some time later the reply came: 'Dear Johnny, I received your box of manure, ducks flown.'

I am also reminded of the lady politician whose agent was asked to stop her speaking of manure when addressing farming groups. 'Ask her to say "fertiliser"?' 'If you only knew', said the agent bitterly, 'how long it took me to get her to say "manure".'

But we need not stick at imitating the bottling of Malvern water or kidding the mugs with bottles of London fog in the old mode of mendicant friars with the Virgin's milk and St Peter's foreskin.

What is more nostalgic than sound? You can't bottle that of course but, while some of the sounds last, some could be taped. I know that much is lost in taping but if I were deported or wrecked on that desert island I would give much for some of these Merseyside memories in sound.

Some dockers' nicknames

Sam Goldwyn. He keeps saying 'Lissen, lads, I'll put yer in the picture.' (Was Sam – the creator of the immortal include me out, who had the mucus of an idea, which wasn't just colossal it was mediocre – of Scouse origin?)

The Reluctant Plumber. He won't do a tap.

The Bewildered Minstrel. Mister White whose daughter is singer Cilla Black. Wonders: 'Am I Black or White'?

The Unknown Soldier. Dockers lived in community, went to same church, patronised same church, pub, bookie, pawnbroker. He was a stranger. And he wore a long khaki (Army surplus) overcoat.

The Auctioneer. When I complained to a shed foreman that I'd nearly been sent a-over-t by a bogey-driver he said, 'We call him the Auctioneer – he'd knock anything down.'

The Mangy Kitten. When told to go to remote dock calling for a bus ride he says: 'I haven't got no fur.'

The Lonely Cat. Hard to put it in writing. His father also works at docks and when he looks down a hold hoping to see his ould feller he says. 'Me-ow-l feller down dur?' Gerrit?

Stanley Matthews. When he joins three others to man a hatch he says: 'I'll take dis corner.'

Blessed Art Thou. A great lover. From the opening words of Ave Maria '. . . blessed art thou among women.'

Phil (Fill) the Cot. Father of many.

The Vicar. Keeps saying 'Eh men –.' Hard taskmaster, he'd have you on your knees.

Lino. He's always 'on the floor' (short of money).

Ink. He's always in the pen (the 'taking on' point).

The Chemist. Loading a truck he says 'There's more f'yer'(morphia).

Piano. He thinks he's put on. 'They're playing on me.'

Lazy Solicitor. He went to sleep on a case.

The Good Shepherd. He took the carcase of a sheep out of the docks.

Sheriff. Foreman who says 'What's the hold up, lads?'

Jellypex. He's only got one coat.

Harpic. He's clean round the bend (daft).

Wallpaper. He's up the wall (daft).

The Baker. Keeps talking about 'me and me tart' (girl, wife).

Surgeon. Keeps saying 'Cut that out.'

Lame Kangaroo. Hasn't had a jump (sexual intercourse) for years.

Bird Doctor. Says: 'This lark's no good.'

Contented Diner. 'I've got enough on my plate.'

Pontius Pilate. He's always washing his hands.

Midwife. He's always on deliveries.

The Blood Donor. A very pale fellow.

Sore Finger. Always wants sympathy.

Frightened Fish. Won't handle a crane.

Rattler. He has false teeth.

The Parish Priest. Works every Sunday. (Overtime pay for Sundays is so high it's called The Gold Nugget.)

The Lenient Judge. A foreman who keeps saying 'Let 'er go' or 'Let dat guy go' (a guy being part of a sling for cargo).

The Spaceman. Says he's going to ma's (Mars) for dinner.

The Destroyer. Always after subs. (Wage advances.)

Wonder Boy. A looter. Looks at cargo, says, 'I wonder what's in this, I wonder what's in that?'

London Fog. He never lifts.

Balloon. Foreman who says 'Don't let me down, lads.'

The President. Always in the White House. Drink of the house is cheap Australian white wine and the docker who pinches pals' drink (a minesweeper) is called

The White Hunter – and

Cinderella says 'I gotta be away by twelve.'

City of sight and sound

Fifty or so years ago there was a medley of sounds which was Liverpool. For us lads, and for our elders, it was a perfect, however unmelodious, background to the wonderful, and entirely free, panorama which the great seaport presented and still, in its way, presents to the eyes.

In Manchester Street, not far from the Wizard's Den, which

has now 'disappeared' elsewhere (it advertised Useless Gifts last Christmas!), was a taxidermist's, in the window of which was a realistic stuffed cat which must have fascinated hundreds of office boys, hurrying to Harry Petty's cheap lunch, and little boys like me.

Everything fascinated me. It happened that shortly after I arrived here it was St Patrick's day and I saw a procession of the green-and-gold coated Irish Foresters, many in saffron kilts, their brass instruments a-gleam under a sudden watery sun. I had never seen such in Ireland itself and I thought it magnificent and later missed it greatly. I recall too how, after the First War, the Eighth Irish marched, many of them Boer veterans, along Shaw Street and the ranks, behind the pipes, stretched for a mile, led by a very tall, handsome, much decorated colonel. They marched again this year, on the Sunday, but how small a group it now is!

The Orange still march and make a grand show. When, as has happened in Belfast, they and such as the old Foresters all march together through our streets it will indeed be – a great day for the Irish.

Soon followed my first election, and surely no kids get the fun now of marching behind makeshift bands, using bin-lids, old biscuit tins and all sorts, waving printed slogans given us by the candidate's friends and singing, 'Vote, vote, vote for Whatsername', and finishing by consigning the opponent, 'ould Whosthis', to the dock. By the Cock.

But there were less noisy scenes to witness than marches. Many individuals were providing gratuitous amusement. A bearded old boy with a queer scaffolding of window panes hobbled along with the catarrhal cry 'Winders, winders!' and it does seem to me that more windows were broken in those days than now. One certainly saw more drunks, including women. Once I ran home to tell my aunt I had seen 'two ladies fighting!' After the *Lusitania* riots and the 1919 anti-Negro riots no sight should have surprised. For that matter I had seen men releasing rats from traps in a street off Islington for dogs to chase, and unsqueamish readers of my age will of course also remember seeing cattle being driven through the streets to the bloodstained alleys behind London Road where unhygienic slaughter went on all day and we lads could get bladders from kindly slaughterers, which were much better than a tin can or roll of paper for street footballs. Of course we could not afford a full-size ball ('casey'), not even a half size ('tanner megger', for they were only sixpence-ha'penny).

33

A poor fellow used to go about the streets then who always wore different hats. I have seen him in a fireman's helmet, a busby, a 'straw gussie' and a real Spion Kop peaked cap in one week. One does not see the weak-minded and hard-up person so much about these days and also, after the last war, you don't see the crippled still in hospital blue and peripatetic bands of ex-Servicemen.

The barrel-organs have almost gone. The father of a famous local boxer used to let them out on hire for so much a day and had to keep changing the tunes. *The Sheik of Araby* would have to replace *Give Me a Little Cosy Corner* if the shopping crowds were being slow with their pennies.

Best places to find entertainers working without contract except hope were outside the theatre queues. An ex-jockey, 'Kruschen', would do feats of contortion astonishing for his age. A one-man band might perform his marvels ('We once were six but down in the Strand, We clicked for a bob and five got canned . . .'). The elocutionist ('Cannons to lift us thim, cannons foreninst thin') also sold sheet music (*The Tears of an Irish Mother* – One Penny).

I loved the salesmen in the street, some of whom are still to be found with the beshawled 'sage or mint or parsley' vendors. Gone, alas, and just like our youth, is the brandy-snaps man ('Oh, they are nice') and the cough-sweet peddler, himself hoarse.

Who would want to run home to telly then when the Negro still had a puppet show in Scotland Road with his famed butter-milk rhyme? When a happy families display of dogs, cats, monkeys all living in one large cage was to be seen? When in most streets were the ballad-singer and the sellers of sandbags to keep out the draughts? And coal-bricks (as in Dublin, O'Casey giving the call dramatic force in one of his tenement plays) mingled their cries with 'Here you are ladies, ripe bananas, four for a bob, buy me last one an I'll give youse six!' Not to mention coal, salt and rags, a bone, a bottle.

There is many another sight or sound I could recall, but a loudspeaker van has just gone past and, whether it advertises an election or a vacuum cleaner, I'll never know. One should remember even street noises in tranquillity.

In the doctor's insulting room

You give me the wrong conscription, doc.

I haven't been able to masturbate me food.

The other one ordered me a dose a courtesan.

I had a large abbess on me knee.

I was getting ejections.

There's something wrong wid the cornelia of me eye.

I had castoritis, coroner's trombonis, murgatroyd arthritis, bronical chest, pewmonia, combustion of the lungs, plumbago.

I need some paralysed gauze.

Paradised all down one side.

I was dat embezzled, he made me sthrip right off.

He's a diabetic and has to take insolence regular.

Ad a bad accident at the docks, doc, I tink compensation has set in.

It wuz a congenial injury, lucky I wassen decapitulated.

She had her overtures removed (could be).

He got conclusion of the brain (could be too).

Quicko Cough Cure's the ting, youse'll never get better.

The other doctor told me to pollute it wid water.

Said he'd have to seek a second option on my case.

He's one of dem plaster surgeons.

I was in pearl of me life.

His little phoenix was hurted.

He had his independence removed (could be).

I had to have me head X-raised, and was ultra-violated.

So I took the description to the chemist, smart chap, he's got diplomats on the wall.

I took it wid a glass of Helter Skelter.

Put the powder in the palm of yer and, he says, and ignore it.

I swallered a couple of tabloids.

And (Ben Trovato?) she asked for an animated picture of Queen Ann (ammoniated tincture of quinine).

The doctor used a hypothetical needle.

Lorra smallpox about, tink I should get the kids humanised.

So sore, tink I ought to put some imprecation on.

Can't take that meddysin, I'm lethargic to it.

I got an ulster in me mouth.

Comes out a hospittle tomorra, he's had a post-mortem. (Luckier than the fellow who was took to the symmetry to be created?)

PART TWO **Proper Dicky Sam**

Proper
Dicky
Sam

Dad – a Scouser's life

I still have all my own teeth. Quite a feat in Huyton, where, even at 16, you can lose the whole lot while minding your own business. I'm 60. I had no teeth at all when I was born. My family lived in Ireland. But my mother popped over from Tralee where me dad was making black puddings – an art unknown to the Irish, who still love to eat them – to make sure I was a Scouser, like my dad.

She, of course, was Catholic. He was, then, a Methodist, born off Scotland Road, son and grandson of a master mariner. I was born in Canterbury Street, off Islington. The house is now a betting shop. At four, I went to school and my first teacher had a beard; she was a nun. I came back with Dad to the 'Pool during the First World War to witness the street riots round Canterbury Street, where we went to live again, after the sinking of the *Lusitania*.

Besides butchering, giving birth to me and turning Catholic, Dad did some professional wrestling. He wrestled Hackenschmidt one time at Liverpool Hippodrome – with six others. Hack put 'em all down in minutes. In the ring, Dad wore green tights and used my mother's maiden name – Murphy. All his family came from North Wales, on the paternal side originally from Scotland, and some had been civic leaders in Liverpool in the 18th century. Names of streets like Shaw Street and Shaw Brow (now William Brown Street) recall this.

My grandfather was drowned at sea after having fought, for reasons best known to himself, in the American Civil War. My grandmother was killed by a motor car while going to collect her pension – it happened in Shaw Street! Dad, educated at the Quaker School in Islington, went to work for uncles in butchers' shops round Great Homer Street. There are no longer Williamses and Robetts with butchers' shops around there, but the family still exists as auctioneers, builders and the like. My mother's family, all farmers, lie buried in a small graveyard in Co. Wexford, and she and my father, God rest their souls, in Yew Tree Cemetery, West Derby.

It was in the Forties, after the war, that I developed, without any conscious effort, the image of being The Scouser. Dad, after all his years in Ireland, was the complete Dicky Sam. He assumed the name of Murphy when wrestling because he didn't want his strict Methodist uncles to know of his extra-shop activities. It has always astonished me that this industrious apprentice, chopping meat, boiling the blood for the black puddings, filling the sausage skins, and serving in the shop, was never exposed as a secret wrestler. Nor for that matter as a man-about-town.

Dad was always fixed in a *Pink 'Un*, yip-I-addy, penny cigar atmosphere and wore a curly Liverpool bowler (or 'blocker') at a jaunty angle all his life. He loved music halls and took me to them from an early age, as well as to boxing matches and, of course, Goodison Park.

When he was wrestling in small halls, his shortness and pugnacity went down well with the crowd, win or lose. If he won, of course, his opponent always being taller, they were delighted. I always feel a bit sorry for the Goliaths of this world. One thing I can't bear to see is a little man bashing a big slob. A little woman is worse. But though he was, I've been told, very useful at the then popular catch-as catch-can, he seldom finished up licking the Philistine. For that matter he had, facially, little resemblance to the conquering David in the typical Academy painting.

Dad had a big head which early shed its hair, pale blue eyes, small ears, a hooked nose and a prognathous jaw jutting in those days from a sweeping red moustache: it was grey in my time and, in later years, he shaved it off, as I did mine.

The main wrestling hall, the Adelphi, was in Christian Street – a predominantly Irish area. In those days young ladies did not go to places like the Adelphi, but on one occasion my mother (then courting my father) went to see him wrestle Cannon. Cannon was a most handsome man and was displaying his admirable body in the centre of the ring when Dad came on looking, she said, like a big-chinned leprechaun. A woman in front of Mary Murphy said 'Here's Murphy now, isn't he an ugly booger?', and my mother started a rival wrestling match in the body of the hall.

He married shortly after he became a master butcher – as proudly borne on his marriage certificate as master mariner on his father's – chucked the wrestling a year or so after as pay improved and moved to Tralee at the turn of the century. The following years till, with me and ahead of the family, he returned to the 'Pool in 1915 were his best, though he fully enjoyed every period of his life. For my mother, though she wasn't fond of Tralee itself, it was her most prosperous period. I recall very lively parties almost nightly.

A few years ago I did a piece in a Tralee newspaper about those days and a correspondence ensued from Tralee people alive in those days. One was from 'Ireland's Strongest Man' as an enclosed professional card, a very large piece of cardboard, green as Dad's tights, proudly proclaimed. This man, now living in Dublin, was still touring the halls. He recalled my father, then in his forties, accepting the challenge of a big tough young wrestler in their troupe when they played Tralee, and putting his man down in a minute. I had never heard the tale before, but quite believe it.

Another correspondent, a missionary priest in Pretoria, told me how my father, in 1913, outside St John's church, Tralee, outlined to him a scheme for making money which, said the priest, was simply what is now the football pool, one of Liverpool's leading industries. I could believe that. Dad was full of schemes but nothing whatever came of them. He bemoaned the fact that he had no capital. I doubt if it would have made a difference.

Some men are born to be Littlewoods (actually Moore), or Lord Vestey, who started off as a butcher's boy. Some not. A rich man needn't be unhappy. But it is easier for a poor one. Dad never gave up hope. He just could not take the first step, which often needs no capital at all.

At one time he and some other English chaps in Tralee, who used to meet at the Munster Fusiliers barracks, had plans to win a big prize in a newspaper contest, twenty-four results for £500 or something like that, by a system of permutating. They bought dozens of copies of the paper, spent all Sunday permutating, all week waiting for the result, and never won a tosser.

One of the syndicate's wife was seriously ill. She was having

41

an operation and my mother, meeting him, asked how things were going. 'No luck again', he answered. He was the coupon checker, and could not imagine anyone talking of anything else.

I sometimes wear the Shaw clan tie. Bought it in Glasgow during the war. They'll fix you up with a clan tie in Glasgow if your name's Tatarski, and they'll make Cohen into Colquhoun at the switch of a sporran. My eldest brother went into this and affirmed the Shaws were out in '75 as my mother's folk were out in '98 – she was supposed to be a descendant of the hero of Vinegar Hill, Father Murphy (not direct, of course, in the circumstances). Why is it that everybody wants ancestors fighting the English, the nicest folk in the world? All sorts of people without a drop of English blood claim to be English. English folk always want to be Irish or Scottish except for the large minority who, on thin ground, are proven gypsies.

One thing I do assert. Don't, like so many of us foreigners, knock the English in their own country, as so many Irish, real or imaginary, do. Whose bread I eat, his songs I sing, Damon Runyon said. This is not a council of subservience; it is plain justice. It's the little fellow belting the big one again, most unfair now as England is no longer a Goliath itself. Paddy may be only four foot two but John Bull is no longer six foot three. To his credit.

Tom McInerney, the English wrestling champion, who at one time had a famous hotel, The Feathers, where you could meet every sportsman, told me Dad was quite a good wrestler, and would have been top class if he'd not been short. I don't suppose he was three inches below my five-ten.

When he wasn't talking about Everton football club, the old Everton toffee-shop in Everton Brow, Kier Hardie, making black puddings, and women at whist drives who kept their trumps, Dad would always revert to Liverpool's waterfront Gordon Institute where he learnt his boxing and wrestling. When his sons are asked where they learnt their wrestling and boxing they answer at the Jack Shaw Institute. He left nothing when he died. He left us wealth beyond counting. He taught us modesty too. I am most grateful for the large numbers of periodicals he bought – a most varied collection from *Titbits* to the *Sunday Chronicle*. Dad could talk nineteen to the dozen. But I never heard him say anything against anyone, except, of course, Liverpool goalkeeper Elisha Scott, some disappointing jockeys and Stanley Baldwin.

Education of a Scouser

There undoubtedly is a younger generation wearied by tales of oranges four a penny and so on about which, though they do not doubt the narrator, they do not want to hear. And I have to remember, much as I always hung on Dad's reminiscing lips, there were those among us then who couldn't care less about getting five pints for a shilling.

The young reader or the older satiated reader must tolerate one emphatic recollection of the elder. The punishment given to young people fifty years ago by teachers and others was criminal. Nobody cared. We say it did us no harm. I wonder?

When the church, to which our school was an adjunct, was built, almost in the country, there were scarcely any Catholic families except those of Servicemen. What there were were of middle class, sound Lancastrian yeoman stock, whose ancestors had resisted the Reformation through their own fortitude, and the distance from the centre of Government in the days of slow transport. And let us be fair, the Christian tolerance of their Protestant neighbours.

Most of the names at our school were English. It is true of course that many of the mothers, many more of the grandmothers, were Irish but, at that stage, the poor Irish were staying in their ghettoes. Among the names I remember, two were German (their fathers interned, in no way looked sideways at), one was Italian, the Chinese family (Irish mother) were itinerant actors. Compulsory education made strolling actors send their children, of school age, to school. Thus Charlie Chaplin, it is said, was once a pupil at our school. Maybe he was. I saw the register giving his name when he, as a boy, performed in Liverpool.

The name of the Chinese boy, Anglicised as it was, I don't remember. Nor that of his lovely doll-like sister who, if alive, would now be 70. But we did have another acting boy at school. When made to kneel in front of the class, as punishment for some default (and were those boards dusty and splintery and well within reach of a casual switch from the teacher's ever-ready cane!), he used, when teacher turned to the board, to perform behind his back from that position the most elaborate contortions for our amusement and his own eventual lashing. How we suffer for our art! Anyhow we had, carefully restraining our giggles, seen his toes behind his ears and, as he faced us grinning, his narrow buttocks pointed directly at the bald back of teacher's head.

One group of boys at the school were of most varied origins

and had no parents to refer to. Many had been given their name in much the way Oliver Twist received his. In one way they needed no names – they were not individuals, they were orphans. Kept alive by grace, sustained, educated by charity. And those were the days when charity was at its chilliest.

The unhappiest days of my life were at that school. What can it have been to them? How much any good fortune since must smell the sweeter, thinking of those days. How easy to bear the worst of misfortune in comparison! It is the smell of the Home Boys I still recall. They were so sunk in apathy, so beyond resistance or rebellion that they accepted punishment readily. There was probably no fun in it. Lads like Yowds who simply refused to learn, disobeyed every school rule, walked out to the stinking slate den in the yard we called the lavvo without wagging a permission-seeking hand, seemed genuinely surprised at being punished.

They pulled their hands away at the last moment, tried to snatch at the cane, swore and kicked out and still showed surprise at the further whaling this brought. And, when it was over, they put on for the delight of boys and teacher, a most exaggerated pantomime of punishment, reeling as if just off the rack, dancing with pain, holding hands under arm-pits, groaning the while.

There were mission halls where you sang hymns for your supper, but most of the administration of alms-giving was secular, cold, almost clinical, impersonal, truly disinterested. There were police clothes. The working class, at any rate in those days, and with much justification, hated the police, dreaded police-stations. But if a boy had no clothes it was a policeman you had to ask for them, it was from a police-station you must collect them. The corduroy breeches and clogs and jersey were very distinctive garments, so that seeing someone wearing them you knew where he had been given them. Just as if you saw a woman carrying a *six pound* loaf you knew she was on the 'Parish' (the old name for the Poor Law, Public Assistance, Social Security lives to this day). In case this improvident woman, thinking a good plate of scouse might do the lad more good even than corduroy kecks, tried to pawn the clothes, they were specially marked in addition to warn the pawnbroker that this was public property and must not be taken in pawn.

There was the Dinner House. School dinners were, of course, decades away. Yet some boys, where absolute need could be proved beyond doubt, went at midday to a gloomy old building where they were grudgingly handed a bowl of cheap, substantial and temporarily satisfying, stew. For this they were released from class

44

a few minutes before us. So the command rang out, 'Dinner House Boys', and out they tramped. We said our prayers and doubtless expressed thanks to the Creator for seeing that our dinner of herbs would be served with such semblance of love.

A few years ago a Labour candidate for Lancashire County Council was, surprisingly at that time, elected. When called on to give the vote of thanks to the returning officer he turned and waved to his delighted supporters, made a vulgar gesture to his opponents and his followers and, grinning broadly, confined himself to a few words: 'No bad, eh, for a dinner 'ouse lad!'

Hardly the right form, but one can see how he felt. A few days later he was on the board of governors for Merchant Taylors.

Backward children, including spastics and others, quite intelligent, but physically handicapped went to special schools which we, without malice, called soft schools. ('Soft lad your mother has' was one of our derisory shouts.) But for minor disabilities there were special classes. Stammering, for instance. 'Where's X?', a teacher would ask. 'Please, sir', he would be told, 'it's his day for the stuttering class.' I often thought of exaggerating my slight stammer (since self-cured), but on the whole one never wanted to be special.

*   *   *

Short, broad, with a dark piratical look, formally dressed, K looked strong enough. The cane was never far from his hand. I think he was as good a teacher as you'd get in such a school in those days. I would say much more capable than the average in similar schools today. Most of the teachers at the school were, all things considered, pretty good teachers. It was unfortunate that for lack, one can only believe, of someone better he was as well as a class-master, the senior boys' teacher of singing.

Perhaps all the teachers did not like beating us so much, perhaps at other schools there was less beating. Memory could exaggerate, but though I liked learning and acquired a fair amount between the ages of seven and eleven, before a miraculous release, it seemed, in the senior school, I was getting at least a hiding a day, often with no knowledge whatever of why I was being punished.

They tell me some of the alleged aphrodisiacs work, but only in the mind-controlled way placebos do. I want to tell any schoolboys that if the cane is still used, resin is as big a myth as oysters. It isn't easy to get. But if you could get a slice of resin you had the

infallible way, it was once believed, for breaking Teacher's cane.

If your dad worked at the Boxing Stadium you might get a bit. We ex-boxers recall the smell of it put on the floor to prevent slipping. (So it caused the cane to slip? It broke it, see? I see, said the blind man.)

Dockers' sons could also get a bit. The bronzy shiny substance used to sharpen billiard cues doubtless played a bigger part in British industry; on some parts of the docks it was possible to pick up slivers. Of course at Liverpool docks it was dangerous to pick up anything. A man once had three months for picking up a rotten apple: by law all property lying round the docks, whoever brought it in or should have taken it off, belonged to the Mersey Docks and Harbour Board and it was by them you were charged for picking up unconsidered trifles.

I could get resin by going down to the Liverpool Exchange in the evening with my cousin Denis Dunne. His widow mother cleaned a block of offices. There were four floors. There were no lifts. She had to lay fires for lighting in each office. Denis (who had a morning newspaper round) and I, who had a colossal homework schedule every evening, went down to help her carry up the coal from a cellar to the top of the building.

In one of the offices to which we carried coals, samples of different types of resins were laid out on window sills. Denis and I could purloin pieces without any difficulty – while his mother was pinching bits of soap, a piece of coal, lumps of sugar (I also got some sheets of paper, but there wasn't much left loose, and carbon paper – 'tracing paper' – which all kids lusted for, as we were great ones for copying pictures from comics). Denis, who collected toy soldiers and was a very useful lad at making forts, could pick up the manager's empty cigar boxes (Romeo and Julietta) which I used for my hopeless attempts to make a one-string fiddle in three easy lessons. We, of course, also nicked the odd cigar stump.

Denis and I made a copper or two, a few cigarette cards and the like, out of resin as well as the cigar-stumps, and were, like a bookie's runner, sold on the thing itself. But as a way of avoiding sweet little scorings across the palm of the hands and frustrating Teacher – it just doesn't work. The cane can slip. That only means he'll beat you under the hand to knock it up or get you on the wrist. I never really solved the bimomial theorem. But I do know something about the cane.

Every morning after I had served my Mass, before running home to breakfast, I would go round to Our Lady's chapel and pelt her blue-cream statue with prayers that for this day only I would not get belted.

Teachers could find so many reasons (or shall I say excuses) for giving you the cane. There was the Monday morning assembly of defaulters who had missed Mass on Sunday. Whish, whack, whish. A boy who had been up at six in the morning to deliver newspapers or milk or out all the evening selling chopped wood (chips) yawned at three in the afternoon and was walloped for not paying attention. I could not sing. Neither could K. But I could get walloped for a wrong note. I'd no voice but I could hear and, for all the flourish with which K abstracted a tuning fork from the fob pocket of his snuff-stained waistcoat, I knew he didn't know B Flat from a bull's foot.

I was an incurable blot maker. It was partly through nervousness, partly through being left-handed but, try as I might, I could not avoid making blots. The nibs on the pens supplied in school, often used by the rougher elements to torture respectable types like me or as darts when teacher was absent, did not help; nor the watery ink made of powder. But sometimes I would really try, holding the ruler firmly in the centre with one hand while drawing the line neatly with the other; at the final moment the ruler would slip. I assert that I tried hard to do all my school work well including arithmetic which I never really grasped. But even when the work was otherwise satisfactory – as most of the teachers, from the beginning, found my English, even K – my blots let me down. To this day I cannot draw a line properly – the ruler always slips. I think the man who invented ballpoint pens should be canonised.

There was a school medical service in my day but in all my years at school I was never medically examined. (This goes for the grammar school too where, at puberty, tales were told of glass hammers and the order to cough. But somehow they missed me.) I have been bronchial all my life, an affliction which nearly had my entry to the Jesuit Order blocked. I know now that I had slight astigmatism – a hindrance to activities calling for precision. In the Home Guard I could always hit the other fellow's target. I can miss the wastepaper basket four yards from this desk nine times out of ten, however I try not to. I was from birth left-handed. I must thank the nuns in Ireland, who rapped my knuckles till I used the right, for making me ambidextrous.

I accept these days with complacency the lack of co-ordination between hand and eye, my deficiency of manual dexterity. So do my relations and friends. As did my colleagues in the Customs in my youth. The melting of wax for a Crown seal, the use of a jemmy, the use of a Board of Trade tape-measure for cargo . . . my cack-handedness in all these activities and many more is accepted. In fact it brings me the sort of special respect the village idiot gets in some Latin countries.

But I never made anything. I wrote poems and things of course but I mean *make*. Poor Dad, as unhandy except with a butcher's tools as myself, once bought me a little carpenter's set and another time Meccano Number One. What more had Edison or the Wright Brothers to start with? They were in no danger from me.

But Dad had faith – my mother didn't. My mother only wanted my hands to be used for handling the Host and giving a blessing *in nomine patri et filio et spiritu tuo*. She just wanted me to keep at the Books. 'What do you want a fretsaw for? You haven't finished the *Lives of the Saints* yet. Musha will you not be moidering me to make paste for you, I've better to do wit me flour, you can't ate cardboard trains like pancakes, your father'd kill you if he saw you using his razor the like of that. Away up to the sacristy and get a bottle of holy water, take the big bottle in the panthry.'

Dad was quite annoyed when Mr D, four doors up, showed him a cardboard van with a cardboard horse in the shafts and a cardboard man holding the reins and the words Good Shepherd Laundry on the side. It was a model of the van Mr D drove in which sometimes he gave his son Jimmy and me a ride. Jimmy, after my two cousins, was the first lad I'd chummed up with in Liverpool. A pale little fellow, slightly older than me but in the same class, who wore a sailor suit and had a fringe of hair such as Mo in The Three Stooges had in later years and after him, the Beatles. He was very handy, though otherwise as thick as two short planks. (He was also a very good violinist, took professional engagements in later years but I've never seen him since those days.) He had made the model van.

'It's (Mr D averred) a exact repplerkah, even down to the least little thread in the horse's tackling, all in perportion. Course the man's not like me but the horse, the van, every –'

Dad (shooting me an ambiguous glance): 'It musta took him a fortnight!'

Mr D: 'Not a tall, not a tall. Just a couple or three hours one evening.'

Dad: 'Away in now, Frank, and write another grand composition like that one Mr Blakeley read to all the school.'

Jimmy's father went so far as to buy him the *Rainbow* comic, which was dearer than others like my *Lot o' Fun* – and posher. This paper went in for cut-outs which involved some pretty nimble and precise work with the scissors, cutting along a dotted line here, turning at precisely right angles and cutting along there, then a circular piece, turn flap A into flap B and there you are, you had a model of the *Flying Scotsman* or the *Mauretania*. Or Jimmy had. I had a clew on the ear and an order to clear up all the mess and let me lay the table for your, God help his head, poor man, to think you'd be annything but kithogue all your bound days. (*Kithogue*, lefthanded, clumsy, Gaelic, cp *gauche, sinister, gammy*).

For all most of the instructions meant to me it might be a pattern for a knitted manhole-cover. I got the first part all right. You were told to gum the whole thing on to thin cardboard. All right, get some thin cardboard. Getting anything in our house was never easy. It was all right for the Editor of the *Rainbow*. He probably just opened a drawer and there was piles of thin cardboard and his mother didn't jump out with a yell as soon as she heard the drawer open. 'What are you rooting at now?'

The least curious of men, as a kid I was always nosing into cupboards and drawers, opening tins, going down pockets, all activities summed up by my mother in one word – rooting. But she couldn't distinguish. Rooting was done when she was out of the house, though later she invariably detected it, which, at the time, I thought uncanny (at a very early stage I really did believe a little birdie, a feathered clat-tale, had told her. It was, of course, simply that I put things back left-handed. By the same token I can always tell when right-handed people touch my things). To find a pin, a pen, a piece of string (to replace a shoe lace whose loss I daren't report), any trifling domestic object which in many households would have its own precise place, meant a major hunt which decidedly observed superficially resembled rooting. One must always judge by the motive. I was looking, *looking*, for some particular object, not following a young person's instinctive interest in all objects which, admittedly, could be termed rooting.

If I did find the thin cardboard it was probably in the kitchen cupboard where she kept my dad's blue aprons and red spotted handkerchiefs, the bits of hair she added to her own on gala occasions, under some spring onions and a cobbler's last. While she was talking over the back wall to Mrs Walsh I had slyly to withdraw her scissors from the private drawer where she kept her rosary, prayer book, field postcards from Dick, insurance books, a sovereign purse (unused), boot protectors, seidlitz powders, Dick's allotment book ('the ring book' – from the circular frank made in the post office when the seven shillings was paid) and Frank in his velvet communion suit with the ducky lace collar.

Then to my bedroom to find the remainder of the flour-paste she had made for me a few days before when I was sticking pictures in my scrapbook (an activity she somehow approved of, perhaps because it had something to do with a book – it was Dad who was the danger here when he suddenly yelled out when he found Bombardier Billy Wells had been clipped out of his *Mirror of Life* and *Boxing World* before he read the fiddling paper). I had an old, almost hairless, blacklead-brush. And now my troubles would begin.

I could only operate when she wasn't there. I had the gum out of sight down by my chair and in a convenient position a large opened atlas to put over the scissors and the rest if she suddenly appeared. That sort of thing was unlikely to lead to a neat model of Canterbury Cathedral but, undaunted, I spread the paste on to the cut-out thinly and evenly. But try as I might – my tongue sticking right out as on all such tricky occasions – to stop applying it just short of the edge, so that when it spread slightly on application to the thin cardboard it would stop precisely at the edge (oh, I knew the technique of the thing right enough from observing Jimmy do the job correctly – and without maternal disapproval), it would still remain uneven under the cut-out so that parts stood up like hillocks, and it always flowed over the edge in a black phlegm stream running on to the protective *Meat Trades Journal* underneath (more wrath from Dad). And if I had to jump up to answer a knock on the front door I would kick over the glue in its old moustache-cup, ram my cap on my head and leave home as I did at least once a week, returning about an hour after when I felt hungry and mother cooled off. Knocks on our front door were constant throughout the days – fellows selling salt, coal bricks, knife-grinders, a neighbour borrowing a cup of sugar, beggars – we had about a dozen of these a week and they all received something if it was only a slice of jammed bread.

*   *   *

The Jesuits had carpentry on the syllabus and we occasionally went to an unused room right at the top of the school to receive some half-hearted instructions from a disillusioned uncertificated lay master who did other odd jobs of teaching in the school and on prize night was, in his civvies in the gallery, keeping us in order while in the main hall among gushing parents the other lay teachers swayed round in academic gowns of most varied furs. Fr. Melling, our head, was in no way interested in our learning carpentry. We did not regard ourselves as future manual workers. We young gentlemen spent much of our time in that class throwing chunks of wood from the window at people passing along the street.

Those were days when I was always chronically short of paper to write on. I could not always raise the penny to buy a 12-page exercise book or, when I had a penny, was tempted to find some other use for it. Two of my sources were the fly leaves of books and the exercise books given us in the schools. There were no fly leaves left in any of the books in my home nor in those accessible to me at school. To tear a page out of an exercise book was a folly the teacher could always spot. But, by levering up the pins holding the pages together in the centre, a feat even within my capacity, it was possible to remove two attached sheets, press the pins back and, in the ordinary way, the removal would not be spotted.

But in our absence at woodwork K, instead of lounging in the teachers' common-room, had been through our desks and examined the exercise books closely. So, of course, I was detected. When I went in the classroom next day I saw K's sour look and shivered. It was worse than the day he overheard Sammy Yowds mimicking the strange lisp he had when singing so that 'Home brewed brown bread and a cottage well-thatched with straw', a pastoral of which I recall no more than those words, became 'Home bwewed bwown bwead and a cottage well thashed with stwaw', reminding us of Arthur Augustus Darcy of St Jim's in the *Gem*. As soon as prayers were over and a few questions answered from the Catechism, K, obviously in a hurry, twirled the cane in the air and dragged me from my seat in front of the class and – well it can only be said, in the words of an old city council friend, he went bismarck. Some of the hard skins among the lads even yelled out protests. He threw me out into the passage. I could hardly walk home.

In those days, in that area, nobody told Dad anything. Had I told my dad he, who hated bullying, would have done the same to K. If I told my mother, I knew she would go to the school, the head would send for K and her Irish temper would lead to a scene observed by the boys from the door of their classroom in which she would appear ridiculous. I did not think she would punch K up and down the passage as Sammy Yowds's mother did while the gleeful and grubby Sammy kept yelling 'Go on, ma, 'it him one for me, ma.'

I had to tell her something to explain my state and to be kept at home for at least the afternoon beyond the reach of that madman.

*   *   *

I don't know whether Liverpool was worse than other big cities for bullying, but its history would have made it unlikely that there were many gentle souls among the working-class male population. Dockers were treated like dogs, which bred a deep resentment still felt today by their prosperous grandsons. All they had to sell was their muscle. Resentment found its external expression in mad lashing round. Every Sunday morning men, stripped to the buff, had fights on the Lock Fields by the canal, to bloody finishes. (From the custom maybe comes the phrase 'have down the banks', for 'have a fight'.)

There were plenty of boys at our school whose fathers had better jobs than the docks or going to sea (a brutish existence even in my time, especially in the firemen's foc'sle – the hardest working men in the world, Liverpool firemen, were little more than animals while coal-burning ships still existed). But there were many whose fathers knew no law but the fist, the head, the boot. Like father like son.

A number of boys had persecuted me in my first years at school and I was a sitting duck because when I was about seven or eight I never suspected perfidy. I still had a thick Kerry accent which made the boys laugh, and my attire seemed to them a little bizarre. I talked my mother out of sending me to school wearing a round hat such as Chico Marx later affected and I hid the button-up tweed knickerbockers in the Black Hole where my mother never ventured. But she rather favoured Eton collars, to be worn on top of a gansey (jersey) knitted by Aunt Nelly, who always left an excessive amount 'for growth' so that I looked a bit like the Michelin man. I put a stop to the panama hat for Sundays; it was attached to the lapel of my velvet Communion jacket, which mercifully, since Aunt Nelly had had no hand in its creation, I quickly outgrew. Getting into my bed one night and reaching for the holy-water font before putting my candle out, I knocked the candle on the hat and had quite failed to save it by the time my mother, hearing a yell, reached the room.

By the time I was 10 and due for the senior school (the big boys), I trusted nobody, my garb and speech conformed and I had become quite useful with my natural straight left after much practice with my father.

One boy, however, had me scared. He had a very large head with close cropped red hair and a large ever-open drooling mouth. Like many half-wits he had great strength. He often came upon me suddenly and would twist my arm or give me a dry shave – vigorously rub his knuckles up and down my scalp – or kick me with a large hat pin shoved through the toecap of his boot. For a short cut up to my home from the woodwork school I had gone through some filthy back cracks beyond Soho Street and our church. This was Indian territory for the better type of lads round our way. Not a pane of glass was in the windows, behind the cardboard in a window frame one saw toothless hags with mad eyes. Herds of dogs fought round offal thrown in the gutters, babies in wooden boxes were wrapped in bundles of sacking and tattered rags, with red bugs crawling round them, men lurched round scowling, their hands plunged into broad leather belts with large black buckles.

In one foul corner among old mattresses, bad oranges, human excrement and a dead cat I came on the big-headed boy. He pushed me on to the ground face down and sat on my head, rhythmically thumping me on the small of my back. Then he turned me round and placed the stinking seat of his breeches on my face. How long this went on for, five minutes or an hour (it seemed hours) with nobody interfering, I don't know. He spoke only when I was standing again, succeeding in keeping back the tears, ready to run. He could not articulate words properly but I gathered that he would cut my throat if I clatted and he flashed the pen-knife he had stolen from me last time. (A sad loss because it was *magnetised*. A pen-knife was magnetised by placing the blade at an opening in one of the street standards which carried the electricity for the tramcars, after which the blade really would pick up pins and such small metal objects, and boys without such a penknife were sick with envy.)

You can't think properly when you are aching all over. I didn't want my mother to make a show of herself and I knew that, anyhow, K and the others (we regarded all masters even the most decent as united against us) would wallop me again.

So I told her raggedly about Big Head, but said I didn't know his name, where he lived, what school he went to. I knew all three.

'I'll go and see Mr Blakeley tomorrow with you.' She just

wanted to make it clear why I'd been kept home in the afternoon. She realised it couidn't be one of his boys. I'm pretty sure he realised it was Arthur Meadows of Rokeby Street, in K's class No. 71. He gave me another day off.

*   *   *

When I came back next day I found that the class was being taught by a demobilised soldier we called Cunny. He spent all morning telling us about life in the last weeks of Germany's defeat and the afternoon in the yard teaching us football. K, not at all the man to go sick, had not turned up. He was indeed to be off many weeks, by which time I was going ahead for my 'college' education.

The visit of my mother the day before was known of course. She was a powerful woman in our parish. It was assumed she had reported K, especially as she had left with the rector, the school manager, 'arging' to him with energy. (She always debated with energy and, on this occasion, was doubtless arguing about whether another two shillings should be spent on the whist drive prizes.) It was, however, assumed that the blessed absence of K was due to her visit.

I had no more trouble with Big Head. In fact he gave me back my magnetised penknife. Of course I did not want such childish things in the coll. But I suppose he played his part in my primary education in Liverpool. He was killed in 1942, coming back from a pub in Islington, when a bomb blast sent a pane of glass across his neck and took his head off.

Lick the plate

I fully contend to do so.

You aren't listening to what I'm gunna tell yer.

He's a great fisherman, a thrue disciple uv Isaac Newton.

He only thinks he's ill – he's a hypodermic.

The building was raised to the gutter. (In letter).

Dis job's killing me, but it's constant.

Sly Bacon they call him, 'cos his real name's Cunningham.

She must starve the poor fella; he looks proper emancipated.

The whole place was permanganated wid the smell of fish.

Our team was illuminated in the last round. (Could be).

They had twenty years of martial bliss.

The regiment was manuring on Salisbury Plain.

A Dicky Sam Mayor

The first Mayor of Liverpool, in 1351, was William FitzAdam. John Shaw held office in 1794 and 1800. When many of the citizens were hungry he seized a cargo of fish which was brought into the 'Pool and gave it to them.

He also refused the allowance of 100 guineas, a goodly sum when beer was a penny a quart and coal 24lb. for a penny. He lived very frugally and gave no formal banquets. Once he asked a magistrate how many shirts he wore and receiving an answer said: 'What a dirty hide you must have. I can make a shirt last a fortnight.'

He is described as being slovenly and unpolished but he was 'an impartial, active and excellent chief magistrate'. It seems so long he was good he let who would be clever. When it was suggested that more brains were needed among the aldermen he asked: 'What is the use of so many clever fellows? There are Dash and Dot and me already!'

Who called the Mayor a - - ?

1663, Port Moot Court. Wee present Robert Bicksteth for a great and heynous abuse and injurye done to the wor'pp[ll] Mr Peter Lurtin Maior of this Corporacion since he was elected Maior upon the xviii[th] day of October instant, to witt, that hee, meaning the said Mr Maior was a thiefe and rogue & had robbed a house in Formbie . . .

(Bicksteth was fined five pounds, though he was a poor man, but he recanted. However, Moore in his *Rentals* says of Lurten: 'He is a very knave and hath deceived me twice. I charge you never trust him . . .')

1667 Oct 28th. At a Port Moot Wee present Mr Edward Moore of Banckhall for much lyinge against his croft in Dale Street vj[d].

1671 Octr 23rd. Order Edward Moore shall cause water course to bee made to carry the water from Castle Street . . . or if not done shall forfeit xx[d].

1672 Octr 28th. Edward Moore for dung lyeing in the street Item Edward Moore for not paying his leys.

1673 Octr 27th. Wee present Edward Moore Esq for rubbish lyeing in Phenix St.

1674 Octr 26th. Wee order Edward Moore Esq for much lyeing at Tithe Barn Street.

1675 Feby 7th. Ordered Edward Moore, Knight, doe for his street between etc. upon penalty of xi[s].

1677 Aug 13th. Wee p'sent Sr Edward Moore for increaching on the town's waste . . .

From Moore's *Rentals:* 'Never trust them (the burgesses) for there is no such thing as truth or honesty in such mercenary fellows . . .' It was an old game.

1685. Att a Port Moot January 11th. Wee p'sent John Lurting for abusing Thomas Tarleton Maior by calling him a cheating rogue. Item of George Prescott for abuseing Mr Maior the 13th day of June last . . . useinge very opprobious and base speeches sayinge a f--t for Mr Maior the Aldermen and Bailifes and all the towne.

1624 Octr 25th. *At a Port Moot.* Wee present Richard Rose now Maior for keepynge his swine unringed.

Wee present Mr Mannering for abusing Mr Maior.

1624 June 27th. Wee present John Mainwarring for abuse upon Thomas Seftan.

Item for calleing Ballive Wood rogue . . . Item for abuseing the fast saying . . . hee wold keepe none, nor cared bot a f--t for it wth dyvrs other revyling speeches and especially against the minister.

PART THREE Liverpool Packet

PART THREE

Liverpool Packet

Folks

What has anything to do with folk singing? What has folk-singing to do with anything? Especially in a book about Liverpool? Unless you realise that we are all minstrel boys, or girls, in the 'Pool you cannot understand us. And if you say you don't want to understand us I have to take me coat off to you. To the world the Beatles may have seemed a unique phenomenon. Not to us. It's the Irish and the Welsh in us. We are all singers in Liverpool. Even if we can't sing.

For folk singers, tone deafness can be an advantage, or at least it's no great hindrance. Some of them sing well. Florrie Brennan for instance, though thinly like so many Irish singers, male and female, including the great McCormack. Glyn Hughes has a trained voice and comes from a long family of singers and musicians. Bill Moore has a good voice but he strains a bit, and folk songs don't need that – no top notes are needed; a monotone is best.

Stan Kelly and Pete McGovern are great to listen to, especially when Stan uses the brogue, though where the hell he got it from Lord knows. His old dad, the plumber, was as Scouse as Scotty Road's Pete Mac. Neither are McCormacks.

Much is in the attitude of the folk singer. Casual and easy-going (as, I now recall, were Kerry Jim and Creeper Stinks). Those two fellows are as relaxed, when they sing, as two rice puddings. I know that easy writing, as Sheridan said, is darned hard reading, but Sheridan like myself must recall occasions when good results come from just letting the pen run away with itself like on a ouija board. Stan and Pete let their voices run away with themselves. But there must be some art, artfully concealed, to it. As there was, I certainly know, in Michael Holliday's seemingly artless singing.

My Judy's down the Mersey

(Words, Frank Shaw, Music, George Dickinson)

> Me judy's down the Mersey,
> > With a fella that just met her,
> I'm sitting at the Landing Stage, trying to forget her,
> > So it's Oh, what the hell,
> There's other girls about
> > And if I cannot find one . . .,
> I can always do without . . .
> > But it's Oh, what the hell,
> As I sit here by the river,
> > If only she comes back to me,
> I'll kiss her and forgive her.

Resign, resign

(The Drunken Liverpool Alderman)

> Hear the sad tale of my cousin,
> Alderman Perceval Punk,
> Who went to the Lord Mayor's banquet,
> Absurdly, uproariously, send-her-victoriously,
> Rather rude-chorusly, very ingloriously,
> Pickled, paralytic – well, drunk.
>
> He loudly abused the headwaiter
> For removing his seaboots and rattle
> And surveying the evening-dressed ladies
> He loudly described them as cattle.
>
> He patted the Mayoress's dimples,
> Emitting the most bull-like roars,

Said her face was like Katherin Bergman's
And her figure far better than Dors.

He sat down by Pastor Longbottom
And whispered lewd jests in his ear,
And waving his hand to the Town Clerk,
Shouted, 'Hurry up, whack, with the beer!'

He gave the Archbish his goloshes,
Saying, 'As a man sows he shall reap',
And bestowing a kiss on the Borough Surveyor,
Went down in the cellar to sleep.

It's disgraceful to think of a J P
An O B E too – almost Bart.
Riding home from a Mayoral function
On top of a coal-vendor's cart.

So they've passed by unanimous verdict
And sent a unanimous note,
At his district committee to tell him,
Four Exes could lose them the vote.

A strong note was sent to him also
From the Bootle Young Whatsits Brigade,
Demanding he hand in his baton
Or keep sober when on parade.

They recall a more shocking occasion
When his conduct did much to annoy
For he consorted with his inferiors
Playing Toss with the new butcher's boy.

And yet with that stain on his 'scutcheon
And even worse things they won't tell,
When called on for his explanation
He told them to all go to hell . . .

So learn from him, all ye young zealots,
If you're anxious to be a success:
Get as drunk as a lord in your own place,
But in public – well, curb your excess.

Oh, come back Maggie May!*

Perhaps I sound a fool, I'd a' thought that Liverpool
Was the right place to produce dat 'Maggie May',
It was there she shed her glory
In that ancient marine story
We traditionally sing of to this day.
Oh, Maggie, Maggie May, They have taken you away,
Dis is something that we find 'ard to forgive,
For they've shipped our dear old gal,
Up the Manchester Canal,
And in Coronation Street she'll have to live.
Oh, Maggie, Maggie May, They are leading you astray
Our emotions are almost beyond control,
It is sad our famous filly
Should parade down Piccadilly
When down Lime Street was her regular patrol.
Will they now shift Canning Place
To Belle Vue? It's a disgrace,
That our best known local lady's been shanghai'd,
And that Scouseport's own son Owen
Her romantic life is showin'
Many miles from where she was the sailors' pride.
Oh, come back, Maggie May, Say tarrah and run away
Back to Park Street and the bevvy will flow free;
Every whacker must feel moody
When the seafront's best-known judy
Is an exile and so far off from the sea.

*A variation of this song is given on page 186.

The Sis Song

'You whipped me panties off the line, Sis –'
'Well, I diden think you'd cur,'
'And them nylons, aren't they mine, Sis –?'
'Well, I 'adn't gorra pur.'

'And yer going to a dance, like,
Do yer think yer playing fur?'
'Well, I thought I'd take a chance, like,'
(Very roguishly) 'All the fellas will be thur.'

66

'And what d'you think I'll do, like,
When you're at this flash affur?'
'Well a fella in a car, Mike – an' I wish you wouldn't stur –'
'So you pinched me fella too, like,
You're a queer 'eel, I declare –'

'No I'm only kidding, Maggie,
And I wish you would prepur –
For he's calling for *you*, Maggie,
It's your birthday, Sis, you know,
And he's fallen for you, Maggie.
And I'm going to let him go.'

'I've a better lad called Lance, Sis,
Coming here with me to pur –
And *you're* going to the dance, Sis,
HERE'S SOME BRAND-NEW UNDERWUR.'

The Ballad of Norris Green

(After ta, to Paddy Roberts, The Ballad of Bethnal Green)

I tell the tale of a Scouser male and a judy of sweet sixteen,
She wasn't dumb an' she lived wid her mum
In a Corpy in Norris Green;
She worked in a shop for a rich old Wop,
Wid her ould fella on the dole,
An' her one delight was, on Saturday night,
To go for a rock-an'-roll.

Chorus: Wid a rid fall lal, tiddy fal lal

Then one fine day in the month uv May,
   She found her big romance,
He was dark an' sleek an' he lived in Speke
An' he wore them narra pants. She said, 'My dear,
It will be the gear, Wid you through the years to come' –
For she loved the gay and nonchalant way,
   He flipped his chewin'-gum.

Chorus: Wid a rid fall lal, tiddy fal lal

67

It started well because he fell for all uv her girlish charms,
Until the day, In 'Ackins's 'Ey, he copped her in someone's arms;
He said, 'Look here, you know me dear, yer goin' a bit too far',
An' he went quite white an' sloshed her right
    In the middle uv a cha-cha-cha

Chorus: Wid a rid fall lal, tiddy fal lal

He was up las' week, before the beak, who said 'Dis will not do,
I've 'ad anough of dis sort a stuff, I must punish the likes a you',
An' she was peeved when he received a longish term in clink
So she married the Wop, now she owns the shop,
    An' 'er panties are made a mink.

I was a Gunmoll for the Peanut Gang

But I haven't always been
I never even clocked a cop till I was seventeen.
I started in a convent and now I often muses,
When doing a little lifting up at Owens's or Hughes's
That instead of hanging round for hours outside Walton Gaol
I might have been a better girl and even . . . Took the Veil
Since then I've took a lot of things but one thing, this is straight,
I've never took no nonsense from a fellow, boss or mate.
I never seen me father, me mam seen him the once,
She never got his name that time but thinks that on his bonce
He must have had fur hur like mine (No frizz!)
    But can't be sure of dat
She never went with fellas that didn't wear a 'at.

Me brother works in Lime Street, floggin' ciggies what he stole,
One sister's on the lorries, the other's on the dole;
Me Auntie lives in Sefton Park, she's gorra lovely flat . . .
The Uncle's on the council . . . but we never mention dat!
(Come from a good fam'ly, y'know,
    me grandfather kept two boozers, me Mam and me Ant)
The first time I was naughty it was wit' a Argentine
He took me for a choppy sue . . . these fellas they're not mean,
He wanted me to rhumba, in my shimmy, I sais 'OO-ey'
An' whipped his wallet from his pants an' scarpered up the cooey,
Since then I've met some fellas, I've even met a Greek.
A Prince from French Nigeria, a Irishman from Speke,

Two Swedes, a Pole, a Geordie, a golfer and a Wog,
   and a Big six-foot Alsatian – *he* was a dirty dog;
A Corporal from Burtonwood but the medals on his chest
Would tickle when he jitterbugged and tear 'oles in me vest.

Reely, in the end, y'know, I feel perhaps it's best
To stick to local fellas, like, though some as you'll have guessed
Won't be round again for years . . . inside or gone to sea . . .
I'm drawing three allotments now . . . Sometimes I'd like to be
Inside meself or in a home . . . The Sailors' Home of course,
There's a lorra trouble for us girls now that there's on the Force
These tarts that look like softies, but each has took a course in judo.
Only yesterday I was steppin' out a Yates's
I seen a barman who I knew refused dhrinks to me mateses,
I clocked him one, a female cop said
   'Don't do that, me lass' ('me dear')
I said 'shurrup' an', honto crise,
   next' thing I'm on me ass (me ear)
I always thought I wassen bad, at scrappin' I'm no duffer,
I don't mine sparrin' wid a man but not a female scuffer;
So if tings get no betterer I'm gunno, strike me silly,
Emmiggerate, tarrah well then, see yer in Piccadilly.

It's a laugh

I give dis feller a lift in the priest's car to the Catedral from
Skelmersdale an I'll go to the closet if he doesn't excuse himself
four times en root. When at last he hops off in Hope Street I says,
'D'you tink dat feller's one a our's, Father?'
   'No, me son,' he says. 'No', he says, 'I tink he's a Urinatarian
or a Episscopalian!'

When I was married I was virgo impetigo.

I was wearing a brazier too tight for me.

He burnt his hand on a hot girdle.

He took me out on the miranda.

I was absolutely prostituted with the heat.

He took advantage of me in the virginity of the barracks.

He was very ill. He had to have erections regularly.

He was sitting there having a tater-tater.

Now I don't want no more kids. He'll have to use a prerogative.

D'you gerrit?

It's the Irish in us. We're full of bulls, orally incontinent. We love words and we don't always pause to think what they mean. The resultant Irish bull suffering from foot-in-mouth disease, these oral near-misses, often create a wild new meaning of their own. I hear so much in my home town that I called them Mala-pudlianisms, and another writer about and performer in Scouse, Peter Moloney, later called them Merseypropisms. Between the two names you'll know what is meant:

He was on the horns of a diploma; She was suffering with Murgatroyd Arthritis; You felt a big soft ting on yer honeymoon; We came here of our own violation; They paid me a great condiment.

Knocking round Liverpool for 40 years, mostly at the docks, I've kept my ears open. I became learned in docksology and gained my M.Sc. (Master of Scouse). I didn't keep a notebook open or I'd have had my eyes shut. I had to trust to memory or jot a note on a corner of toilet paper and, if suddenly observed, pretend I was making out a betting slip.

I know such expressions can be heard elsewhere – the howler, from schoolboys and others, we have always with us. But I claim that the art of almost hitting a phrase, sometimes over-used to point of wearing out, and staggering on to a happier, newer one, is reached *in excelsis* where the dear old Mersey's flowing. Just one or two may have been created by a cunning wag; it isn't difficult. But the best humour is unconscious and most of the sayings herein heard by my own ears – or those of reliable friends – were spontaneous and naturally slipped off the tongue with no intention to amuse.

In fact I have had to hear them with the straightest of faces or it might have been made crooked.

Had a shockin crossin on the ferry to Birkenead, I wus glad to get me feet on terra cotta.

He's been living on her immortal earnings.

I useter be left-anded but now I'm ambiguous.

She bought it cheap from a lady in seduced circumstances.

He went real mad; he ran bismarck.

'Distinguish dem headlights', said the bobby.

He was working like a truncheon.

He's hand in blouse wit dat barmaid.

I went into a brassiere for me supper (could be).

Pleeceman on the docks gate asks him if he's any pornographic literature. He says I haven't even got a pornograph. Laff!

I took the dog to be consecrated so he won't contaminate with other dogs.

She was castin incinerations. I'd a hit her at the slightest prevarication.

I cudden hear a word the priest said. The agnostics was so bad.

The cheeky faggit, I sent her away wid me tongue between her legs.

We still got gas, you know, and I can't find any shops selling indecent mantles.

She had triplets and got the Queen's Pardon.

Me daughter's quite uninhabited.

She hasn't arf got a interferiority complex.

Bring yer back a shillelagh from Dublin, la? You'd never be able to play it.

Merseyry rhyme

Three blind scouse,
   Three blind scouse,
See how it goes;
   Their mam give the three uv dem dat every day,
It all went down the same ould way,
   Was all she could give on a docker's pay*–
Three blind scouse.
(*in 1930)

When oranges were four a penny

Two lists of food prices dating from good King Edward's golden day and culled from two very different sources, both prove you had a good deal for your pound in those days. If you had the pound.

The first is from the bill of fare at the Atheneum, off Church Street, where Disraeli dined and Salisbury supped. It is from a photostat copy kindly given by Liverpool Records Office.

Soups, 5d   Scotch Broth 4d
Sole 8d   Beef Rissoles 7d   Chops and Rice 9d
Irish Stew 10d   Mutton cutlets 10d   Fricassee of Chicken 11d
Savoury and Shrimp Omelettes 8d   Boiled Egg 2d
Rice Pudding (Hot or Cold) with Stewed Fruit 4d
White or Brown Bread and Butter 1d   Lunch Cake 2d
English and French Confectionery 1d & 2d
Tea, Coffee, Chocolate, with Cream and Biscuits 3d
Natural Lemonade, Milk and Soda 3d

I have omitted a number of items in the sweets, confectionery and egg dishes line and think members must have huffed and puffed a bit about *Roast Beef 10d*.

My next exhibit I found at an old people's exhibition organised by the Rev. Murrell at the Domestic Mission in Liverpool's South End. It is what you would get from a Christmas Club, in a shop in that district, for 6d a week for 18 weeks (9s total). A turkey or goose. 1 peck best potatoes. 1 peck swedes. 2lb carrots. 2lb apples. 2lb nuts. 10 oranges. 2 bundles sage. Package of best peas. (A peck, I believe, was 7lb.)

You know, not 50 years ago I could buy for my mother five pounds of potatoes for three-ha'pence, and a cabbage and the essential potherbs for the same to go with two-penn'orth of mutton to get stew such as you could never taste now. I did not think then that I'd ever be emulating those who spoke of the prices 60 or 70 years ago. My orange for going to the shops cost a farthing.

Such quoting of food prices, without reference to wage and salary scales, is I suppose pointless. And is the poorer taste of food a further delusion of old age? No doubt my grandchildren will be recalling the days when you could get a cabbage for two shillings and a good lunch out for ten and six each; 'And now it's five pounds for one vitamin pill alone.' And the vitamin pills won't be half as good as the ones *we* could get *at any chemist* – 'no need of notes from the Health Commissioner in 1971'.

Five pounds of potatoes (three-ha'pence), a ha'porth of pot-herbs (and change out) would be the basis of the dish. Next ingredient was a penn'orth of bits – for the dog.

Whether England is a nation of shopkeepers or not, to me, when I was a lad, Liverpool was a town of shops. Tralee had had some, but none like this. Soon I was going inside them, as well as delighting my eyes at their windows; for, in those days, children did all the shopping. (The Liverpool housewife, grown up, still calls shopping 'doing me messages'.)

Of course I was already going for my father's tobacco (fourpence an ounce) to Johnny All Sorts where the fine Irish snuff, beloved of shawlies, jostled boiled ham, upright gas mantles, shammy leathers and sweets. A ha'penny could get a bag of sweets such as I had not found in Ireland. Toffee in large flat slabs, hammered to the required number of pieces before your eyes. The old lady with the bonnet, the gamp and the Cranford gown advertising Everton toffee was then known as more than a mascot for Everton. Boys solemnly told me, in my first school, that the word 'CONTENTS' in a book meant 'Conny Onny Naughty Tommie Eating Noblett's Toffee Sticks'.

After toffee, for me came American chewing nuts. Was the word the attraction? America was already a sort of Tir Nan Og, as England had been. It still fascinates me. I was soon to see real Americans.

Row on row, steadily marching up Islington and London Road from the Landing Stage, packs low on their spines, stetson-hatted, the doughboys were headed for their camp in Knotty Ash, where, for years after the war, the huts were occupied by houseless Liverpudlians.

Girls who had scarcely seen a young man for years cheered wildly from the upper windows of shops, old folks wept happily seeing in this the ending of the long agony of their own men in the trenches. We kids ran alongside the soldiers yelling, 'Any cents, Sam?'; more mercenary than, though just as cheeky as, the youngsters of this last war with 'Any gum, chum?'

Chewing gum was a novelty frowned on by grown-ups. No doubt an adult inspired the rhyme children chanted:

Chewing gum, chewing gum, made of wax,
Has brought me to my grave at last.

It was the new jingle, the fresh catchword, which caught my ear instantly, and they have stayed there ever since, when the book read yesterday or the TV play seen this evening have already faded. 'Any broken biscuits, mister? – Well, mend 'em!' 'Any empty boxes? – Well, fill thum!' Shopkeepers existed to be annoyed. You smacked the sides of bacon hanging outside grocers, tipped over bins, opened the doors to make the bells ring before scarpering down a jigger, over the dead cats and discarded mattresses.

As we roamed the streets on errands or otherwise we heard echoes of the war and saw plenty of men in the blue uniform of the wounded. Dardanelles, Hill Sixty, the ould Kaiser, 'Kitchener isn't really drowned'. Songs more evocative than *Tipperary* are *Paddy McGinty's Goat*, with a reference to submarines and *Boys in Khaki, Boys in Blue*. Who now remembers: 'Twas the night of the charge and the Lancasheers, Stood with faces, stern and grim', finishing with the Colonel announcing, 'Ee, lads, I was born i' Lancasheer, So remember one and all', etc.?

Teachers told us the names of our great leaders, some since not glowing so brightly, of VCs like Michael O'Leary and Jackie Cornwell, and taught us the anthems of the Allies, including Russia's noble *God the All Terrible*. If one undertook the long trip to bungalow-town, Moreton, one might find German prisoners exercising on the sands in patched grey uniforms. There was a blackout, searchlights sliced the night sky, there was a rumour a Zeppelin had almost reached Liverpool; every evening the *Echo* had page on page of casualties.

But our lives were most affected by the growing shortage of foodstuffs and, before rationing came, the hunt from shop to shop for sugar, butter, spuds; the last being most elusive of all. We spent hours in queues. I fainted in one eventually – one of the first victims of the 'flu epidemic which was to kill thousands.

All else I recall of those times is seeing Uncle Don, formerly of the Eighth Irish, clad as a 'khaki docker' and a slogan, now deprived of meaning, 'John Hughes won't save you!' (John Hughes, it was alleged, could get his Irish immigrant shop assistants exempt from military service.) The joyous Armistice Day is even misted over, though there was something about the Kaiser being burnt in effigy in the grounds of Crosse's Menagerie at Otterspool. Books already meant more to me than tin soldiers and cardboard forts. Long live Kensington Free Library!

*　　　*　　　*

I still had to do the shopping. Half a quarter of rhody (streaky) bacon, a penny cup of red jam, a large twopenny loaf which – if the baker knew his business – he topped with a 'jockey' of cake or biscuit for the young shopper. When mother made her own bread in a scoured panmug, you took the dough in a clean pillow-slip (which, anyhow, had probably started life as a flour-bag) to the bakehouse – what a marvellous smell! – and you must not forget the metal 'tally' in receipt.

A lad would no more patronise a baker who forgot the jockey than a barber who did not give away a 'blacklead'. A cobbler I loved to visit displayed gory drawings from the *Police Gazette*. The fish shop gave us wood for 'bonnies', as Guy Fawkes Day approached. Greengrocers lured us with bargains in 'fades' (damaged fruit) and might even give one a sound apple or pome-granate. (I preferred raw carrots myself.) Best buy in the green-grocers were the sweet beans called locusts. The hard cases among the boys went to the docks and got this or brown sugar by nimbly vaulting over the backs of lorries, unless a rival lad wickedly shouted to the carter 'whip behind!'

On the whole, there was little crime and 'Basil' and other bobbies of the time ('Basil' means fat – from 'barrel'?) had a short effective way with the delinquents. A few pebbles in a white glove was better than an appearance before the magistrates. How mothers feared a raid on the ubiquitous gambling schools! A 'good rent book' might have to be borrowed for bail. The 'hurry up van' might drive offenders away. A summons 'blue paper wid a duck on ut', might even result . . . Just part of the daily tragedy of the working-class woman, which she somehow lightened with laughter. 'Cheer up, lad', one shawlie said to a glum tram conduc-tor, 'you'll be a man before yer mother!'

Whackerishi's whizzdom

It's a long lane widout a lump of dog muck in it.

There's never one door closes but two shut.

People who live in glass houses should undress in the dark.

The existence of the good old days depends solely on a bad old memory.

Girls run in our family but not very fast.

When your woman gets to forty – change her for two twenties.

'Ah', asks the Wise One, 'what has four wheels and flies?'
'A Liverpool corporation muck-cart.'

They live in a posh district. They 'ave salmon tins in their dustbin.

When I was playin' panto at the Pivvy, Robinson Corkscrew, I was so 'ungry one night I ate the parrot.

I says to the bobby, 'what are yer takin' me in for?' He says 'Drinking'.
I says: 'Ta very much, I could just do wid one.'

He's got a nose on him as long as the Corporation housing list.

Told me to chuck him out. How could I? He wus the Guest uv Honour.

Homesick among Scousers?

In 1964, with this heading, the *Liverpool Echo* printed prominently this letter: 'It was very interesting to read the account of the Indian Day Celebrations at the British Council, in your esteemed paper. As the person behind the slides of India . . . I would like to say that my intention was to give the local public a glimpse of the diversity in India along with the appropriate music. It never occurred to me that there might be a few Indians feeling homesick, especially when we are in the midst of the most kind hospitality of the Scousers. As a matter of fact most of the slides were kindly lent to us by a Frenchman and a few by an Australian.
     – T. Sreenavasan, Department of Electrical Engineering,
     The University, Liverpool.

Printers at play

. . . she had no intention of ever marrying Mr C. She said that all the time she knew him she was going about with her ex-finance, John D. – *Liverpool Echo*, 1967.

For him and others with a wrist measurement which is a vital sadistic – *Liverpool Echo*, 1967.

If a woman is under 45 a mini-skirt makes no odds . . . She will be just as attractive whether she wears it or not. – *Liverpool Echo*, 1967.

She will be a member of the crew compromising girls from all over the country. – *Liverpool Echo*, 1967.

He is a retired docker and has been all his life. – Item about Liverpudlian in *Northern Catholic Pictorial*.

Pastor George Wise (militant Protestant leader) lectures tonight at St Domingo Hall. Don't fail to miss this. – *Liverpool Express*, 1913 (a pape among the compositors no doubt).

A rowdy do
This is our house and we'll all 'ave a do in it

'Is it a party in a parlour?', asked Wordsworth. (Can't see him as a chairman, can you?) It may be in a parlour. It won't stop there, it will be into the lobby, the kitchen, through back door and front door; the doors have never been closed anyway. They've been 'on a jar' all evening for any belated guest. It is notable that uninvited, or at any rate unwanted, guests rarely arrive and that some people, not necessarily poor relations, never enter the front door. It can be a sign of intimacy with the family to enter that way – the front can be formal. In both cases a knock is expected and an announcement of who you are.

One sees on films of American social life how neighbours walk in without warning in the suburban areas. It wouldn't do in Dingle or Scotty Road, and the rule still works when these people are deported to sad and similar suburbs from their warm homes.

'Is this the house where the does do be?' (Traditional facetious.)
'It's me, Maggie, can I cum in?'

But as the night goes on the doors are open wide, so that neighbours get the benefit of the song and music if, for one reason or another, they can't be present. No neighbour complains of the noise; they either like it – most do – or tolerate it till it's their turn. The motive of the party-giver is mainly altruistic but there is an element ('We'll show that misrible ould one at 23') of one-upmanship – I'll bet *you* couldn't have as noisy a do as this!

The time to join is when ale is being carried from a nearby pub in cases and demijohns. In these degenerate days the draught ale would be in the newfangled cans. In my do-going days the ale would be in old wine or spirit bottles, but mostly in demijohns:

it was a long process for a barman in those days to fill these up from the barrels. The procession would move from the pub, maybe with a stave or two of *Nelly Dean* (the drinkers' *Internationale*) led by a boilermaker or some such hefty type with a ten gallon cask on his shoulder and mincing like Rebecca at the Well in a Victorian lithograph.

Someone might be carrying a gramophone. It would not be called portable then – they were all portable – and the comic of the company, the mark, would wear its horn like a firebobby's helmet. There would be some spirits for the old 'uns. Not much; it was already getting too dear, 12/6 a bottle in the early 30s, and throwing a do (the verb had not long come from the US to England. Liverpool, as usual with Yankeeisms, being first – e.g. *jane* for a female with whom to have a *date*) did not mean you were well off. Usually the do-giver was helped out in the purchase of drinks by comrades, though if you were his mate, one of the lads, and skint you were not made ill at ease.

The scoff was left to the lady of the house, who may well have gone into debt or had recourse to the pawnshop. But she would not lack helpers, and tablecloths, cutlery and plates would be willingly lent by neighbours. The meal was buffet, though the word was not used except among the pretentious, the 't' not being silent. (These pretentious types would be the sort to call the parlour, lovely old word, the 'sitting' or 'drorrin- room' and the lobby another beauty of ancient and sound English lineage, the 'hall'. Of such more elsewhere.) If it was a house without a parlour, a two up and two down, food would be piled in the kitchen, leaving the other room for the song and dancing. When there were three rooms the kitchen would be the bar, the middle room for eating, the front room or parlour – all easily breakable objects removed – for the do proper.

Into the kitchen, anyway, the beer was carried. Stout for privileged ladies, usually elderly, maybe mulled by plunging into the glass an unwiped poker from the ever-glowing fire. Not that everybody got a glass, all sorts of objects which would hold liquid were pressed into service – cracked cups, jamjars, any suitable object you could imagine and some you might not have thought suitable or imagined.

In my time there were no minerals. For strict teetotalers there was port. Children, even babies, if they didn't take tea, of which there was plenty (good solid stuff – the kettle was on the hob throughout the night, with plenty of 'conny onny', condensed milk), had beer or nothing. There were nearly always children and babies, of course. The beer drinkers drank tea too, as a rule.

It was a disgrace not to have plenty of beer, the draught being consumed first as a rule as it so soon became flat. A credit to the do-giver was for a guest to tell friends next day: 'It was a gear do, the wuz beer for dogs.' What phrase could better suggest plenitude? The neighbours next morning would have many ways of telling whether the do was a success or not but, in the oral Court Circular the main criterion would be: 'owmuch did she get on the empties?'

The host, his almost ambassadorial suavity on the do night itself now shed, is now on the sling at Huskisson Dock, muttering about a scrougin crowd a bastids who wooden lift a 'and if you wuz dyin a thirst.

I remember getting into an afternoon do, following a wedding, by taking on the task, without being asked, of assistant ale-carrier from the Bootle Arms to one of the narrow streets behind Bootle Town Hall. Ted Fyland, landlord of the Bootle Arms and husband of my first girl friend, God rest his soul, told the other bearers I was a good and willing strong lad capable of carrying ale in any capacity.

I spent most of the afternoon being lushed up in the kitchen. This was a house with three rooms on the ground floor. The wedding feast had been held over the Bootle Arms and the happy pair had gone on their honeymoon from there. The middle room, next to the kitchen, would have snacks for the evening laid out and at the moment was being used to entertain a few special guests. One of these would be the priest. Presently the priest looked in the kitchen.

'Anyone seen Mick Duffy?' he asked.

'He's at the back, Father'. That meant he was in the bog, petty, closet, if it hadn't been the priest asking. (Later the pretentious went on to *toilet* and now it's that horrible middle class *loo*.)

'Is he? I'll wait for him then. Hullo, Frank, what brought you here. Long time no see.' We had been at school together. 'Come on in here, don't be rottin yer guts with that stuff.'

He saw I had a couple of John Jameson's from the mantlepiece and introduced me to others there, including the Grand Master of the Knights, grand man, who decided he must be off for Confession that evening ('And when did you have your ould kettle scraped last, Frank, you shocking sinner?') Mick Duffy or no. He was seen, with some fuss, to the door and I went back into the kitchen. My status had been extremely elevated. I got served in a glass now and some baby's napkins and other wet clothes had been swept off a backless chair by the sink. Sitting there I heard that Mike Nolan, the priest's houseboy, was in the backyard, down the old air-raid shelter, with the blonde Sadie, barmaid at the Bootle Arms, whom I'd been idly jesting with before joining the wedding-party.

I went in the front room where the wedding guests were sitting all round the wall, the middle of the floor being entirely cleared of furniture to facilitate dancing. The finery of the girls had a temporary look; there were anyhow only a few of them. The men, docker types, in tight blue serge, necks bulging over unwanted collars, looked, with silver-grey ties, and brass-trimmed geraniums, even tougher than in normal garb. There was no space for me round the wall and nobody would make any for me. Nobody spoke.

I sat on the piano stool by the piano. One spoke. 'Gunna give's tune, mate?', and giggled. No-one joined him. There was some muttering at the end of the room and with my Customs Officer's ears I gathered the giggler was engaged to Sadie, that they blamed me somehow for Sadie's absence. (I was the only male in the kitchen when they'd left and Sadie was talking to me, her gorgeous bosom balanced on my lapels. She was wanted to play the piano anyway.)

As they muttered they glanced at me and I felt like Captain Bligh when he saw a group having a chat with Christian on the deck of the *Bounty*. 'I don't know him', said one, 'no I diden bring him, he just helped us carry the ale.' Sadie came in, stood by the stool and went back into the kitchen.

I'm going', I announced. 'Have one before you go, mister.' I had a couple and set off for the bus station. It was a long journey from Bootle to Huyton. Buses rarely ran and I wasn't quite sure of the way to the station from this street. It was already getting dark. I'd have little time at home before setting off back for a ten hour night watch. We changed over from day watches on a Saturday night for seven nights. (These pampered civil servants!) I had to run for the bus and step off again briskly. I'd left my library book. With difficulty, going by ear rather than sight, I found the house.

'Have another before you go, mister.' I had – dregs. And Sadie who was resting from the piano smuggled me in a drop of Irish. And gave me a quick kiss. Just as two blokes, typecast for First and Second Murderer, came out of the parlour en route for the shooting-gallery.

It was chilly out as I hastened through the little streets. At the Mersey Bar fog horns groaned. There was nothing hymnal about Bootle's night sky. The canal was a trickle of snot with feathery breaths of fog dangling above it. The town hall, slowly being wrapped in the fog looked like a huge Victorian widow in her weeds. The power grids at Millers Bridge were etched silvery in lights against the unhappy sky. I'd a long wait before a bus elbowed its way to the stop. 'Good job I got the book', I said to myself as I shuffled on with the other lost and silent souls. Jaysus, I hadn't got the book. I'd not go back, I'd pay the library. It would mean at least a quid up my shirt – a big life of Cardinal Newman, God stiffen it. And when I eventually reached home Sadie's lipstick was still visible.

*   *   *

After someone had sung a song, the chairman would lead the assembly in –

> A jolly good song, jolly well sung,
> Cheers for the singuh ever-ee-one
> If yiz can beat it yer welcome to thry
> But please to remebuh – the singuh is dhry.

When this had been rendered if no volunteer jumped up (which could happen, even in Liverpool, early in the festivities) someone would be peremptorily called on and, vowing he would ne'er consent, consented, sometimes dragged to his or her feet with the mock coercion involved in the establishment of the Speaker of the House of Commons. Most of us could do something (as an encore to my recitation of *The Road to Mandalay* while the room still echoed:

> Ship me somewhere East of Suez
> Where the best's just like the worst,
> Where there ain't no Ten Commandments
> And a man can raise a thorst

and the *blotto voce* interruption 'You don' after go all dat far, whack.' I usually gave – no, I mean rendered – The Green Eye of the Little Yellow God by Milton Hayes). But most well-met was a pianist, then a good singer, any instrumentalist. Nobody came to the party with his uke or fiddle or squeeze-box slyly left in some obscure corner outside the parlour, without being asked to play. I do recall one fellow travelling some distance back home to get his instrument. It was a pair of spoons.

Few brought music, few knew music. If one did it would still seem to be 'putting it on' to bring it. There is in Liverpool a rowdy style of singing as distinct from a refined sort. The latter, deplored by most, was the style of Liverpudlian Ann Ziegler in her duets with Webster Booth. To hear the rowdy sort at its best you need only listen to Cilla Black. It projects like a ship's horn, drags and slurrrrs, biffs you over the ears back and front. Rowdy, by the way, does not signify making a noise. A rowdy is low class, a rowdy may be quite a nice person, quiet even, though the working class is noiser than the others I suppose. She may have her house almost worthy of appearance in *Homes and Gardens.*

'She has a luvlee place, luvlee, you cud eat off a the floor.'

Outside, the paint of the door has been washed with vigour, she has a well-polished brass step, the fanlight, maybe enshrining a white marli horse, bootscraper blackleaded, step red-ochred (we prefer red-raddled), 'flags' scrubbed right to the edge of the side-walk, the 'parapet'. She will be praised for being 'rowdy but neat'.

But rowdy she must stay as irrevocably as an Indian Untouchable, accepting it like him as her destined caste. All attending a rowdy do and describing it so do not necessarily class themselves as rowdies. It is just not one of those a la posh parties. It is one where the females sing like Cilla Black, though not, of course, so well. And as she belts out her top note it is not only permissible to shout out 'WE-ELL' but almost obligatory. My own habit of following this old and good custom has brought me sidelong glances not only at soirees in good-address households but at folk clubs where the atmosphere favoured is that of a welsh bethel and that sort of audience participation is without favour.

> And the an-gels above
> Taught the way-a how to love-a
> To Dat Old Fashioned Mudder a Mine
>
> WE-ELL.

A singuh who could not inspire a WE-ELL was just not on. In a little pub near Scotty Road, you can still hear it on a Saturday night, on the corner of Juvenal Street (three syllables for Juvenal, please) going towards Cazneau Street (as before for Cazneau) when a stall-holder from nearby Paddy Market gives out one of her ould ones.

What makes a good musician is not so easily defined. But it has the same quality of assault. I have heard that the first jazz was heard in this country from the Dixielanders in Liverpool. It is sure that no place in the U K welcomed it and its recusive ragtime as the Liverpudlian did and, of course, from it all came the Mersey Beat and the best known exponents of it – what's their name again? I write as one recognising a fact, not one who likes all that sort of noise. But then I am not a pure Scouser. There are times when I don't even care which team wins or loses, *don't even know after the game which one has.* Mind you, any noise is better than the soprano recalling where her caravan rested, or barrel chest impersonating the Company Sergeant Major or the Toreador, or a 'Madam, will you walk' duet of which at church concerts in aid of I had a bellyful in my Liverpool youth.

*   *   *

Playing an instrument in Liverpool you must tackle it as you must tackle life, with a deal of pugnacity, show it who the master is. A pianist need not be a great executant and can neglect niceties. (Unlike the wife of a concert pianist of whom her husband, a ship steward mate of mine, said: 'Arpeggios, Frank, she pisses over them.') But her audience expects her to approach the piano as a training heavyweight champ will approach his punch-bag. If you have a squeezebox – squeeze it. Set about with the bow as if you would saw the fiddle in two. Live music was preferred to the gramophone, and of all sources of music the Liverpudlian preferred the old joanna. There was a time when most households in Liverpool had a piano. Unused for most of the year, it was what we'd now call a status symbol, aspired to by the lowliest as never even the telly aerial or the Cortina was.

The really aspiring fringe of the working class bordering on middle had shy daughters taught by some poor spinster for coppers a week. The big thing was for the girl to get her Final Certificate, treated as a graduation and unjustifiably called her Cap and Gown (she might even be photographed at Gale's in London Road, 3 for 6d., as a sort of girl graduate. For this the garments were on hand).

My sister went through it, on an excellent German piano which went in a 1941 air-raid, out of tune, unplayed for years. (They did not go to the extreme of having me taught the violin.) It was like buying a set of encyclopedias from a doorstep salesman. It all came to nothing, in most cases. (I suppose someone, some time, has opened one of those encyclopedias?) Few of the *soi disant* Cap-and-Gown girls ever again touched the piano, few boys who had tormented neighbours by torturing Rachmaninoff handled again a violin. At dos, the pianists were almost always completely self-taught, knew nowt of musical theory, played bravely by ear and with success, bullying the melody out of the mute beast. To me as mysterious a faculty as dowsing or keeping the score at darts is the ability to sit at a piano, or to pick up an instrument and perform at once any popular tune (I said *tune*, I said *popular*). Or the more difficult task of accompanying, not correctly perhaps, but to everybody's satisfaction.

The piano is a most complex factory for combining sounds and I am told that many instruments – like the guitar – are not so difficult to vamp on. Yet there is no room in the modern house for a piano and our Treesa no longer Takes Lessons – not in pianoforte playing anyhow. There is room now only for the radio and TV set and the tape recorder and the cocktail cabinet, all hostile to the gusto of a good old rowdy do which still, here and there, survives. 'No do without the ivories' was the motto of Joe Cassell, whom I nicknamed the Singing Plasterer. Joe, a hefty bloke who spent all his working life in the building trade, had a terrible stammer. But when he sang the misfortune disappeared. (This is a well known phenomenon, but I have noticed that some of the worst offenders against Standard sing in good English and often when they don't it is the illiterate song-writer:

> Under my umber-ella
> Upon my word I am a lucky fella . . .

who is to blame.)

Joe was a basso-profundo, self taught, whose party pieces were *Old Man River* and, with me on his knee, naked but for an improvised, carelessly-fastened nappy, *Sonny Boy*. But he must have piano accompaniment. On this occasion there were all the makings of a good do, with professional barmaids from Joe's local in charge of the bar temporarily erected in the bathroom. Plenty of food. A good sporty crowd. But no piano and Joe's missus present, one of the best ivory-rattlers in the game.

Joe, however, recalled a friend who had a splendid piano and he only lived about half a mile away. He and I and some other male went round to the house. It was not easy to break into the house nor to trundle the piano out, down the garden path and into the street.

> Last night we had a do,
> Some chipped potatoes too . . .

A snatch of song made the task of transporting the piano lighter. We had gone winding round suburban streets under the sodium lighting, which makes the gayest of groups look ghastly, for about a quarter of a mile, now grunting a bit and not helped by Joe's stuttered instructions, when coming towards us, we met the owner of the piano with his wife. He took the fourth corner and she tagged on behind us. We knocked a hole in the plaster just inside the front door almost through to the neighbour's but the do was one of the best ever.

After music and beer for dogs good scoff made a good do. All the time you could drink. Some did nothing else. They posed as servitors, even affected aprons, as self-sacrificing types who, much as they longed to join the singers and the dancers, stayed on in the kitchen to attend to the needs of others – an attitude which became less convincing as the night wore on and thirsty latecomers were bundled out without ceremony.

You could snatch a bite at any time. But, if only to rest the pianist, there had to be a spell of non-desultory eating or else the hostess was offended.

'Muck in, lad, you're at yer grannie's.'

'Don't be backwids at cummin forwid.'

'By gees, I'd sooner feed you for a week than a fortnight.'

'You don' eat much, mate, but you shift a lot.'

'Not as if she showed it, not anough fat on her to fry a egg . . .'

'No, no, missus, I'm full up; I've had a currant.'

'Evryting I eat flies to me stummick.'

'Throuble wid you, mate, you've on'y got one ass-hole.'

How, without a formal meal-break, could the familiar litany be recited? One Birkenhead docker, noted for obtaining the food for his hoolies from the store-rooms of outward-bound ships, had an original addition:

'Muck in, lads, don't be fright, all passed by the Board a Trade.'

Huge cobs of fatty ham overflowing down the sides of doorsteps of well-margarined bread, tinned salmon sarnies, corn dog abnabs. Some of the old 'uns had crubens, pigs' feet. As with spare-ribs, the younger girls discouraged their beaux from food which would make their fingers prematurely greasy. Boiled ham was a must for the rowdy do or wake. On occasions it appeared for both in the same week at the same house – 'Thrift, Horatio, Thrift' – especially after the First World War, during the terrible Spanish Flu epidemic, when a returning soldier might face a funeral before his own welcome home do.

Oh, to think of it, oh to dream of it, in a time of chipolatas, crisps and Babycham! On with the dance! Not just yet, after a supper.

Complimenting the hostess with a civil belch, the self-appointed chairman surveyed the possibles, issued his fiat. There was a breathless hush. Would Bill, as he did once before, sing Joe's song? I have often told the stranger in Liverpool that the quickest way to the hospital is in some areas to make some slight chaffing remarks about the Pope, in others to give some credit to Everton FC, anywhere to have a good word for Liverpool public transport or – to sing the other fellow's song.

'The wuz skin an' air flyin, Josie is giving *Paddy McGinty's Goat* an' issen Gladys sittin right next her? Proper yor ol goat, I don' mind tellin', ho, ho, ho.'

The chairman must prevent such contretemps. He has to have a good knowledge of protocol in these matters. There is, for instance, what is now called audience participation:

'The singuh is on he's feet. Quiet please! Order puh-lease, give order, give Arry Lauder. Give a little ush PUH LEASE!'

He obtained order. But hardly had the singer started when someone from soft humming joins in the words, a shush runs round the room and from the chair comes a peremptory 'Second time, please'.

The singer must be allowed to sing solo first time. Then others could, were expected to, join in and no whipping-up, Florrie Forde, 'all togethuh boys' devices were needed. Anybody could be called, most were, most would be disappointed if they weren't. But we couldn't all sing. A piano solo displaying some flashy virtuosity, better a piano duet with tricky manual manouevres miraculously avoiding digital collisions always went well. Very favoured, giving everyone a chance, was a medley of old favourites, with all joining in after the first few bars of each tune and the pianist cleverly moving from one tune to the next. There was an almost compulsory routine, from *Daisy, Daisy, Tweet, Tweet* via *Roses of Picardy, The Miner's Dream of Home, When Irish Eyes* to *A Bird in a Gilded Cage*. A little of what was called 'classical' music never went amiss. But this had to be heard in respectful silence like the singing of Gounod's *Ave Maria*.

*   *   *

So if the uninvited guest was a musician he was unlikely to be turned away. Which reminds me of a semi-rowdy do in the Kensington area of Liverpool, near in fact, Bessie Braddock's home – no slum area. It was a cut above my own district, and it hasn't even been demolished yet. Why Liverpool uses London names for some of its components is not easy to answer. In my father's youth Kensington was called Kensington Fields. Building had not started. But Islington was Folly Lane. Why change it?

On the other hand our Haymarket, Cheapside, Covent Garden, Drury Lane are as old as London's and, in each case, quite different from the metropolitan places. From the Kensington Carnegie Library, Liverpool, I borrowed my first library book. In the park near the library, called Kensington Gardens, and then worthy of the name, I, a rosy-kneed stripling on a bench, had my first encounter with a dirty old man in the traditional raincoat. Not exactly first (I had been a bit of a *roué* round Salisbury Street at nine) but an early, much extended knowledge of the differences between the sexes I acquired in my teens at a cinema there, now an ice-skating joint.

I often wonder if any teenagers saw the pictures? I often wonder did anyone over the age of twenty for second house Saturdays ever enter this Temple of Venus, for juveniles only? Remember that we teenagers were conscious of the big difference between us and the older generation, though we might not call them squares. We favoured the triangular, razor-edged trousers lying like twin pyramids on the pointed shoes. But the older generation took little notice, though Press and Pulpit as ever up till then tut-tutted on behalf of the elders about the excesses of modern (or flaming) youth in the Jazz Age. The difference between then and now is that we hadn't two ha'pennies to rub together. Nothing more. The Beatles would have died broke in 1928.

The lights in the pictures went out and soon giggles and grunts and the tearing of flimsy lace mingled with *Ain't She Sweet* and *Black Bottom, We've All Got 'Em* from Mr Stokes's Orchestra

(Stokes was a distinguished popular musician who had rather come down in the world. He churned out what us kids wanted and, if he ceased for a moment, muffled murmurs came from under the seats: 'Stoke it up there, Stokes!') Maybe then the operator, the manager, male and female staff joined the carnival.

In those days few of us had regular girl-friends unless we met one who liked an open air life and a follower without even the penny for the tram-fare. They usually went for older boys in jobs, with pocket-money. Somehow we raised the ninepence or so for these Saturday nights. And naturally we didn't bring a girl.

We youths arrived while the first house was on – during which, I've heard, films actually were shown to an audience of serious film fans – and bought our tallies. A tally was an hexagonal piece of metal about the size of a five-shilling piece, which had to be handed in at the cinema on entry. It was something to do with Entertainment Tax then levied by the Excise, a substitute for paper tickets.

Before the first house let out some of us lads, greatly daring, would go in the pub opposite, if we had the fourpence for a pint. On this evening Jack Gordon and I somehow had five bob between us (perhaps from one of our occasional raids with a nimble knife on the Foreign Missions Box on our kitchen dresser). It was eightpence for two pints, and Jack, a very sweet treble, gave an almost muted rendering of *Bonny Mary of Argyle*. (Singing was absolutely prohibited in Liverpool pubs.)

'Good on yer, lad', said a blowsy-looking shawlie, now in a mottled astrakhan coat, one of a group of gay old girls, already half seas over. Jack, while I keenly kept douse for an objecting barman, proceeded to Nirvana and we had two more pints.

'Don't you sing, la?' she asked me.

'No,' said Jackie, 'he's a violinist.'

'Oh, well we're going on to a do from here. Would you like to come, you to sing, la, him to play?'

We had to get to the cinema before the lights went down – the period in which the lads paraded up and down the centre aisle like young pashas surveying the knee-displaying bobbed, shingled, Eton-cropped, apparently disinterested judies, deciding which lucky one would have our company. Babette, Colette, Leah (with the slight moustache and bells on her garters), who? We just made it.

The old girl had asked us to come round after, gave us the address, asked us to bring our instruments. Jackie could be very

90

good on such occasions. He said we were in the cinema orchestra, that was why we must dash, he played the piano, couldn't bring that could I? 'Oh, we got a piano, you can bring your fiddle, la?' 'Well no,' I said, 'Mr Stokes doesn't like us to take our instruments away.'

We had forgotten all about it when we came out of the cinema. From the pub came a group of young fellows, slightly older than us, jolly, but not actually rowdy types. Well-dressed, they were carrying a fair amount of ale, 'jars out', the evidence of a do. We politely offered our assistance. The offer was not refused but not accepted with any great enthusiasm. They turned into the street the old doll had named. We entered a well-scrubbed house with pink lace curtains on its bow windows.

As we put down the jars and cases the old doll herself appeared. 'It's them two fellers', she said with delight. 'Proper good turns they are.' (For Jackie the evidence was slight enough. But me?) 'Give 'em a drink, Arnold. Sit down, lads, and sup up – fill yer boots.'

Arnold, a tall pink lad in a green whipcord double-breaster and a shirt with blue vertical stripes and long-pointed collar with blue diagonal stripes, a tiny green bow, green hanky in his breast pocket, well-waved yellow hair and a perpetual blush, brought us glasses. Most of his companions were tall like himself. From another room came the comforting chatter of females. Beer and females, punch and judies, the Scouser's delight. We could enjoy ourselves here and, after the old girl's gushing reception, the young chaps were much more friendly to us. They were, it soon appeared, her lodgers, and this was a prosperous household. Biggish late Victorian place.

'Well', said the old girl, 'you can give us a few tunes, Jackie. And we'll find a fiddle somewhere for Carl here.' (Why I chose at that period to be known as Carl and why I wore horn-rimmed spectacles with plain glass in them, there is no point in pursuing now.)

'Peg,' she said to one of the girls, 'you know where that Bonetti woman, the Italian, lives, somewhere down near Boaler Street. I'm sure she's gorra fiddle. Ass her if you can borry it, say it's for me.'

I pleaded with her not to trouble the Italian lady. I found it almost impossible to play on any fiddle but my own – it's like a sewing machine (never seen the sewing machine I couldn't use), it could even be valuable, Italian heirloom, a Stradivarius, I'd be frightened of my life of damaging it . . .

Peg couldn't find Mrs Bonetti, but other fiddle-owners were recalled and cheerfully enough Peg started off. I said it wasn't fair. I'd recently hurt my right arm jumping on a tram, couldn't really do, hadn't really played the violin that evening, just the triangle (my God, I suppose she knows someone who has a triangle).

The search for an instrument for me came to nothing – half a dozen times in a life one has these unjustified moments of good luck – and the lush was flowing very freely. Jackie, at the piano, wasn't doing badly. He had a fair repertory of old and new songs in which others could join and he could sing a song himself as he played, though he knew no music. It crossed my mind that someone there must think it strange that a professional should play with two fingers. This may have gone unnoticed, because Jackie could play and sing a group of songs which, at that date, were considered rather near the knuckle. And when the older ones had left us to it, around 1 a.m., Jackie played to fox-trot tempo these tunes, breathing out the rather suggestive words in the manner of Whispering Jack Smith. The young couples danced, guffawed, giggled. I stood aside looking as always (I hoped) rather Byronic, but I occasionally obliged by switching out the lights for a few minutes during which Jackie hit more wrong notes than usual and his voice was like a serpent's hiss in the darkness, the light from the gas fire catching occasionally the shadowy movements of the couples, the shine on men's shoes, the flesh colour of girls' stockings.

'Oh, Charlie, take it away, oh, Charlie do what I say?'

'Ma, he's making eyes at me Ma, he wants to – marry me, Now he's got me on the fender, Now he's broken my suspender Ma----- he's KISSING me . . .'

'Put your skirt down, put your skirt down, put your skirt down, Mary Ann, Just because you've got a dimple on your knee, It wasn't put there for the world to see, Put . . .'

How greensickly harmless they all seem now! Can it be that the permissive age may one day seem as innocent as the so self-consciously sophisticated, emancipated Jazz Age? Jackie must have a rest, it was decided. Just a few tunes on the gramophone and then, said Arnold, seemingly a sort of accepted leader, postman's knock. (Girlish giggles.) Arnold had been dancing with an astonishingly beautiful tall redhead, whose eyes glinted. She had slid out, as Jackie had. He always had a great gift of being with you one moment and next nowhere to be found. In time his friends came to expect this.

'Where's Lily?' asked Arnold looking slightly annoyed, but he had chosen a record and placed it on the whirling circle, still winding away. No tune came. There was no needle.

Jud, a broad beetle-browed type with whom Arnold had been very matey early in the evening, had the packet of needles, but Jud was nowhere to be found. The old ones in the kitchen said he'd not been about for some time. Maybe he'd gone down to Erskine Street to the Territorial barracks. There were long sessions there on Saturday nights in the sergeant's mess. Jud liked to go there for a game of snooker. Funny he didn't tell Arnold, though.

So, no needles, no gramophone. Postman's knock. This was simply a pretext for putting the lights out and gathering in couples on the stairs. I found a partner who was not at all bad but she had buck teeth and wanted little besides kissing. While she sucked my tongue almost into her tonsils, she held my hands firmly while pressing her plump, bare knee rather painfully into my groin. I was lucky, I suppose.

The last I had seen of Arnold, he was gazing sadly at the gramophone. He and the other chaps here were a cut above Jackie and me. They had clothes, knew how to deal with girls, had money in their pockets, could afford these good digs. Jackie was wearing a plum coloured single-breasted suit with trouser-cuffs of only eighteen inches. It was a botched, machine job. (I'd had a spell of being a tailor.) My mother had bought it for him on a 'cheque', two shillings a week. Of the material I told Jackie that, if ever he wanted to be a penitent, he had only to wear this suit and find some ashes somewhere.

My own suit, my only suit, was morning style, striped trousers, black jacket, a rather lowcut double-breasted waistcoat, cloth buttons. (It was not made for me but it was a bargain second-hand, when not claimed, in my tailor job.) My brown spats went rather well with this rig-out but, as I was out of doors a good deal trying to sell vacuum cleaners, my mother insisted on my adding a rather loud woolly pullover of which about four inches appeared above the waistcoat. Which even I knew was hardly the thing.

We sat on a low step; she wouldn't go further up, although others were constantly stepping over us to do just that. Giggling from behind told me that others were doing better than I was, but this was usually the case. I edged off her knee and tried without success to press her lips closed with mine. I was glad when Arnold switched on all the lights. He looked at each of us, clearly looking for Lily. She wasn't about.

The girls gathered in the front room tidying themselves, rather silent. The men went into the kitchen, where the old ones were dozing over a dying fire. There were half-empty glasses and part-eaten pies and sandwiches in every corner. We found some beer, filled glasses and headed towards the parlour. Down the stairs came Lily, smiling cheekily. Behind her, looking very pale, came Jackie.

Arnold rushed at Jackie, threw a punch and missed. I jumped in, Arnold belted me, breaking the glasses, and I rushed at him head first. The others grabbed us both, to which I made only a slight show of resistance and Jud appeared mysteriously and said, 'Cut it out, Arnold, cut it out all of you, or the old girl'll have the Super on to the lot of us on Monday morning.'

I might have guessed. They were all single bobbies. The girls had screamed slightly and were all preparing to leave. I heard one say: 'They broke that fellow's horn-rimmed testicles.' 'Sir Kreemy Nut in the pullover, d'you mean?' said one with her. It was the girl I'd sat with on the stairs. 'Don't think he's got none.'

They left quietly, Arnold and I shook hands, the ale was finished but it was only five o'clock. 'Let's have a couple of hands of cards till the trams start running.' It was pontoon; Jack and I steadily lost. About seven o'clock we were ready to go. They were all going down for a morning swim. A few of them gathered round Arnold and Jud in quiet consultation a little away from the step. We had to move aside at one moment for an old boy going into the house, who waved tiredly at the cheery greetings of the others.

Jud came over from the group with a handful of pence. He told us the old boy was the old girl's husband who worked nights at Lister Drive Power Station. 'Uh,' he went on, a little bashfully, 'bit of a misunderstanding tonight, best forgotten, eh, eh? Now listen. You two lost all your money tonight, we guess, so, well – can we offer you your fares home? I mean we don't want to in—'

'Quite all right,' said Jackie.

Jud started to count out pence. 'Where have you got to get to?'

Promptly Jackie replied: 'Birmingham', and Jud put the pennies in his pocket and brought out some silver. They left.

'It was him', said Jackie.

'What?' said I.

'He was the one, in the bedroom at the top of the stairs. I could hear them both. All the time. I was in the petty being sick.' (Jackie was always doing this at parties, especially if he played piano.)

'I saw Lily anyhow; I was still spewing when she come in. He was just going back into the room when I came out, he'd seen me. Otherwise Arnold might have seen him walk down behind her. A bit of luck for Jud.'

We were about to close the door behind us and find a place to get a cup of tea when terrible yells came from inside the house. A voice was screaming 'I've been stabbed, I've been stabbed.' A man's voice. Women's voices soon joined it. We dashed back in. The explanation was simple. As soon as he stepped into bed he found the missing gramophone needles. As we passed the park and the library, a chill morning sky scudding over the roofs of Kensington, the first bell for Mass at Sacred Heart was sounding and Jackie softly sang; '*And when the jazz began I got a surprise, You could tell their thoughts by the look in their eyes. And if that's what they do when they're dancing – What happens after the ball?*'

Laff!

'Can you tell me where the urinal is, mate?'
'Ow many funnels has she got?'

Merseyry rhyme

Little boy blue come blow on your horn,
    While little boy Red swings a rattle.
If both of the footee teams failed to turn up –
    We'd still have a flippin good battle.

In the classroom

He's been doing long decisions this term.

Speaks the Latin like a native.

Like one of dem public schools where the scholars wear bloaters.

He speaks French fluidly. (Eh, what's the French for eau de cologne?)

Cosine? Dat's the aunt's son, i'n 'it?

Went to a lecture on Keats. Wooden know a keat if he seen one.

He sat the exam under a consumed name.

In the school play he took the part of a Chinese mandoline.

Solomon had a thousand wives and a hundred cucumbers.

A sentence wid the word oyster? Oi stir me tea wid a spoon.

Wid the word bewitches? Tarra, lads, I'll bewitches tomorra.

Ben Trovato's quiz

What are rabies, and what would you do for them? – Rabies is Jewish priests, I wooden do a bloody ting for them.

What did Julius Caesar write? – Latin I s'pose.

What did Henry VIII do for Wolsey ? – He made him a cardigan.

Name two ancient sports – Ant'ny an' Cleopatra.

Why was Our Lord born in a stable? – Because Bethlehem's 'Ousin Kermittee wuz as bad as Liverpool's.

The Pope lives in a vacuum and is supposed to be inflammable.

The Three Wise men wuz Gold, Frankinstein and Meyer.

(OK, OK, but I did hear a docker define an indentured apprentice as a feller wid false teeth before he was twenny-one!)

Is the 'g' in 'margarine' soft or hard? Soft in summer, hard in winter.

Einstein? He wrote a the'ry about his relatives.

Corny gags in Paris

Dick the Docker took me. On'y fair. It wuz me dropped the case on he's foot. Tuk me cos I can speak the lingo, anyhow. But the wuz dead tick in the hotel. I kept askin for a nother piller, they keeps givin me the gardener's wife. We et well, wid loads uv the red ink. Chops wid likkle collars on like choir boys. And we finish up wid a demi tasse – be all right if the'd use a big cup – and a glass uv benediction. Then off to the night club. Them judies in their topless tingies. Ever seen anyting like dat, asses Dick. Not sense I wuz weaned, I says. But, eh, lissen, here back in the 'Pool wid dat red-eaded barman spilling all the beer and putting the change in the wettest part, wid dem dustin round yer boots a quarter of a hour before closing, and the barmaids wid faces like farmers' asses d'you t'ink I'd change me likkle Liverpool ale house for one of dem French joints wid good service till all hours and the girls dishing the plonk out in topless d'you tink I'd rather be in Paris? By geez, I wud. But tell yer what. If the waiters in Lime Street didden come for the money till you'd finished bevvying eh – the'd after ave runnin-pumps.

Gerrit youse?

Come out Hughes, said the teacher. And the whole class walked out.

Me father took me to school. He had to, he was in the same class.

Accent
Exceedingly
Rare

PART FOUR

Accent
Exceedingly
Rare

Scene, a blasted heath*

Three shawlies are bent over an earthenware pot, or panmug, canting into it.

    First: Eye of newt and toe of frog,
Second: Six spare-ribs and some Mersey fog,
   Third: Ringo's ringlets, Lennon's larynx, Glottal stop from Cilla's pharynx.
   First: Smoke from the Rile Iris funnel[1]. Contract ticket for the Tunnel[2].

---

*No reference is intended to any Prime Minister living or half-dead.

Learned Notes

1. *The Royal Iris* is now a motor-ship, but her smoky old predecessor (the third since the first won the right to the prefix, with the other Wallasey ferryboat, *The Royal Daffodil*), was well-beloved. It was famous for fish-and-chip suppers on evening river cruises. ('Oh look at the mist on the Mersey.' 'That's not mist, it's the fishan-chips on the Rile Iris.') The Mersey Ferries are centuries old, the first was run from Birkenhead by monks, and are likely to be scrapped in one more outbreak of bureaucratic busyness in which, in an effort to make Unique Liverpool just like any place else, public feeling is never considered.

2. Season tickets are always 'contracts' to the Liverpudlian. Liverpool writer Richard Whittington Egan noted in his life of the Birkenhead-born poet Richard le Galliene (his father, a brewer, was plain Galliene. His actress daughter also affected the French article) that, for all the years he lived away from Merseyside (mainly, like his sister, in the USA) he never called a season ticket anything else. It was the old tickets on the under-water railway made clear, a contract between the holder and the carrying company.

Second: Dixie's football boots, who'll beat 'em?[3]
          God's amount of spuds – we'll eat 'em.
 Third: Wet nella[4], olley[5], and a kewin[6],
          Jungle juice[7] and mother's ruin.
 First: Rhody[8] bacon, foot of pig,
          Bessie's bustle, Laski's wig[9]
Second: Cob a chuck[10], a gill of ale[11],
          Warder's key from Walton Gaol.
 Third: Sargent's baton[12], docker's hook,

---

3. The great Billy Dean hated the nickname Dixie given him in his 'teens by an Everton supporter who yelled 'Give it to Dixie', referring to his thick woolly hair and dark complexion. Now every male Dean is, to his mates, as inevitably Dixie as Miller is Dusty and Murphy is Spud.

4. The great Liverpool boxer Nelson Tarleton hated to be called Nel, as he was always billed at the Stadium, or Nella. But the cake, made of dried fruit placed in a doughy sandwich and made wet with burnt sugar, was called a Wet Nella after Nelson cakes. They were first made in Nelson, Lancs. Hard to get these days, but the name has a great nostalgic quality for older Scousers and they regard the wet nella as our invention and sole property. As indeed they do (lob) scouse, which is only Irish stew, though it is said you can make scouse out of anything – and that's the point of this poem.

5. With us marbles are olleys. Corruption probably of alley, another name for marble.

6. Kewins are winkles. Said to be after an old winkle-seller named McKeown. Doubt it. Don't forget your pin and remember you buy them by the pint. Bring your own cup.

7. Jungle juice is rum. Ships trading from Liverpool to the African Coast used to issue it to the crew daily – an excellent practice, alas, now scrapped, as in the Royal Navy. Their crews first nicknamed it so and dockers spread the name. It is the spirit Scousers prefer, but the only drink stronger than beer consumed these days is cheap Australian 'sherry', called Aussie white.

8. Can never find out why streaky bacon is called rhody or rhoded and a Liverpool shopkeeper just can't understand what else you could call it. With cabbage it is, after spare ribs, our favourite dish.

9. Justice Laski was the first judge to serve when Liverpool got its own Old Bailey. Formerly a barrister in Manchester, brother of late Harold Laski. Very strict and full of humour.

10. Cob is a piece, chuck is bread or any food. Rolls are called cobs – what else? I stayed at the very posh Brown's Hotel once at a conference and my Scouse companion, missing a roll on his side plate at breakfast, shouted across the breakfast room, 'Eh, whur's me cob?' To be in a temper is to 'have a cob on!' – as it were a chip on shoulder. Chuck is sailor talk. A cob of coal, of course, is quite standard. By extension – a lump of owt.

11. As elsewhere in the North a *half* pint is always a gill. It's a word unrelated to measure and simply means a small glass. It will doubtless be so under decimalisation.

12. Scousers who never went near our Royal Philharmonic were proud of Sir Malcolm's years of association with it.

Pages from a ha'penny book[13].

First: Locusts[14], chewy[15], fireman's sock[16],
    Everton toffee, Roby rock.
Second: Echo, mid-day, one o'clock gun[17],
    Punch an Judy[18], Lots of fun.
Third: Pug in gob[19], clew on ear[20],
    Sunday's salt fish[21], it's the gear[22].
First: Pennorth a fades[23], a Marli horse[24],
    An ould Corpy tram of course.
Second: A tickling stick from Knotty Ash[25],

---

13. If you talk rubbish you are told 'you're talkin like a ha'penny book' (actually 'bewk'). From the days when cheap and silly literature was even cheaper.

14. An edible African bean we kids loved, especially if stolen from dock shed. Not in greengrocers in 'Pool any more, but still imported by ICI. Funny to note that in Germany this sweet, liquorice-like food is called John's bread. Wasn't it locusts John the Baptist ate – the insects?

15. Chewy is chewing gum, typical Liverpudlian apocope. Y'what?

16. When ships were coal-burning, the tough Liverpool firemen who manned the stokehold were the hardest working men in the world and proudly boasted they had the sweatiest socks.

17. For many years, at one o'clock, an old gun was fired at Birkenhead. When they heard the bang all watch-owners checked the time. Liverpool-born Augustine Birrel writes about a political meeting in the city where the speaker, a stranger, was disconcerted to see each man in the audience looking at his watch, all at the same moment. The gun had gone!

18. Young or old we love Mr Punch. Three generations of 'Professor' Codmans have run the show using a set and dolls supplied by a local art society. Like him we talk through our noses, and aren't all Liverpool girls Judies? His toughness suits us too. For years it was presented in the centre of one of Liverpool's busiest streets but there was public uproar when it was ordered to move on, as a hazard to traffic. A safer place had to be supplied nearby, a much better site.

19. Pug is a punch, a puck, word of Gaelic origin like some other bits of our slang.

20. A clew is another sort of punch. Gob is mouth, Gaelic too. Saying, 'I'll put a fluke's gob' (the fluke, a fish, has a large, twisted mouth) is a threat.

21. Salt fish for breakfast on Sunday, to give a good taste to the midday ale, is a tradition. The harder the better.

22. The Beatles made the phrase 'the gear' or 'gear' famous, but it is quite old, is of shipyard origin, found in Clydeside as well as here and long used generally by musicians to express excellence.

23. God be with the days when a bundle of rotting apples could be bought for a penny.

24. A white or Marli horse in a fanlight was a sign of respectability, particularly favoured in Orange districts because King Billy's horse was white.

25. Liverpool comic made the tickling stick famous. His home is in Knotty Ash.

Harry Petty's saus. and mash[26].

Third: Gansey red and gansey blue[27],
Jars out from a rowdy do[28].

First: Vaughan's gussy[29], foreman's blocker[29],
Old jokes from Ted Ray's golf locker.

Second: Askey's speck; say 'ay then you!'
From each cathedral take a pew.

Third: Shawlie's handcart, jacksharp[30], Liver bird
Dollypegs[31].

First: Amino acid chains three miles long.
DNA will make it strong.

Second: Cobblestone from Scotty Road,
Orange drums that Papists goad.

Third: Togo stolen from a shed[32],
With a pig's foot from Birken 'ead[33].

First: Rose Heilbron's briefs[34], a pair a kecks[35]
Spice-balls, let's not mention sex[36].

Second: Tommy's gags, a jest from Robb,

---

26. Generations of Liverpool office-boys, including young Tommy Handley, had excellent lunches at Harry Petty's cheap restaurant. It was part of a number of eleemosynary activities on the part of this rich Edwardian.

27. The red and blue jerseys of our two football teams have an almost totemistic quality to the fans, as I record elsewhere. We got gansey for jersey from Dublin (Guernsey?).

28. See my *Rowdy Do* herein.

29. We call straw hats gussies. Gussy, as with Arthur Augustus Darcy of *Gem* school stories suggests poshness. Frankie Vaughan – and Chevalier – must be among the few who wear them.

30. We fished in park lakes for tiddlers – jacksharps in North Country dialect. We call them jackies. In Ireland, kishawns, which is almost literally sharpjacks. Some wrongly associate with the elusive speed of once famous footballer, Jack Sharp, Liverpool businessman, Everton director.

31. Used with dolly tub to wash clothes, the process being called dollying. (North Country generally.) Saying she's dirty when she's dolly is a feline insult.

32. Togo is brown sugar.

33. Irish cattle are slaughtered at the lairage in Birkenhead.

34. First woman judge, we are proud of the learning and beauty of this great defence lawyer, who practised in the Liverpool area and was born and bred here.

35. Kecks are trousers, from old thieves' lingo *kicks* – from (they say) the final kicking on the gallows.

36. Spice balls are savouries made from spiced offal.

Lovelee orangies four for a bob.

Third: Coarse apron well below the knees[37],
and after you with the vinegar please.

First: Stink bomb from the Wizzid's Den[38],
Splinter from the dockers' pen[39].

Second: Here's a scuffer, scarper douse!
They taste brew. Good gees, Maggie, we've invented
Scouse!

*　　　*　　　*

If I have a party piece, this is it. I have added to and subtracted from it on the air and concert platform, at dinners and giving talks to various bodies, the change being often based on the purpose of the gathering, the names of people present, the day's hot topic locally. First time was ten years ago on the club ship *Landfall*, tied up in Canning Dock, one of the port's oldest, near Maggie May's parade, Canning Place. The menu consisted solely of scouse and other dishes we love such as Paddy wack (pea soup), wet nellas, kewins.

This last time was in 1968, when I had dinner (similar menu) at Warwick University and Stan Kelly asked me to use, for fun, the amino acid and DNA phrase. Many laughed. But I've no idea of the meaning, and never asked.

I had three excellent witches when this was done in my *Plate of Scouse* revue at Everyman Theatre: Stan Mason, Sheila Donnahey and Tess Griffin (Stan was the one with the beard).

A Scouser describes the Nativity

Jesus was born in a back-yard in Betlem in Judea but he wuz the saveyer uv the whole world. His mother Murry wuz a virgin, come fum a good famly. So did er husbind Joseph who become Jesus's foster-father.

When e wuz courtin Murry in their home town of Nazrit whur dey

---

37. Barrow girls favoured sacking or hessian for their aprons.

38. Well-known Liverpool 'Joke' Shop frequented by many generations of school-boys (of all ages).

39. Before decasualisation, dock labourers used to stand in the pen waiting for work. Selection was arbitrary – while some men usually got work, others seldom did.

wuz very poor, im being in the carpentry in a small way, an eers how she wuz he's proper narked at the first. Den he gets a direck messidge fum God and he understands.

... The town wuz choc a block. The baby wuz due and they cudden even ger in a likkle pub. So the baby wuz born in the back-yard among the animils. But wise men an ordnry sheppids come to see um an dey knew he wuz no ordnry kid.

– Gospels in Scouse

Flynn serves scouse*

In memory of the 8th Kings Regiment, disbanded March 1955

'It doesn't look as if he'll come now, Sergeant.'

'No, sir.' Sergeant Dunn, heaving his big form from his chair with a poor pretence of reluctance, tried to twist his wide red face into a look of regret.

'I suppose there's nothing for it but the oul canteen.'

Flynn and O'Hara were on their feet almost as quick as he.

Captain (now Major) MacNabb remained seated.

'Siddown,' said the Sergeant, slipping back himself.

Lance Corporal Flynn, product of a Liverpool slum, short and swarthy, was a smart soldier, uniform neatness itself, black hair close cropped, able to avoid detection, slyly insulting and a great success at unarmed combat which, compared to life in 'are street' – where, he declared, they played tig with hatchits – was kids' stuff. Plump, ginger Private O'Hara, from the same area, a fellow-seller of fruit from handcarts, was not so adept at keeping out of trouble. In civil life he had graduated from Borstal to Joe Gerks (Walton Gaol). His admiration for Lance Corporal (now Private) Flynn was immense.

'I feel, Sergeant,' drawled the Captain in his best Rossall, 'we must keep these voluntary educational efforts going or, well, really, we'll all go to seed, won't we, I mean? So my idea is that one of us gives a talk. Each of us must have some subject in which he specialises and by expounding which I mean he can enlighten the rest of us and – Yes, Sergeant?'

---

* Naturally with acknowledgments to Alan Hackney's marvellous *Private's Progress.*

Dunn was indicating that such was exactly what he had in mind himself.

'Now I don't suppose you want to hear my little talk again on the fine points of polo?' Silence. 'No, rather thought you wouldn't. But surely, Sergeant, we have one among us interested in some special subject. Yourself, for instance, you must have a hobby?

No one could possibly have noticed O'Hara's lips move as he muttered 'Yis, beer', and the Captain's eye was still oozing mateyness as it swept the room.

'Stamps, etymology, coins, economics, philosophy – isn't there anyone – um?'

No ripple disturbed the sea of expressionless faces. Flynn was again on his feet.

'Siddown,' said the Sergeant in a whispered bark, no easy feat.

'What's up wid you, yuh big pudden?' asked O'Hara almost soundlessly through closed lips.

'I'm going to give a talk, sir,' said Flynn.

'That shook yuh, Sarge.' (from the ventriloquist.)

'Excellent, excellent, I am most pleased.'

Flynn had started before Dunn could do anything about it. He scorned conventional openings.

'Now, lissen, youse,' he began, 'a lot a youse are in dis rigimint under what you might call false pertences. We're sposed to be a Liverpool rigimint, sposed to be, see. But one arf a you issen Scousers a tall. I'm goin to teach yez how to talk proper. Liverpool talk. Make whackers a you, So youse'll after foget your fancy talk or yer Cockney or Geordie an all like dat. Right? Well, lissen.'

'Let him proceed, Sergeant.'

'Yes, sir.'

'Siddown, Basil Belly,' seemed to come from the map dangling from a pin under the light bracket on the green-distempered wall.

'A few essamples for a start.' Flynn pushed his little chest out and linked his hands behind his head in the manner of a recent visitor from Caius whose talk on the Far East brought it no nearer to his audience but had provided, for the friskier ones, a dozen catchphrases and postures to cause hysteria in the wet canteen along towards closing time.

'Sposin now you was skint, adden the coppers, was broke. Can't go to no pics, aven't even the splosh for a ciggie, dependint on yer mate for a nicker or fag-end an yet you want a bevvy, a drink. Do you stand outside the canteen waitin for someone to mug yuh? Youse'll ave a long wait, lad: No you aveter go in see.

It's bess a course to ave a few meg or a bit a silver, for a latchlifter like, your entrance-fee, but if you aven't you must go in just the same. Nex ting you mus' do is find a mug, a big-earted sucker, as it might be the sergeant here -y know- who'll mug you and you tap him for a gill. Praps you don't so you goes minesweepin up an down the bar. Now what d'you call dat? Tell them, O'Hara. Moodying. You are said to be moodying up and down. If you get a dhrink you wait talkin a lot a crap and wipin your glass all roun the counter like, waitin' for another mug. An what's dat called? Hangin the latch. Correct.

'To pass from bevvyin to scoff, food or chuck, not wit'out regret, 'syou might say, youse'll find dat all Scouse or Frisby Dyke sayins is equally approperate. Take scouse if you can get it. You can't get it in dis mob. Cooks, I've shot um. But evybody eats scouse in Liverpool dane night. An what is scouse? Nothink more or less than stew. Quite right, O'Hara. Come to me fer a oly picture after the class. No yew can't leave duh room, Corpril Stern.

'Plenny a vegtbils is the secrit. You can ave less an less meat till the's no meat a tall. Dat is blind scouse. But wit good stewin meat – like when the ould dolls, shawlies, Murry Ellens useter come to the markit askin for two pennorth a meat for the dog anough to make scouse for five a dem. Scouse, pigs' cheek, spur ribs, salt fish av a Sundy mornin, all gear chuck. Dere's a word. The littlest child in the 'Pool knows what the word means yet I spose the's some a youse here wus four yeers a more in Standard Six an you wooden know what it was. Well it's like smashin', or (screwing an imaginary glass in his eye) "jolly rippin". It just means somethink good, see. You go to a do, lots a ale, jars out, plenny a talint to dance wit, lots a chuck, a real rowdy do. Afterwids you meet a fella and you say, "Ello, there, Jud, you should a went, it was the gear". Or you get a new suit, what we call a whicker, an your pal likes it. Does he say, "You look smashin"? No, he says "You look the gear", or "Dat is a gear suit, whack".

'Now, gentry, spose the Sergeant ere wus demobbed – Take dat appy grin off-a yer moey O'Hara or I'll marmalise you – will he wur a bowler on he's big ead? They'd aveter build im one at Cammel Laird's. But if he's in Liverpool it won't be no bowler, friends. What'll it be, O'Hara? A blocker. B-l-o-c-k-e-r.'

Dunn was unmoving but the Captain's hand flew along his notebook. Flynn paused to let him complete his last note.

'Bossis on the docks – such as some a youse cud never be so long as you got a-siwasaying, bossis down dur wear a blocker in case workers over 'ead accidentally drop such tings as ammers, rivits and etcetera as the bossis pass. If I wus to be demobbed – if, a big if – and was daft, doolally or mugs-for-rags anough to wanna work not being a boss I'd be espected to wear a decker, a peaked cap, with a big peak becos of our Scouser motto 'If yer can't fight, wur a big at.' The peak is offen called a letting-board a espression as comes from pigeon fancyin of which I'll do a bit as well as fancyin other birds, tarts or judies.

'As to fightin you may be s'prised to know that in Liverpool the is a certain amount a violince a times. Two ladies may fight over some janglin, or gossip, carried on in the wash-ouse – dough now the almost all use these here laundryettes, y know – but the fellas will fight over anythink. If you jus wake up wit a cob on, in a bad temper, no chuck in the ouse perhaps or yer judy assen pressed yer kecks or you aven't the price uv a bevvy or the footee coupons as let yer down again you'll go out an dodge round the jiggers, likkle streets, till you meet some other nark and before you can say Bessie Braddick you'll be down the banks knocking the bells outa one another. Well in dat case youse'll ave to know some insultin remarks an a course vary dem, cos what would do for any oul rowdy you met on a lecky – tramcar dat is – wooden do for a Paddy Kelly, scuffer or cop. But the jus issen time for me to give youse esamples of all dat in dis place. But if any youse studints ave the price – or even if you aven't – me an my shacker here, O'Hara, will on'y be too pleased to give yer the benfit. Right. And now, dough there is much, much else I cud tell yer, I see the Sergeant lookin thirsty –'

Looking down at him, he murmured *sotto voce* to his whacker; 'Don' some mothers ave funny kids? An the Captin is lookin at he's watch. So, wit he's permission we'll close. Did you like it, sir?'

'Siddown, sconehead,' from O'Hara as the Sergeant rose.

'Most certainly, Flynn, and I am most obliged. It was absoloutely the gear.'

Potherb

Gorra big job at the docks y'know, has men under him; he drives a crane . . . Bad tempered, he'd start a row in a empty ouse. Light-fingered? He'd steal the stripes off an ould night-shirt. Well known in Joe Gerks (Walton Gaol), they keep his needle threaded.

A Scouser's catedril hymn

(*At the opening in Liverpool of the Cathedral of Christ the King, Whit Sunday, 1966.*)

On Brownlos Ill a workhouse stood
Now it's the ome of a great worker:
With Mary back in Nazarit
And Joseph Jesus was no sherker.

The lad grew up, in later years
E done good work, E does it still.
The greatest work E ever done
Was for us all upon a ill.

E said the poor and meek E'd bless,
And peaceful folk would know great peace,
An dem that suffer on dis earth
In Eavin for ever find release.

After E'd blessed the bread and wine
E prayed, then calmly waited till
The soldiers come wid Judas an
A cross soon stood on Calvry Ill.

Into a cavern, Jesus put,
Jesus come out again. The wimmen found
The baby clad in swaddlin clothes
Ad left Is burial clothes behind.

On Whitsun Day Is followers
Instruction got on many a ting,
Dat's why dis Whitsun finds us in
The Werker's ome, now E's a King.

An as I kneel in it an pray,
My eart wit great rejoicin fills,
To think the greatest werker sent
Is blessin from the Seven Ills.

So now we know no evil can
Destroy our soul against God's will
So long as wid a umble eart
We visit Im – on Brownlos Ill.

112

Sermons in Scouse

An old lady in Everton told my mother years ago: 'You're for ever pushing that lad on to readin the lives uv the Saints. He'll be finishin up a bloddy at'eist.'

It didn't get as bad as that. I have, however, hobnobbed with Anglican clergy. When, before making my first Communion, I was being taught the Commandments, the teacher, Miss Connolly, quite cleverly interpreted sins in terms suited to children. Religion should be much more than a source of good conduct, but it should be at least that. Teachers trying to make young savages fairly civilised used it to that end.

'Taking the Lord's name in vain' covered vulgar talk like bum and bugger. Adultery was dirty talk or, maybe, Flashing it. Kids' fibs were false witness, 'Thou shalt not kill' meant you mustn't go round belting others over the ear-hole.

Religious instruction for British Catholics is no longer governed by the *Penny Catechism* – which is a loss. Catholic children acquired much more than a code of belief and conduct from the little yellow book. This simplified digest of Aquinas's mighty philosophy gave them a mental advantage over non-Catholics.

I will not suggest that Catholic dockers having a pint prefer to chatter about transubstantiation or the hypostatic union instead of the subjects other dockers prefer. But that he once heard of such mysteries gives just a little bit more *shape* to his life. It is unlikely that the bo'sun on a banana boat, as he lays himself down for the night in his bunk thinks of the 'Four Last Things' – Death, Judgement, Hell and Heaven. But, if he squandered it all long since, he once had his share of that patrimony of which those four things form a unit and, though many of its coins are spurious, gave simple souls a life with meaning which the cleverest cannot otherwise discover.

But of course teachers who were not trained theologians could be plain ignorant or evasive, poor souls.

Blessed art thou among women and blessed is the fruit of thy womb, Jesus. – '*Miss, miss, miss, what's a womb?*'

Incredible to relate, this could once embarrass those spinsters. The Catechism in the section on adultery spoke of 'wilful pleasure in the irregular motions of the flesh'. For a long time this meant to me enjoying a visit to the lavatory because of a teacher's mumbled explanation.

So, when Miss C, teaching us the Commandments, was asked

what making a graven image meant, she said 'Going to Protestant churches and mission-halls', and passed on to other things. My hobnobbing with Anglican clergymen has led to just that. (Mind you I never believe for one moment, deep down, that they are *priests*, any more than Queen Elizabeth did, at any rate the married ones. As the weary old jest has it – 'What, im a father? He's got six kids!'). I have read the Lesson in a Protestant church. I have been in a Protestant mission-hall and come out without a scratch. My archbishop would not mind if he knew; if I went to confession I'd say nothing about it. That is all very well. What would my mother say? *What is she saying?* I bet you thought that was only thunder.

When German bombers forced my mother to attend a church manned by secular (she preferred circular which could be correct in a way) priests instead of her beloved Jesuits, she had the strongest doubts of the validity of their faculties.

Roman Catholics attending churches and halls of other faiths, and vice versa, has become so usual since the reign of good Pope John that it is at this date difficult to recall the former unlikelihood of what my local Anglican vicar called 'mixed bathing'.

Evangelism was, rightly or wrongly, in the minds of many R Cs, associated with attempts at proselytism. A hungry Pape would starve before he would go for free pieces of meat or bread to the South End mission-hall (now an inn patronised by the *avant garde* from the nearby university) conducted by Gypsy Smith and nick-named Cob Hall from the pieces of bread and meat Smith gave away.

My mother always called anyone who gave up his belief in our brand of Christianity a 'souper'; for, in her native Ireland, in famine times, it was alleged, hungry people deserted their faith for a bowl of soup.

I had a good strong cup of tea and some delicious home-made scones, but it will be Mass not Matins for me next Sunday, as in Miss Connolly's day.

My visit to St Athanasius' Church hall in the North Docks area of Liverpool, not a Kop shout from the soccer ground, is a trifling incident in the growing serial story of true ecumenism between Protestants and Romans in this one-time battlefield of rival regiments of the Church militant, both claiming sole allegiance to the Prince of Peace.

Why was I there? For years I have been writing about Liverpool in our peculiar Scouse dialect which I have spoken through my nose on concert stage, in clubs, on radio and TV – just for a fee-earning laugh. More or less since I left a Jesuit novitiate and married and became a Customs Officer, it put jam on my bread and butter, helped educate my children, gave my wife holidays abroad, kept me out of the billiard halls.

When in London, at the BBC, giving readings from another Scouse book, a very secular publication, *Lern Yerself Scouse*, a producer showed me a par in a paper about an Anglican clergyman in Liverpool who was writing bits of the Gospel in Scouse for his parishioners, notably the young ones. They were receiving it well and he had approval from his superiors. I contacted him, and over a coffee we decided to write a book to try to get home the Great News to people who would not listen to it in its traditional form. We accepted that through the ages in art, the theatre, drama and architecture (as witness the new Liverpool RC Cathedral) the story of Jesus must be retold to new generations in new forms.

And we felt sure that Jesus, though he could converse with learned rabbis, would have spoken, as a north country working-man himself, to his followers and *not without humour*, in their own lingo. (Aramaic, I am told, is a sort of Scouse dialect.) When the first Christians spoke with 'tongues' wouldn't one of the tongues be the slum speech of Jerusalem? The educated St Paul, being all things to all men, would, when appropriate, use 'hippy' language in swinging Athens.

The first purchaser of the book when it appeared, and who now asserts that I hailed him as 'whack' when presented to him, Liverpool's Bishop, said it made certain things clearer to him than the traditional testaments. So it has been. We set it down not in pride but in humble gratitude for being inspired – I do not jib at the word – with folk all over the UK, and in other countries, laymen and cleric, Protestant and Catholic.

This book is no literary masterpiece but that it was written and printed (by a Jewish firm who are most proud of being associated) and published and its words heard on the air, in homes on a record, read in USA, Japan, Australia, used in senior schools in Liverpool (and one in Belfast), quoted in churches, in quality periodicals, religious and otherwise, is a minor miracle.

Jesus was a provincial workman. The tradition is that he worked for his foster-father who was a small town carpenter. The carpenter may not have been poorly off and Jesus, who after all at an early age argued with elders in the synagogue, must have had some education. Everything points to an ordinary workingman – as certainly most of his closest followers were. Anyhow, he left home and lived, with his followers, the life of a tramp. He was a tough 'un. He could ride an unbroken donkey, he could drive traders out of the temple single-handed.

He went up to Jerusalem with his mates as a Liverpudlian might go to a Cup Final. The provincial speech of his followers made them a joke in the capital, his accent betrayed Peter to the high priest's servant. It is not likely that Jesus, speaking to these working class types, telling his little tales, would speak in a language they didn't understand. One can sense the colloquialisms, the sly private jokes even in the written versions all these years after.

I visualised a Liverpool workingman who knew his Gospels but was otherwise illiterate telling their story in his own words. I thought this was worth doing. I had no call. I lived just as disreputable a life after writing it as before. (My collaborator became a Rector.) Des O'Hare, who spoke as Jesus in the recording in words of crudest Scouse said more or less the same thing. We had a moment's grace. It passed. But I can say that though I went on to write about Liverpool using Scouse in its more normal form, nothing I've ever done has satisfied me so much as the Gospels in Scouse.

A visitor, asked what religion Liverpudlians practise, described the Sunday morning pastime at the tough Bullring on a Sunday morning. The Minister (he reported) stands among them and casts coins into the air, which when they descend, all bow to and all but the minister say 'Good Christ'.

'If Jesus came to Liverpool?' asked a wayside Pulpit. Pencilled below was 'Ian St John would have to go inside-right.' On another was: 'If you're tired of sin, come within.' Pencil comment: 'If not, try 124 Thingy Street.' That's my Liverpool. For one little illuminated moment I'd had a glimpse of another.

The Good Samaritan

'Who is your neighbour?' they asked Jesus. 'Lissen', he said:

'The wus a fella goin down the road, as it might be fum London Road into Lime Street, when he got set on be a gang a buckos who arf marmalised him and skinned off, leavin im on the flags. Along comes a clergyman, sees him, does nowt, just carried on. Den a city counclir itself: norra blind werd, jus carried on. Nut a black fella offa a ship, e elps him, first aid an all, an pays fer a taxi to get

116

im to ospikkle quick. Now, even if the clergyman lived next door and the counclir wus is first cousin – I don't after tell *youse* who was the reel neighbour, do I?

– *Gospels in Scouse* (Luke 10, 25-37).

The Prodigal Son

Dis boss ad a son, two in fact, but one's a proper tearaway. So e gets all the dough e can off dad an skins off leavin the other brother to look after the business: e liked werk. Meladdo spends the lot in clubs an bettin shops, up to all sorts a low tings wid all sorts. E falls ill, e's skint. Decises to go back ome. Says e's sorry, reely is now, an maybe e'll be let back in. When is dad sees him he says Gear, he's come back. Nor on'y lets im in, he throws a big do for him and asses evryone for miles round to join in wid the celebrations. The udder son didden care for it but you saw see ow the old feller felt – God, who made evryting, knows anyting, can do anyting will forgive us wen we go off the rails an say Sorry. He's a Dad. The udder son still ad the business.

– *Gospels in Scouse* (Luke 19, 11-24).

'I'm just as ignerint as what youse are!'

Of all my sources of information about my townies' mangling meanings, the city fathers – and aspirants to the honour – gave me the most. For instance, the maker of the above proud appeal to the electors added: 'I wuz in Standard Six five years' – which had him elected.

On the council he often delighted me whether *on the horns of a diploma* or making *an impassive appeal*, after which he told me with delight he was *undulated with letters*. Off to a conference from Princes Dock for Belfast he complained to the chief steward that his room was so small he had *no room to perform his absolutions.*

I'm a pheasant and the son of a pheasant.

I believe we should let the status quo stay as it is.

Now let's boil this whole ting down to tintacks.

I will pefy anyone to agree wid me.

I always try to be unscrupulously fair.

I take evryting the opposition says wid a dose of salts.

I take no connivance of the opposition.

Dat's a horse of a different feather.

They have milked the golden eggs.

Their whole policy is redundant to me.

The bankers pockets bulgin wid the sweat of the workingman.

I want youse all to sign a partition.

You have been falsely misinformed.

Calls hisself a repperee-sentative; he's only a siphon.

I had no symphony from the audience.

I can corrugate dat statement.

The opposition is sticking its head into the ground like a kangaroo.

Liverpool
Gentlemen

Liverpool Gentlemen

The dastardly attack on the Punch and Judy Show

Professor Codman is a very good man
    And so was his father before him;
If on a fine day you are down Lime Street way
    You'll see how the children adore him.

On the George's Plateau in the old puppet show,
    May it play there for many a year,
He displays the wild life of old Punch and his wife,
    And for pennies will give an encore.

It's not just the lads and the girls but their dads
    Who still grin as their dads did before,
Seeing Punch with his stick give a bobby a lick
    And poor Judy's bonce get a crack or two more.

For you'll know that a whacker is never a slacker
    At belting a cop or his judy
And it maybe that she will hit back instantly
    And he'll boast to his mates: 'She's a cracker.'

From Italy Punch came – Dommer's Dad did the same –
    But quickly a Scouser he grew
And right out of his nose the famous phrase goes,
    'What's the mattuh wid yew?'

The baby, the doc., the hangman, the croc.
   And the dog generations had loved
Till one very sad day the Town Council did say:
   'Mr Punch – he has got to be moved.'

But — they hadn't allowed for the bold Scousers proud
   Who loudly cried out 'No, no, no,
'If old Punch's abode is stuck right in the road
   'As a menace to traffic – the traffic must go!'

A crowd a mile long on that day they did throng
   And determined down Lime Street they trod,
Proud men of the 'Pool to defy the new rule,
   Led by Ted Ray and angry Ken Dodd.

Their plans went adrift. Old Punch had to shift,
   But he's now in a far better spot.
While lawbreakers are tried in the Hall he's outside –
   Still old Punch gets away with the lot.

Codman

When, in the very year it was celebrating its Royal Charter, Liverpool Corporation told Professor Codman the Third to take his Punch and Judy show away from the Quadrant they were defying much more than public feeling, which itself was strong enough.

Old Punch had been in the city centre for 150 years. In *The History of the English Puppet Theatre*, Liverpool had been commended as being the last English town with the old puppet show in its centre as a regular attraction.

Punch and Judy had already almost royal patronage. Charles II refused to ban the puppet showmen from St Paul's Churchyard. Queen Ann decreed that the puppets could be presented anywhere where there was a market – which Liverpool had from earliest times (in fact the port grew round the market). The first Royal rights were the rights to do business; a Freeman of Liverpool was simply a man who could go to market to offer his wares. The famous King John Charter was really a pedlar's licence.

Tommy Handley used to describe the George's Hall as being behind the Punch and Judy Show. Codman first used the Quadrant site. The first Professor Codman (the title was self-bestowed as with Lord George Sanger, King Levinskey and Duke Ellington) died about 20 years ago at 87, after entertaining Liverpool kids and their parents, and visitors to the port, for nearly 80 years. At one time the city had eight open-air Punch and Judy shows. Richard Codman the First spent his early years touring the country in a caravan with his circus-bred father, and he was born in Everton. He retired to Melville Place, Liverpool, in the Forties.

He did his first show at 9 years of age and made his puppets out of driftwood found on the beach. His son, Richard the Second, fared better. Nobody ever thought of shifting his dad, but there were already murmurs when he took over in 1923. There was always a strong Puritan tradition in Liverpool's Council Chamber. Actually Punch and Judy, with its touch of anarchy and anti-establishmentism was a good foil to the autocracy of Liverpool Council, self appointed for centuries, often in defiance of central government. Unfortunately for Codman, people didn't have the coppers. As a kid, I often shuffled off ashamed when the lad, with Toby, came round for the penny. I felt truly sorry for the adults who had to do the same. Codman the Second was a hero to think he could still get a living a few yards away from where men had their heads battered for wanting another sixpence to keep their families alive.

The puppets were falling to bits; he had no money to repair his little theatre – Liverpool's first civic theatre after all – when an assembly of Liverpool people interested in the arts, with a well-established Victorian history, rallied round and roused the better-off citizens. The Sandon Studios, still going, in Liverpool's loveliest building, The Bluecoat, behind Woolworths in the main shopping street, raised the money for a new booth.

Liverpool artists did the work for nowt. It was presented to Richard the Second by W. W. Kelly, one of the city's great theatrical managers, and, like the Ark, carried through the city in triumph. (Sandon Studios have always renewed the puppets.) Subscriptions from the public, in the then down and out city, were not lacking.

Richard the Third appeared before royalty in 1916 when he was in the army. His grandfather, who had toured in the USA as well as over the UK, had previously performed for Queen Victoria.

I saw Richard the Fourth the other day. I was strolling round my parish in Huyton when a car whizzed past me. I didn't notice the driver, but in the back I could see some grinning faces. I recognised them at once, as would my kids and grandkids. Punch and his nihilist tribe. I looked towards the driver's seat and saw their master grinning. Toby – how many predecessors must he have had – seemed to grin at me too. They were obviously off to make somebody, some group, old or young, happy – reviving or giving them memories.

Jimmy Riddle

'What was he doing in this street. He didn't live in it, it wasn't a short cut to his home.'

'I suddenly wanted a Jimmy Riddle', said the young fellow. (Justice Laski did not imitate Stipendiary Stewart Deacon in similar circumstances by asking 'Is Mr Riddle in the Court?')

'I went up an entry and there was a fellow there with a girl. Well, you know, I didn't like stopping.'

'So you withdrew. Very gallant, very discreet. So you used the gutter. Now when you were put into the police van what reason did the police officer give for detaining you?'

The lad looked astonished. He had never heard of the police giving anybody like him a reason for anything. Laski pushed on.

'Well, what did you think when you were put in the van?'

'All I wanted to do was to dodge the nut-cracker.'

'Did you not ask him what you were being charged with? What did you think the whole thing was about?'

'Well, all I thought was – they're making a lot of fuss about me having me chopper out!'

Laski was delighted with this. I have no doubt that, from that moment, he was resolved to let the lad go. But he insisted on the whole case being gone into thoroughly, with both counsel giving their spiel, the bobbies being recalled, the lower court depositions gone through thoroughly.

All the time he kept going back to the prisoner and asking him again: 'What did you think the whole thing was about?' And he almost openly chortled when the young chap gave the same reply. The case against the others went on. The jury were told to dismiss this case, no evidence.

In the public gallery was a civics class from one of the local convents. Laski looked slyly at them once or twice. I wouldn't have liked to be the teacher the next day: ' Please miss, what's a chopper?'

126

Draw your own confusions

'Blind the cat, Maggie, all dem kids.'

'Well, he doesn't smoke or dhrink. The day he wuz married he put all he had in the world in me hand.'

'It's a pity you diden keep it there. Why don't you get him a French letter?'

'Jeesake, he can't even read the *Liverpool Echo.*'

Everyting was in a state of kiosk.

He bought her a cartoon of ice-cream.

I strongly dissemble that remark.

He's not gunna go away leaving me holding the candle.

We had a visit from the sanity inspector.

I love to switch on the radiator and lissen to the tropics of the day.

He went down into the casement.

It was as smooth as a milk-pond.

I gave him a look of content.

He fought in the Criterion War.

Had a job as a connoisseur outside a pitcher house.

He's thinking of evacuating to Australia.

The road wuz up so he had to make a detroit.

I'm not a bit interested, it's quite imperial to me.

He deserted the army but they caught up wid him and threw an accordeon round the house.

I agree wid those sediments.

He gorra pair uv dem binomial spectacles.

If he wins the next fight he'll be condenser for the world's championship.

The age of shivery is not dead.

He went to the philant'ropic Hall to hear the Sympathy Orchestra (Playing *Aida:* 'Ay durr, you wid the stars in yer eyes'?)

I wish my girl wooden ride on the pavilion of dis fella's motor-bike.

She had a lovely 'at wid a bird uv parasite on ut.

I was dead scared; I stood putrefied.

Now, now, no incinerations.

Me hair turned jet white.

Two negatives make an infirmary.

I want something to move me vowels.

A wonderful musician, you shoulda eard er archipelagos.

Dooley

Arthur Dooley's studio is now a former pub in a select Liverpool pub district – Woolton. At the time, 1966, it was a former shop, one in small street of about half a dozen shops, behind St Luke's church (a mere empty shell now kept standing, on its slight hill, as a memento of the German air-raids). It's a faded, Victorian, peaceful little spot, only a few yards from the city's main shopping centre. Such oases are daily becoming harder to find in Liverpool. This was the very beginning of Liverpool 8. In this vicinity, what culture ever was in the old seaport was born; and now the area, still carrying surprising relics of former grandeur, is the home of minor poets and painters who have created a recognisable Liverpool school, not unknown outside the city.

Hereabouts the sons and daughters of the slave dealers had started a philosophical society, debating clubs, art collections, libraries. Roscoe is buried here in an obscure nonconformist church yard, the Royal Philharmonic and Everyman Theatre are nearby, Gladstone was born round the corner. Redmond the great Irish patriot spent his boyhood hereabouts – as did Larkin the great Irish agitator. I can't think of any part of London, not even Notting Hill, where culture and penury walk so cheerfully arm in arm as they do in Liverpool 8.

It has nothing to do with wealth, for wealth long since fled from these parts, as from Liverpool generally, which never had much of a society for the last century or so anyhow, and was always firmly and unequivocally based on money, fairly recent money at that. (All aristocracies are based on cash, of course, but not all so recent or so inept at concealing origins. We never became a Boston.)

The homes of the former wealthy are still there and by no means so sad a sight as crumbling 18th century glory presents in other cities. We have no Coombs. Our real slums are far to the north of the city or on the Merseyside fringes of Liverpool 8. Naturally the wealthy did not use pubs, and for many miles round Liverpool 8 you could once walk and not see one. This is true round the Princes and Sefton Park even now. But some of the old houses are now drinking clubs, and new pubs are growing up just outside the perimeter of the two parks. Quite good ones too: A few yards above Dooley's studio of that period, near the Police Headquarters and the university, is O'Connor's Tavern kept by Jimmy Moore. (The previous O'Connor's was in Lime Street and was burnt down a few years ago.) Here you will meet the university wits and half-wits.

What native culture Liverpool has does not reside solely in McGough, Henri, Patten and the other wits, but they and the best of their followers are truly Liverpudlian and, commendably, retain their home town, by birth or adoption, as their headquarters.

You will not see Arthur Dooley in O'Connor's. You will not see him in pubs very much anyhow and at no time was he as much a barfly as some would aver. Do those who see a writer, painter, actor – any 'Bohemian' – relaxing over a Scotch and chaser really think he can tope as much as legend says and compete with the really dedicated drinker who has no art to distract him? Besides, we must rub minds together, have plenty of noisy talk and you don't get that in coffee-houses these days.

Dooley is, of course, a poet, in the manner of Epstein at his best (oh my Liverpool Resurgent!) not of a *vers de société* sculptor like Rodin (ver-ee good; at times I prefer it, but it isn't poetry, is it?) Let us hope in Woolton he has enough stored up in him from his Liverpool 8 period to produce even grander poetry in wrought iron and glass than has already been given the world by the apparently coarse and uncultivated ex-docker, ex-soldier.

The strange occupant of Allerton Bridewell

Allerton Bridewell 'lock-up' had an unusual occupant for two nights – being 'bailed out' each morning – during the Liverpool

Show. It was a fibre-glass statue of Our Lady – Arthur Dooley's
Odessa Pieta – which the City of Liverpool is presenting to the
City of Odessa. At Liverpool Show it was exhibited at the 'Gear
Gallery' along with the newly-published 'Gospels in Scouse' by
Frank Shaw and the Rev. R. Williams, Vicar of St Athanasius's
Anglican Church, Kirkdale.

After the heavy storm on the show's first night, Mike Shaw,
Frank's son, travelled in the police van nightly with the statue
taking it to the safety of the 'lock-up'.

Liverpool Catholic Pictorial, July 1967.

Dean

Billy Dean was a big fellow, genial enough, indeed witty off the
field, dour and single-minded on it, but he was not handsome.
Eight pounds a week in those days was a lot for a lad in his teens,
about four times what he could get at the shipyard, and he was
single. He led a gay life, although I know it was a deal more respectable and consistent with the need to be fit than false rumour said.
If he had a vice, it was then gambling. That could keep him out
late. I moved in the circles he moved in for a while and never saw
him drink to excess.

So many said: 'Give it to Dixie.' We folk who are not tempted
should never criticise the dalliance of people in the public eye. If
you are only on the TV screen for a minute or so, the next day
people who have passed you by for years are hailing you by your
first name and wanting a lock of your hair or your trouser turn-up.

It is true that Dean was the first leading player as adept with
the head as the boot, with which, after all, he scored most of his
goals. Those were the days when Goodison Park was first nicknamed, not by unanimous agreement among the citizens, the
School of Science. There was always a very good class of football
put before the spectator. Stylish football in those days was based
on the slow Scottish game, weaving intricate motions, which,
speeded up, is what the best foreign teams now play.

Everton tended to have numerous Scottish players, many of
them internationals. The scout was a friend of my dad, Danny
Kirkwood, a former player, and he liked to find his players in his
native land. They were not headers. Everton had a centre-forward
a year or so before Dean, Stan Fazakerley, who had his hair sleeked
back with a neat parting; he prided himself on leaving the pitch
at the end of a game with his hair the same as when he walked on.

130

Billy Meredith, for years the Welsh choice, said you were no footballer if you could not bring a ball down from your head to your toe.

Dean soon ceased to be just an opportunistic bustler. As the centre-forward position became permanently his, he developed a classy style of play, very swift, though he looked a trifle clumsy at times, brought on by the very classy players he had around him. But if they showed him plenty he was showing them how to use the head. Of course many of them did not have as hard a head as Bill Dean.

He was lucky to have two very fast wingers at a time when the winger's function was to run swiftly towards the corner flag, drawing as many players as possible away from what we'd now call the strikers, making sure the strikers were onside, and swinging in towards goal. How often, when he with other Everton players and defenders soared into the air, Dean's head shot above all the others and the goalie hadn't a chance. Dean was one of the first professional footballers to tuck his jersey into his pants; this was because of the grabbing of the jersey which invariably happened as he soared above the others. If, in those days, the linesmen had had the role of advising the ref, since wisely given to them, Dean would have scored many more.

Dean had many serious injuries during his professional career – from a car accident he was a long time in hospital and was not expected to survive. When Dean had a pub (he now works for a pools firm) it was as necessary for visiting soccer stars to make the pilgrimage to the Dublin Packet, Chester, especially during race week, as for a visiting Communist of rank to visit Karl Marx's grave at Highgate. Gathering dust on a shelf were the caps he had for England (there were far fewer international occasions in soccer in his time). After he had casually shown these he would take strangers aside and show them his legs. There was hardly an inch without the mark of a boot – and pros wore shin-guards in his day. Yet he was never known to retaliate.

Maybe he would in the dirtier game which has developed since, no doubt because so much is at stake now in professional football. But of course now if he were 17 again and playing he would earn more than ten times the highest wage he ever had with Everton. 'I wouldn't live in it', I heard him say at the Plough Inn at Moreton, Cheshire. He changed his mind later. He said in print he'd do as well as before. I have indicated some of the changes, mostly favouring him, though goalkeeping was never so good as it is these days, and I think he is possibly right. He would be trained for the modern method and have with him men similarly trained.

Dom

Dom left the University to go to sea and he was in his fifties before he retired from the sea. 'I had', he explains, 'to stay on working to keep the parents.'

The parents were Italians who came to Liverpool in the last century as so many did at that troubled time. They went to live in a sort of ghetto near Scotland Road – Gerard Street. Dom's father used to play a barrel-organ round Liverpool streets while Mrs Volante, who was to have fourteen children, danced. She was the basis of Dom's whole life. He never married. He didn't drink or smoke either and was a regular churchgoer. When younger he went in pubs and hotel lounges because he loved being with people, especially people in boxing and the entertainment business. For years in a pub between the old Empire Theatre and the old Stadium (where your scribe once made a brief inglorious appearance) there was a framed photograph of Dom boxing Gracie Fields. He liked talking and was never self-conscious.

Many pugilists are ill at ease in company lacking thick ears or in a higher social category. Not Dom. In fact he liked to talk with businessmen and men in the public eye as if they were intimates. He was present at a businessmen's luncheon and he was on his feet as soon as the Royal Toast (the Duke of Lancaster) had been given to say: 'Me and Mister (naming the guest of honour) wish yiz all a appy Christmas.' It was reminiscent of the occasion when the American champ King Levinskey was a guest at a sportsmen's dinner. Levinskey was on his feet as soon as the Chairman said 'Gentlemen, the King', to say: 'Tanks fellers.'

Dom's father moved from playing the barrel-organ to hiring them out for a few shillings a day. More correctly, street-organs. There have been few barrel-organs in the streets for many years. It can never have been a very profitable undertaking: street-organs require a deal of upkeep and, of course, the music has frequently to be changed. (They work very much like pianolas with music on perforated rolls, the music coming from a pin-studded cylinder rotated by the handle. The speed of rotating governs what little *tone* there is.) For the last 40 years or so they have been little in demand, edged out by more sophisticated forms of mechanical music. So much that delighted children in the Twenties has gone from the city streets.

Therefore old man Volante can never have been well-off. As soon as Dom began to get good purses he moved his mother into a house of her own in a slightly better neighbourhood than Gerard Street – Erskine Street, where Noonan, calling himself Tressal, who wrote the Socialist classic *The Ragged-trousered Philanthropist* was lodging, en route for the USA, before he was moved to hospital to die. Neither house has been demolished – yet. Neither bears a plaque.

As a lad going to early Mass I often saw Dom doing a bit of roadwork down this street, heavily sweatered, arms going like pistons, and I always waved my school cap to him. He would grin back. Already his face looked as if it had been stamped on; he smiled with his whole mouth in which there were many missing teeth. Dom's smile was rather frightening. I got to know him rather better when he was going to sea and his conversation was almost always about 'me mam'. Once or twice I was in his home in his seagoing years while his mother was still alive. Her talk was all of Dom. When she was buried the sadness on that battered face was pitiful to see.

Gerard Street was the victim a few years ago of town improvement but most of the Italian families, mainly in the ice-cream, roast chestnut, food and drink line, all very nice people, Fusco, Vermiglio, Imundi, Vario (they produced a first-class boxer too; also a Dom) had prospered and had moved away. Quite a lot of them who had fought in the First World War and had sons in the last were interned in the Isle of Man. Just to record that there are potential stormtroopers in all countries, I wish to say I saw a British officer kick one of them when he was too slow getting on to the Isle of Man boat gangway.

Dom started boxing at an early age and he gave every penny he could spare from his earnings in the ring to his mam. He also gave generously to the church (otherwise Dom is, as we say, not mean but careful). I cherish a memory of an open air procession round the almost entirely Catholic streets about Holy Cross church on the feast of Corpus Christi, which was led by Dom in surplice and cassock carrying a tall bronze cross, the battered face striving to look as angelic as possible.

He left the profession fairly early; he couldn't conquer Tarleton and there was nobody left in the country at his weight to fight (six men he had at some time beaten went on to be British champions).

For a while he had a job in the gym at Liverpool University, but he wanted to go to sea (I often feel I'm the only Liverpool lad who never, even momentarily, had that wish). And at first he went Cunard as he liked New York. (He still works, in his late sixties, as a security man and lives with his sister in a towering tenement not far from where I am writing.) It was during those years I had many talks with him. Nominally he was a steward and on sailing day he was to be seen, with other stewards in white jackets, fearsomely grinning and chatting affably in broad Scouse to the first-class passengers. Most of his work, for crew and passengers, was in the ship's gym. Every morning he did a two mile trot round the upper deck. When he was out of Liverpool the Customs Officers used to love watching him from a spot where he couldn't see them, coming off the gangway and moving past the quartermaster and the bobby on the gate. He moved in so sly and furtive a manner one could have believed he had the Crown jewels on him. Each of them knew it was, every trip, a pair of nylon stockings (on which the duty, if charged, was about tenpence) for, of course, 'me mam'.

Dom first travelled Cunard to New York with Tarleton. They were good friends, though Dom was always a little awed by Nelson, whose face never revealed his profession. Tarleton was a natty dresser, sleek haired, with the parting almost dead-centre, a style much imitated by Liverpool youngsters, and still faintly visible on old heads in places where they gather to recall the old days at Pudsey Street Stadium, of Billy Baker, Ike Bradley, Joe Curran, all from streets near Gerard Street (Joe Curran was as pious as Dom. Once the tough Stadium crowd thought he was being too gentle with an opponent. 'Hit him, Joe,' came a shout, 'he's not a holy picture').

Tarleton was a dancing-man, after the girls, from a slightly better-off family in a slightly posher district. (It was near Erskine Street to which Dom moved his mam.) While still in his teens, and when Dean was at his best, Tarleton was voted in a ballot conducted in cinemas, theatres, hotels and the like the most popular sportsman in Liverpool (I didn't vote for him). As the New York-bound ship lowered the Blue Peter and the gangway was dropped Nelson was on the top deck waving to cheering crowds. Dom went below to their cabin and what happened then I was told some years after by the bedroom steward. As so many Cunard stewards he used American idioms. He had unpacked, as a good bedroom steward should, Dom's one piece of baggage. 'Whurs me clothes?' asked Dom. 'In the closet, sir', said the steward. Dom only knew

134

one sort of closet. 'What a place' (he never swore) he spluttered, 'to put me clobber!'

In New York Dom won the cheers. There is a big Italian colony there of course. But it was in the ring he gained approval. Dom's rough manner suited the New Yorker. Nelson was too elegant, too consciously an English man-of-the-world, his upright stance and classic style of boxing, resembling, my Dad said, Jim Driscoll. Dom's wild fist-slinging, tearaway style suited the New York fans. He won six and drew one of the seven fights he had in the USA. In one at Madison Square Gardens against Harry Carlton, Dom was knocked down five times in one round. 'Come on, Limey' the crowd yelled, 'you'll wear your knickers out!'

The referee wanted to stop the fight. But in the next round Dom knocked Carlton out cold. In New York Dom always visited Jack Dempsey's Bar. Jack always had a soft spot for Liverpudlians but, a half-breed himself, he was all for Dom. He compared that knock-out with his own against Luis Angelo Firpo whom Dempsey knocked out after climbing back into the ring from a ringside seat. (Dempsey says he landed in the lap of a pressman doing his report on a silent typewriter and the scribe said: 'What's the hurry, Jack? You'll see it in the papers tomorrow.') One of the classic fistic legends was my Dad's about the great Johnson, whom he took me to see sparring in Liverpool in 1915. Johnson could deliver his knockout punch when he wished, but he liked to toy with his opponents and give the crowd a fair run. In a fifteen-round contest in which he just appeared to be holding his own, he shook hands coming in for the eighth. 'You don't,' the ref reminded him, 'shake hands till the last round.' 'This is it,' said Jack, clocked his man, and a few minutes after was struggling into his dinner-suit to get into a taxi for the high lights.

New York was a place where many Liverpudlians signing on for the round trip 'took a powder' in the hungry Twenties. They somehow found jobs there. There was an amnesty years later and they could stay although they had landed illegally. I met many on Yank ships during the war. Many became longshoremen and they were always there to meet Dom when he went ashore. Dom was no snob; he spoke to them in the same terms in which he addressed chief officers and pursers and important passengers on the old Brit. (Most of them were ex-Cunard or White Star.) It was an old Liverpool streetfighter, friend of Damon Runyon, Jimmy Johnson, known to promoter and manager as Larceny Pete, who introduced Dom and Nel to the American boxing world. (He was said to have

135

belted heavyweight champs round his office when they quarrelled about percentages.) Jimmy wanted to promote the Liverpool-Italian, who could play mouth-organ, in a big way over there. Maybe Dom could have been Liverpool's first world champion. I am sure he could have mauled Miller, the only man Tarleton couldn't beat.

Dom was unlucky that Tarleton was around at the time. There is something in being a great secondbest and he can think of that as he sits in Woolfall Towers watching his telly, his only off-duty pastime. Tarleton is long since dead.

Arsenal's former manager, Joe Mercer, wrote in a newspaper about the best England team that could have been formed among English players in his time. He included six Everton players, not omitting himself, with Cliff Britton, adding that icicle of a man Warny Cresswell, fullback, and a fine goalkeeper, Ted Sagar. Dean was there of course. But Mercer said if it wasn't Dean it would have been Lawton. If I was Lawton that posting as second would have made me glow. (I agree with it fully. In some ways he was better than Dean.) Dean did it all with a plate in his head. Tarleton had only one lung.

Tarleton was 40 when he won his second Lonsdale Belt. He said he had to have it because his wife had just had twins. Saddest of my days was to see Nelson in Chris O'Brien's Douglas Pub allowing people to be photographed wearing the Lonsdale Belt. One of the twins, Brian, a salesman in Liverpool, told me the second belt was missing. The first was bought by a Liverpool sportsman and sold for a good sum at Sotheby's. Brian now has the second.

As the chairman of a boys' boxing club in Huyton, the Blue Eagles, better known as the public house doorstep with a roof on, I found that the boys were formed into three teams. One was called Cassius Clay; one was called Henry Cooper. I was appalled to find the third was called Frank Shaw. I just wouldn't have it, and I asked them to call it the Dom Volante. Dom was never a champion, but he is a Liverpool boxer whose career was so creditable, though unlucky, as to be an inspiration to young scrappers; the name should not be forgotten. He lives across the road from the club. We asked him over and, though he doesn't go out much, except to work, he was delighted to help especially some little dark boys. Fighting would be finished now, he thought, especially among the heavies, if it weren't for the blacks.

The Negroes are often poor. But in Liverpool our boxers mostly came from two poor districts, North (Dom's area) and South (the Rowan country) and the best fighting was seen at the old Pudsey Street Stadium run by Johnny Best when he could get a mauler from Mugs' Alley round the back – someone knowing little of ring finesse, with lots of guts, ready to give the crowd a show, for a quid or so. Just for a slice of bread and butter, Dom put it. They often had to have a wash before they could go in the ring. The few bob they got they gave away before they got home. Later, in the handsome commodious new Stadium, Johnny Best Junior, an old schoolmate of mine, couldn't get cheap fighters.

His dad could get them when daily one hundred thousand unemployed men walked through the main streets of the city. In the prosperous Forties, when a strong lad could get forty a week at Fords, nobody fancied a good hiding for a fiver. Young Johnny couldn't get cheap boxers so packed it up. The moment, says Johnny, a stable had a good lad, who'd done well a couple of times, he wanted the Bank of England. 'I had to put up prices to pay them and crowds fell off, and I hadn't the jack to pay for a good supporting programme.' It's what happened to the music-halls. A few stars wanting too much.

Even as a star Dom didn't get too much, though he could always draw a full house. And what crowds they were!

Courting

Case dismissed, eff off

Liverpool Magistrates Court has five rooms. Serious cases are taken in Number One by the Stipendiary. The other four are under a lay magistrate.

In the middle of the last war a strange one arrived in Number Two. A seaman ashore after a hard run with plenty of money had gone into the Adelphi and ordered a ------ steak and chips. Said the waiter; 'I beg your pardon, sir.'

'Why,' said Jack, 'you got cloth ears? I said a plate a effin steak and chips.'

'I must call the head waiter,' he was told.

'Why the effin ell? Can't you serve effin steak an chips?'

'Can I help you, sir?' said the HW.

'Can't see how unless you can cook. Don't know why you was dragged in. Not as if I was ordering summin out a de way. All I want is effin steak an chips.'

'I must see the manager.'

'Eff the manager, just gemme some effin steak an chips jilde . . .'

Magistrate (after many witnesses had in detail reported the sailor's remarks): 'A difficult case. The man has been at sea a long time. All he wanted was some food, though it is regrettable he should describe it as he did. It seems in all the circumstances hardly an offence. I am not sure what to do.'

Voice from the strangers' gallery: 'Give him six effin months!'

Magistrate: 'Who's trying this effin case?'

Bowman the showman

When Frederick Bowman came out of gaol as Sir Frederick Bowman, he immediately sued the Governor of the prison and subpoenaed the Home Secretary. Herbert Morrison, the Home Secretary, who had put Frederick in gaol, did not appear and the Governor was found not guilty of having stolen some of Bowman's property.

This failure is the story of the second half of an eccentric Liverpudlian's life, which was never one of success. But he had done many things and was very well-known and those of us who knew him find it hard to forget him. So much of the man was pose and pretence, it is quite possible to overlook the genuine talent he possessed in many fields and the hard work he put into a variety of activities as well as creating a memorable persona, with nothing to start with but brains.

The title was given to him by a fellow-prisoner, the King of Rome. Frederick also had a title given him by an unfrocked priest, who said he was the rightful Pope. And on his visiting cards he was described as 'The Chevalier'. He was a bold chevalier from the time he was seventeen and started to write for comic papers like *Merry and Bright* while still at school until he died in 1970 in complete poverty, without a relation in the world, shortly after a successful television appearance for which he was paid over £1,000.

He had no brothers or sisters; he had never known his father. His mother was also a writer for cheap periodicals. His home was in the then best part of Liverpool, near Mrs Maybrick's home. (He always believed her innocent and shortly before his death wrote asking me for a copy I had of the song about her, *Oh Naughty*

Mrs Maybrick, to quote in a magazine article.) He was writing all his life, but he was also an actor from an early age, remarkably good looking as a young man, and he appeared in the West End of London when he was only 21. His mother was often his leading lady and the plays were often written by him. He also composed music and was an able musician as well as being a singer.

His best performance was being Frederick Bowman or, as he vigorously insisted, in his later years, Sir Frederick Bowman. It was with the assumed title that I first met him in the Forties at a meeting of the Old Boys Book Club held in Crosby, near Liverpool. His face was then a little podgy and the complexion flushed; he was below middle height (as so many actors are), and dressed in a velvet suit with a flowing bow and silver-buckled shoes.

He had been detained in prison under the wartime Act which allowed this for men whose beliefs were declared dangerous to the State and who were released when they were felt to be no longer a security risk. He was a lifelong pacifist, anti-hanging and anti-much more, but insisted that he was no Fascist. He was certainly no democrat, despised the ordinary person, regarded himself as an aristocrat, was a friend of Oswald Mosley and was visited by Hess's son who, misled by the title, thought Bowman could help to have Hess released from imprisonment. He stood for the local Council after the war and insisted on his anti-fascism, but in a magazine he edited about that time there was a definite smell of authoritarianism, even of anti-semitism. He edited many magazines during his life and to the end he had beneath his noble name the title *Kinematograph News*.

His father was said to be a well known Liverpool figure, in the legal profession. But who said it? Frederick was in the law courts many times himself, defending himself with ability but rarely with success. In his early days it might have been said that when he wasn't committing libel he was threatening it.

He called his home Humanimal House. He certainly devoted a large part of his life to the cause of animals, but characteristically he early broke with the Royal Society and regularly collected on Sunday mornings round Liverpool pubs for his own animal welfare organisation, giving no receipts. All that he had at the end was a cat, which he found alive in a rubbish heap (nothing ever happened with Frederick in a normal way) and the house. With thousands of papers and magazines, most of which he or his mother had written for, playbills and programmes recalling performances by him and his mother, often in theatres which he managed, and a few hundred stills of films (he was connected with the cinema in many roles from its beginning in this country).

Although he was a lifelong bachelor, among his effects, many of which I had the melancholy privilege of viewing before they were taken to the city incinerator, was plenty of evidence that he liked a pretty girl, even a pretty boy. At theatres and cinemas, dinner-suited if it was an evening affair, admitted by the flash of his *Kinematograph News* pass or the equivalent, he was usually escorting a smart young girl. The last time I saw him in public was Christmas 1969, when I acknowledged his doffed grey topper as he drove, with a real dolly, past the Adelphi Hotel, in a brougham drawn by a young mare which could only be called spanking.

In his later years this always dressy man became most careless of personal hygiene. A lady at whose home he had lived for years, cared for by her, finally turned him out for this reason. He was not, however, homeless for long. In Wavertree he saw this large empty house. He occupied it and moved his possessions in (most of them, but for the printed material thieves did not value, later stolen, including his very full wardrobe). He rang Liverpool council offering to pay rates. They agreed to accept them but reminded him that the house was the property of the Duchy of Lancaster held on behalf of the Royal Family.

Off went Frederick to London, doubtless passing the ticket collector with the lordly wave he gave to doorkeepers and the like at any public function he chose to attend. Mrs Topham used to send him a ticket for the Grand National so that he could make his annual protest at jockeys using whips. He went to the offices of the Chancellor of the Duchy and sent in his card.

The Chevalier Sir Frederick Bowman

and was allowed to remain in the house at a peppercorn rent.

Then he visited the wealthy Mrs Van der Elst whom he had so often supported in anti-hanging demonstrations. It is strange that a man opposed to capital punishment (as well as being anti-vivisection, opposed to blood sports and anti-war) should have bought the door of a prison condemned cell, Ellis the hangman's rope and such relics of barbarism for exhibition. And among his magazines he circled in red ink pictures and passages referring to boys being flogged.

In and about this house a few months before he died, he was televised, and the result was so good it was likely that he had good prospects of further engagements. Ever an actor.

His last act was tragic, and there had never been much humour in the man. His only friend at the end was a printer (and his assistant) who had a business near Humanimal House. This printer, a brisk, youthful man almost as old as Bowman himself, was a naturally kind man. And blessed with no sense of smell. He regularly visited Bowman and could see he was dying. He begged him to present his vast collection of literary ephemera to Liverpool Library. Like so much ephemera, it could have had considerable value for posterity. But such a bequest suggested death and Bowman did not believe he would die.

In the end, a local policeman, whom this printer brought on the scene, almost physically forced him into an ambulance to get him to hospital. He died there. He had not wanted to go because hospital meant associating with common people and he was not an ordinary man and wanted nothing to do with ordinary people. Only the printer with his assistant and one other were at the graveside. A small sum of money in a bank account has never been claimed. Much was stolen. And of this he would have been saddest about the Court suit. One of his dying consolations must have been, such a snob was he, and so intensely loyal to the Royal Family, that he was, in a way, a tenant of the Queen. A year before his death when he was talking to me (I have a sense of smell but I kept well to windward) his mind went back to his reception at the Court of the Queen's grandfather.

A real title, however trivial, would have delighted the poor pretender. Worse men have been recommended. Perhaps no good reason could be found to give Bowman a ribbon or some letters to put after his name, but in how many cases has there been good reason?

Perhaps one should not grieve for the gifted but silly charlatan. I think of the many parts he played and how he must have been his own most approving audience. On his visiting cards, in the periodicals he edited, in various pamphlets he published, there are pictures of him in many various guises, including the Court dress, morning suit, *le smoking*, evening dress and a hunter's costume (as a bowman, of course). There was even one of him holding a duelling pistol. On a few occasions I was on the verge of getting the story of the duel, but he would switch suddenly to some other character, much like Bransby Williams from Scrooge to Peggotty, Sidney Carton to a Soldier of Waterloo.

Maybe lying in that smelly, dusty, slovenly bedroom in that big house with passages and rooms piled to the ceiling with fading print, he walked the stage of his counterpane in these costumes,

141

and others . . . Bowman at 18, having written a considerable amount of stuff, including a commissioned serial, having his first play *Enslaved by the Mormons* banned by the Censor . . . Bowman producing and appearing in a four-act drama, *The Confession* in 1916, aged 20 (he apparently did no military service in either war). . . . Bowman writing such unrememberable films as *Good for Evil* and *The Mill on the Heath* . . . at the Grand Theatre, Plymouth, 1918 in *Divorce or Dishonour* . . . Bowman, drama critic of the *Liverpool Weekly Courier* . . . Lancashire correspondent to a miller's monthly, film correspondent to *Die Kinematograaf* of Amsterdam. . . . As an elocutionist . . . Founder of the Political League, Liverpool, and unsuccessful candidate as Independent for Liverpool Council . . . Loser in a trial, defending himself, on a charge of libel in his film paper *The Critic* (founder Frederick Bowman) before judge and special jury declared guilty after two days, 1928 . . . As a mimic with a magnificent soprano voice . . . writing the words and music *Love that is Lost, The Prayer of an Irish Mother* etc . . . Organising a National Dog week . . . Editor *Talking Picture News* . . . Manager Lyric Theatre, Liverpool . . . Bowman in the school cadet corps inspected by Lord Roberts . . . Buying a sword at King Charles's Tower in Chester . . . Lunching at the London Victoria with an ageing Ellen Terry and the then Prince of Wales . . . Bowman who had a friend whose father, a nobleman, charged with the Light Brigade and knew Napoleon's gaoler, Sir Hudson Lowe, Governor of St Helena . . . Having himself a friend who was the grandson of Napoleon, Monsieur Juan Buonaparte (he wore his grand-dad's sword at a performance of *The Royal Divorce* at Liverpool Shakespeare: his ancestress was Countess Walewska) . . . Appearing in a realistic hanging scene with Ellis, the hangman, who later committed suicide . . .

Foot in mouth disease

'I just don't understand im, he's a complete enema to me.'

She gets so moody, I says to her, 'Lizzie, it's no good sitting at ome brewing over tings.'

She adter get special compensation from the bishop to get married.

This Indian was wearing a turbine and his wife was wearing a safari.

He claimed he had an ali-baba but the judge says his ev'dince wuz purged.

He was in the Dardaniels in the first war.

My feller wuz in the British Extraordinary Force (could be).

Demoralised in 1919 (as I said).

It wuz enough to make your head stand on end.

He was such an extinguished looking gentleman.

Don't look at me in dat tone uv voice.

People of all transcriptions.

He writes to me reglar but I can't cipher his letters.

The kids was evaporated to Nort Wales in the last war.

The wuz too many fellers on the job and my feller wuz declared repugnant.

But relations between them's quite harmonium again.

The Iron Duke

It was not inappropriate as a nickname for the Lord Mayor of Liverpool, Freeman of the City of Liverpool, Luke Hogan. When I first met him in the Thirties he was working on the marvellous but hopeless task of organising barmen and barmaids in a union. But they, especially the barmaids, in Liverpool, remain among the poorest paid workers.

He was almost the only one who pronounced the first letter of his surname. Some knew they should, but there is, at a certain level among Liverpudlians, the snobbish insistence on dropping the aitch (although most of them put an unnecessary aspirate on the front of the word 'aitch' itself, making it 'haitch'); the commonest solecism, after 'between you and I', of the consciously literate. Most elided the Christian name to give the result 'Loo Kogan'.

There was much that was Iron about Luke, educated in a Scotty Road slum school. He had the manners, speech and appearance of a Duke. Indeed, when as Lord Mayor he succeeded Lord Sefton, many compared his predecessor, on those points, unfavourably with him. Still, it was only rhyming slang – Luke, Iron Duke. As so often with rhyming slang it was a two-way job, like wife, trouble and strife.

Much rhyming slang is just mad poetry worthy of Lear – sister, skin and blister; match, ship's hatch (then just 'ship's', further to confuse the intruder). I suppose there are circles where this secret speech flourishes. It is not solely Cockney. Many Liverpudlians, who welcome all forms of slang, favour it, especially in the villainy and racing sectors.

Luke wanted power from an early age. As our slums create good boxers they create good fighters with their brains. Power for his union, his party, himself, not necessarily in that order. During his year as Lord Mayor, he had much publicity, especially when he opposed the Labour Government's moves to close the very capitalist non-productive body, the Liverpool Cotton Exchange. As a result Luke was cold-shouldered by his old Labour mates of whom now he had completely ceased to hide his low estimation. He became associated with a strange body, bred, I'd guess, of the Economic League, always a crypto-Tory organisation.

As ever, the country was in a sick condition economically. A group, which Luke joined, held a number of public meetings throughout the country peddling the cure. Luke was billed to appear with a leading Liberal and a leading Tory on the platform at the Picton Hall, a wonderful place for mass meetings, and now part of the City Library.

I was having a dockside pint after work with a chap off a ship. When I told him I had to go as the meeting's starting time was growing near, he asked me why and I told him. 'I'll come with you', he said.

'It wouldn't interest you,' I told him.

'It's politics, isn't it?' he replied.

'Yes, but not Irish politics.' He was an officer of the Irish National Union of Seamen.

'Didn't you say Hogan was on?' he next asked; and when I said yes he insisted on coming. The man was a Dubliner, but he knew about Hogan. He regarded him as a renegade. All through Luke's speech he shouted imprecations, causing some members of Luke's bodyguard wearing steward's badges to move nearer and nearer to our seats. I begged him to shut up. When Luke sat down and invited written questions, Nelligan (for such was his name) kept demanding bits of paper, on which he swiftly scribbled, pausing only to ask 'How many rs in "bastard"?' With a commanding manner he passed these to the stewards. Whether they

144

reached the podium I doubt, but when written questions were answered later, none of Nelligan's had a reply. (Luke knew as well as I did the old game of the written question.) Nelligan stayed till the end hoping his tricky stumbling-blocks would be brought forward. When we left the pubs were closed.

Nelligan was a thirsty lad. He was a barman on the night boat to Dublin. Entering port at six in the morning when spirits and other high duty goods would be placed under seal, he had the problem of the optics on the wine and spirits bottles, used for measuring the drinks and always automatically holding the next measure, to deal with. His solution was simple. He filled a beer glass with all the remnants and swigged the lot off before sending to the pantry for his tea and toast. He had serious stomach trouble and had to attend a doctor in Liverpool. Asked to accompany him once in his car (which he had used one day to smuggle ship's stores past the Princes Dock bobby and, without unloading them, to go back for more, being caught on the second trip) I was not really surprised – in Liverpool after all – to find that the doctor also had a pub. To be precise his wife had the licence but, by agreement with the brewery, he held surgery in its back parlour.

Anyhow, after the meeting, Nelligan wanted a drink. I took him to Marybone to the point off Vauxhall Road where Liverpool suicides used to be buried with a stake through their hearts. It is a very Irish area, near the old St Patrick's Cross, and the first Catholic church the town ever had. The pub was called The Maid of Erin. The licensee was the brother of Luke who was a powerful man on the local Watch Committee, well liked by all policemen.

Nelligan didn't know of the Hogan association. His mouth dropped open over his pint when the handsome figure of Luke, with a lady, strode in. His brother, God rest his soul, hailed him and asked how the meeting had gone. One would not have believed Luke had noticed Nelligan as he swept in, though he nodded to me, in front of Nelligan. Or that he could have seen him up by the Picton Hall ceiling, even heard him, from the platform. He replied: 'Oh, it went very well'.

Then he turned to point at Nelligan. 'He did the most speaking.'

Yes, Luke's defunct school of politicians never missed anything.

We could drink after hours because Luke was a magistrate and on the licensing committee. Police, pubs and schools he saw from the outset to be the sources of power and personal repute. One may have genuine social aims, want improvements for the people or have rigid political principles, but you cannot work them unless

145

you have a political nose. Lord Birkenhead said of the Tory Party of his time that those in it who had principles had no brains, those with brains had no principles. Luke could appear the statesman, but he was basically a politician. He could be nothing else in the Liverpool of his day; the combination of both, as with Lloyd George and Roosevelt, gives the owner world repute and Luke must have felt he was working in too small a field, especially as he got older.

Luke knew how to get publicity. He was the newspaperman's friend; he was a member of the Liverpool Press Club for seventeen years and spoke freely there. When he had attained some national prominence he began to make pronouncements about public affairs often only remotely concerned with Liverpool, frequently attacking the Government of his own party. Often he chose these occasions arbitrarily – maybe not the most suitable occasions, a Boy Scouts rally or a convent prize-giving. But it was always on a night or at an hour suitable to the Press, and the speech was given to them in good time. Luke often said he did not make prepared speeches. This, in his Lord Mayor years, was not so. Luke knew the needs of cameramen, so he looked less absurd than most in mayoral robes and wore his evening clothes to the manner born.

He had been active in politics from an early age. His mother was a widow earning a shilling an hour at odd jobs to keep him and other children. These days a bright boy like him could get further education at the State's expense. Luke got by without it, but how many were lost for ever to blind alley jobs and early marriage? He became an apprentice bookbinder but, before he was out of his time, was known rather as a spell binder, having quickly become active in the union.

Of course, he had joined the Labour Party. He spoke on every occasion he could both for union and party, and before very long his facility as a speaker and decided evidence of organising ability made him a district officer of NUDAW. (The National Union of Distributive and Allied Workers, for whom he worked till the year before he died, continually finding odd pockets of unorganised workers who could fit into the Allied category.)

It was 1921, when he was 35, that he joined the small group of Liverpool Labour councillors, but he had already made his mark, not apparently having been required for service in the First World War. He became chairman of Liverpool Trades and Labour Council, MBE in 1931, leader of the party in the council when the Second World War threatened.

Small as the group was, Luke was not without rivals for leadership and later had to compete with as nimble a brain as his own. Joe Cleary was a very young councillor, who became Lord Mayor at a comparatively early age. Like Luke he did not readily accept party discipline, he had a mind and will of his own, but he did not drift as far away from the party as Luke did after his spell in the Town Hall.

Cleary, of Catholic descent, was a Nonconformist lay preacher, which did not endear him to Luke who, however, probably liked Jack Braddock even less, since he proudly claimed to be an atheist. Braddock was a quietly ambitious man, not so clever as Luke but less devious.

Cleary was an MP for a short spell, a role which I am sure Luke would have played perfectly. Cleary won a funny little by-election by beating the official Tory at Croxteth, Liverpool, when the vote was split by the intervention of Randolph Churchill standing on his father's India policy. He never entered the House again, and was eventually knighted.

In 1944 Luke was chosen for the safe Labour seat of St Helens which was in the gift of NUDAW, but he was Lord Mayor the next year and, by the time elections came, he had left the Party.

Luke is one of the many smalltime politicians and union leaders I have met who would almost certainly have made very successful national politicians; it may be to the loss of the Labour Party that so many of their bright young people get bogged down at an early age while the clever dicks are looking out for selection committees before they are out of sixth form. But there are other reasons why Labour leaders tend to be above the average age of their equivalent Tory opponents.

Luke was automatically, in 1938, put on the Liverpool War Emergency Committee, without three hearty cheers from his Labour associates. I have heard Luke deride the whole notion of Air Raid Precautions. Such committees were set up to be a substitute for elected local government if for some reason it collapsed during the war. Such, thank goodness, was never necessary and their main work was civil defence. Here Luke did marvellous work.

Throughout the war years the city had the same Lord Mayor, a mouselike Liberal. I recall standing near him waiting to go on a troopship from New Zealand. Flanking him were the two handsome figures of the King of Greece and Anthony Eden. A New Zealand private said to another, viewing him, morning suited, unimpressive, as Luke would never have been: 'Why does he wear a chain?'

149

To which the reply was: 'Dunno, mate. Perhaps he got away one time.'

The Labour Party was bigger in strength on the council than when Luke entered but the Tories still had the majority. They picked Lord Mayors. The year after the war they picked a local aristocrat and landowner, as Lord Derbies were picked in the past – an unpolitical choice. Personally I think a distinguished citizen without a political past should be the usual choice, but the Labour Party in Liverpool didn't think so. Luke Hogan certainly didn't and was most vocal about it. He said he would have nothing to do with the new Lord Mayor during his year of office. But he did, and he was nominated the next year. Many thought a bargain had been struck.

For form's sake the choice is eventually unanimous but the initial nomination of Luke came solely from the Tories, who had already moved him further away from his Party by making him an Alderman. When the Scotty Road lad received the chain from my Lord Sefton he looked as fitted to wear it as that handsome and elegant gentleman who had had every chance in life. Yet the ranks of Labour forebore to cheer. During his year of office he did not endear himself to some of them. He insisted on his neutrality, and some were annoyed when, as so often, speaking as a national not a local notable, he reproved de Valera for his neutrality during our recent struggle.

He was said to have received threats from IRA men. Nothing more was heard of these. Nothing more was heard of a writ served on him in 1944 by the local Brewers Society, which Luke said he welcomed: it dealt with communications he had made to members of his union employed by the brewers.

Presently he left the Party and called himself an Independent. Once he had declared publicly that he would fly the Red Flag over the Town Hall. He announced now that he was going to run against Bessie in Exchange Ward (her husband Jack was now the Party leader and they were both active in the move to keep Luke off all committees). He did not, in fact, run and gave as a reason for that – 'I do not want to split the anti-Labour vote.' There could be no return after that. He carried on his work on the Watch Committee and on the licensing bench until he died in 1954, aged 68, leaving £614.

There are of course policemen who carry out the orders of the licensing authorities and Council by-laws regardless of persons. Luke met one once. Years before he was Lord Mayor, an afternoon club was raided and Luke was found on the premises. He was a member of many clubs but not of this one. (In his last years he was frequently to be found in the Builders Club near Exchange Station – where I never recall meeting any builders.) He was not drinking or gambling. He defended himself successfully with the plea that, unlikely though it might appear, he had dropped into the club to write a letter on behalf of a constituent.

I was in Luke's company in the Forties with other heavy drinkers in the home of a prominent Liverpool businessman. The businessman was temporarily out of the room. His wife, much younger than he, clearly resented his generosity to us, though she must have known, as we did, that he wouldn't give anything to anyone for nothing. She said: 'I think you gentlemen should pay for your drinks.'

Luke, elegant as ever, carefully put his drink down and looked down at her, murmuring softly: 'Madam, you forget. I am a magistrate. If you charge one penny for a drink in this unlicensed room I shall have to summon the police.'

Watch Committee meetings are normally, I should imagine, shortlived affairs. Not the one held on the last day of Luke's life. It went on for eight hours. Luke died getting into a taxi shortly after it ended.

The principles Luke most firmly adhered to were those of his religion. He was a governor of my old school, which was a long way from St Sylly's in Scotty Road, and also of the convent school my daughter attended in once-rural West Derby near Luke's handsome house, Red Roofs. I know what excellent work he did for both. He defended his faith vigorously at all times, even though he attended a synagogue in his first year as Lord Mayor. He battled especially over school grants, with anti-Catholic elements in his party and elsewhere – I should think Liverpool is the only borough in England which has a Protestant Party. The leader of the Protestants was Pastor Longbottom, who was to have his spell as Lord Mayor. On Luke's desk after his death was found a letter of sympathy from Pastor Longbottom commiserating with Luke on the recent death of his son.

The old jokes at home

Luke Hogan's old school St Sylvestre's was noted for its soccer; many of its scholars became English schoolboy players, some pro-

fessional footballers. I saw Luke shout himself hoarse the night they beat their old rivals St Anthony's (Sin Antnees). They won three – nil. This had a sequel.

An amateur football referee died and appeared at heaven's gate. Asked if he had any special sin on his conscience he brokenly admitted that he had knowingly and with malicious intent given two offside goals against St Anthony's.

'That's all right,' he was told. 'Not to worry. You've led a pretty good life on the whole. Come right in.'

'Thank you,' the ref. stammered. 'It's awfully good of you, Saint Peter.'

'I'm not,' he was told, 'Saint Peter. It's his night off. I'm Saint Sylvestre.'

When St Anthony's was beaten in the local Schools Final by a sturdy team of Orange lads, one of the latter was heard as they went to the dressing room murmuring gleefully, 'There'll be sore hearts in the Vatican tonight.'

Another tough team, in the Wednesday League, was surprised to be beaten by the Shop Assistants eleven, who proved even tougher. As they limped off the ground the captain of the former asked bitterly: 'What sorta shops dem fellers werk in, knockin shops?'

In the Berating Chamber

The pleece must find some detergent for all this violence.

The leopard can't change its tune.

I've never shown no discrimination towards nobody.

I want to state right now – I'm neither a man nor a mouse.

Youse'll soon find you're barking up the wrong end of the street.

It's a bane of contention.

Now I want to make, comrades, the confusion more clear.

An oral agreement, friends; not worth the paper it's written on.

I'll give you a few saline facts to show that it is tantamount to the equivalent.

The whole party is rent with strife and personal fjords.

Widout fear or favour, disregardless of what anyone says, an' ninety-nine times outa ten I'm right, dis is absolutely a completely unique case of content of court and inflammation of character (could be).

I have no envy, no spite, no anchor.

He was absolutely right, friends, to a certain extent.

Comrades, I diden know what to do. I was in an absolute quadrangle.

So he spoke to me, in his own inimical way.

I have always been inscrutably honest.

My opponent's statement is sheer adulterated rubbish.

I put the case fair an' square an' the boss says, 'We acquiesce.' So I called the lads out on strike, no messin.

Crippen's captor

'Dr Crippen is on board.' The famous message sent by Captain Kendall of the Canadian Pacific vessel *Montrose* in 1910 is, as everybody knows, the first occasion when a ship's 'wireless' hanged a man. And a thin wire it was. Pause a while and imagine the message had been: 'Fully confident Dr Kendall is on board', and Captain Crippen had sent it. No doubt Kendall would have been hanged. Yet there is a fate in names.

In the *Magnet*, Skinner and Snoop must be cads, Bunter a figure of fun, Wharton and Cherry, good chaps. Kendall sounds a good chap. A good name for a prefect or the school head. Crippen is a doomed name. The girl Crippen murdered for, if he did, and ran away with, was straight out of a Sexton Blake story. Miss Ethel le Neve. His wife – Belle Elmore, always pictured as a pissy, bullying, blowsy blond, an unsuccessful actress, in strong contrast to the sweet little secretary who lived to die of natural causes. Belle, I've heard, was a normal sort, not a bad actress.

The Scotland Yard man who, on receipt of the message, caught a faster ship to Montreal and arrested Crippen in the St Lawrence River, had just about the right kind of name. Inspector Drew. From an illustration to an old *Strand Magazine* story about Sherlock Holmes, bowler-hatted, walrus-moustached, behind the pilot, looking towards 'Mr Robinson' and his 'son' – 'You are Doctor Crippen.'

Crippen, I suppose, had the right to be called Doctor. Few dentists in England use the title though Crippen had practised in London. Few masters of merchant ships have the right to call themselves Captain. Transatlantic usage in this is strange. Under maybe Teutonic influences you can go for hours in some parts of the USA and not pass anyone but a doctor, much as in a British fishing port every trawler skipper is captain. A friend of mine was a doctor of letters at a Canadian university. He says he was in a Liverpool hotel once when a chambermaid somehow was backed on to the hot pipes in a narrow room; she needed medical care. The receptionist looked up the names of doctors in the register and sent a page to his room telling him what was necessary. He said he dressed like a fireman and was on his way in quick time to the room named. 'I was beaten', he reported bitterly, 'by a doctor of divinity . . .'

A woman, very well known in Liverpool, held a very respected name, not yet forgotten – Mrs (Ma) Egerton who managed the famous Lime Street pub The American Bar and later The Eagle, behind the Empire Theatre, near the station, haunt of pros. She had on her walls a fine collection of pictures of once-famous turns, right back to a boyish Charlie Chaplin, a bust of Leno, herself with D. W. Griffiths and the established Chaplin. She had been a Miss Glover from Dublin (her brother was Jimmy Glover) and about the time Belle Elmore died she was in theatrical circles in London. She saw Crippen one evening in a London pub with Ethel le Neve who was wearing jewellery she recognised as belonging to Belle Elmore, Crippen's wife, who had been 'missing' for some time. She told the police. Her information led to Crippen's house being searched and his flight with Miss le Neve. This led to a further search, where the remains of Belle were found in a cellar. So it was thought Crippen had killed her, and the hunt was on. He was hanged. Miss le Neve lived for many years after, almost as long as Ma Egerton, whom I knew well, and Captain Kendall, who died at 91 in London in 1955. He was one of my wife's family, and lived as a boy in Everton. Henry Kendall first caught public notice in 1883 in pantomime with Marie Loftus. Then he joined the training ship *Indefatigable*. (Another boys' paper name.) Life on those ships was absolutely vile and brutal in those days. He ran away. He was caught. Brutally flogged. Ran away again. Before long he was concerned with murder. At 15 he witnessed a

156

murder off the Australian coast on the *Iolanthe*. Boys, wait for the next thrilling instalment. The murderer, a Negro of course, killed the other witnesses and was about to do the same to Henry when he jumped ashore on to an island and made his way one hundred miles, at the double, to the goldfields at Croydon. After a period of pearl diving off Thursday Island, he edited a local newspaper.

With one spring Henry was back in England on the largest sailing ship in the world, naturally named the *Liverpool*, and soon was commanding his own vessel the *Milwaukee*. His home now was in Liverpool where, first at Anfield, later at Blundellsands, he spent all his shore time for many years.

After the *Montrose* he commanded the *Empress of Ireland*, which was rammed in the St Lawrence with the loss of more than 1,000 lives. In the First World War he was a convoy commodore; after the war an Elder Brother of Trinity and (when I knew him) CPR Marine Super, Southampton, spending his last years at Lee, South London.

It was not he but a steward who saw Crippen kissing a boy on the boat deck – which might not now cause surprise – though Ethel as a boy was rather like Dorothy Ward in Dick Whittington. He told the 'captain'. I wonder what the steward's name was?

A few little antidotes, like

He'd had 20 kids and 40 years with the Corpy. They gave him a piece of silver plate on his retirement which he proudly showed to the bowls club. 'Dat's a funny-looking Liver bird,' says one, 'wid short legs.' 'Dat's not a Liver bird,' says another, 'it's a stork wid 'is legs worn down.'

When the *Liverpool Echo* published a series of jokes from readers in 1962 this was one of the winners: A young sea cadet was carrying a lifebuoy to a show his troop were giving in the George's Hall. It was pouring rain so he called a taxi. Seeing the belt the driver said, 'Blimey, mate, is it that bad?'

'Whur,' she asked, 'can I gerra tree?' I tried to help her and she says, 'No, no, no – I wanna number tree bus!'

She's a proper bucko. If ever they start a Common Markit she'll 'ave no difficulty gettin' a stall.

When TV announced a scene from the paddy fields of China Micky Dripping says; 'Dem Irish, they get ev'rywhur!'

How did I get dis eye? I was just leanin' on the bar, like, makin' some light chaffing remarks about the Pope.

He was bent down outside a notoriously tough pub where today's sawdust was last night's furniture and a shortsighted lady said: 'Fancy a grown man playin' ollies!' (marbles). 'Dem's not ollies, missus,' he told her, 'dem's me teeth!'

In the office

We must think of a system to make it quite foolhardy.

She didn't have a carbide in the typewriter.

Dear Sir, We are unable to alleviate our price.

It's a veritable hive of inactivity.

I haven't read it yet – just glanced through it superciliously.

Who indicted you to walk in here?

Just because he's indispensable he thinks he can't be done without.

Eff-ervescent Fred

In the early Sixties there was a fellow named Fred with a long, sad, pale face, a most unimpressionable physique and a good line of patter, who provided entertainment to passing shoppers in the city centre. He performed on a piece of waste ground near a big department store. The Germans had made it waste while, unfortunately, missing other targets. He performed in a never-white singlet, one of his acts being to balance a paving stone on his chest and have someone hammer it in two. He also tore telephone books in two: at one period there wasn't a telephone-box within the square mile area round his site which had a book.

His glib patter was liberally laced with a big, big eff. Fred knew no other way of talking; he meant no offence and passers, male and female, took none, they just chortled. 'Youse'd laff, wooden you, if I ad me effin ead knocked off. I don' after do this, y'know,

158

me father left me tousinds. Mind you I don't know where he effin well left it.'

Fred's best-paying act was the old trick of getting out of a chained and locked bag. 'I used to put another feller in but the Labour Exchange complained when I ad three uv um died in there in a week.' He made a very convincing job of the illusion and the pennies rolled in.

Fred was quite a good citizen. Some of his associates were well known tea-leaves, had had their porridge, and one was a murderer. He was a good husband and father, living in the rough but fairly respectable Bullring, off Brownlow.

He was belting his wife one day on his doorstep when a police van paid one of its routine visits to the Bullring. Fred was astonished when two bobbies jumped out and lumbered him into the back of the van. An Englishman's home is his castle, isn't the effin doorstep part of a home? And belting his wife, not just any judy. It was nothing but an attack on the liberty of the subject. And he stood like a latter-day, fouler-mouthed Hampden in the court saying so.

Old jokes at home

What are the three oldest jests in the world of the whacker? Easy lead is the shawlie hearing of a babe being christened Hazel. 'Holy Jasus, all them lovely saints in the book and you call her after a flippin' nut!'

'Who painted the Mona Lisa?'
'You know very well Cammell Urds does all dem Islerman boats.' (must be second.)

Try this for third; among our many best sporting ones. The great Liverpool goalie Elisha Scott met Everton's immortal Dixie Dean in Church Street. The latter nodded and Elisha from Belfast dived hands first into the gutter.

The burial of young Moore of Bank Hall

Having another son lying a-dying in the house, I resolved to bury him [a son aged 14 who died of smallpox] between 12 and 1 of the clock at night, in order not to send to the minister or sexton till 3 or 4 of the clock in the afternoon, lest any servant in my house know it till then. And when night came I resolved to carry in my coach privately only with 40 or 50. But, truly, before he went out of the house there were not so little as 800 people. And about a mile from Liverpool, on foot, the Mayor with the mace and wand, the Aldermen and the common council and at least 700 or 800 people met the corpse so that when we came to the church there was not as little as 16 hundred people and number not seen in any man's memory in this church before, and which was much more strange, I believe that like lamentation was not seen before about us; truly I bore the affliction very well till [then]. I thought then my heart would have broke . . . It brought upon me my old pain insomuch that all people thought I should have died. Then in 4 days my youngest son Thomas died, who was buried at one o'clock as the former, with many others that met him.

[*Four days afterwards his son Fenwick died of the smallpox too and ' I buried him also at Bank Hall'*] – **1672, Moore Deeds, Liverpool Records Office.**

Moore, a miller, was a powerful landlord in the earlier years of the town's growth from a village in King John's reign. He kept a rental of his tenants in Lancelots Hey, Hackins Hey and other 'heys' round Moore Fields near the 'Pool – his own home, Bank Hall, was some distance away. He would send notes advising the rent collectors about tenants – for example: 'Lancelot is a drunken fellow.' These heys, Fenwick Street and much more of the whole town are scheduled for destruction under 'improvement' plans. Hey seemingly was a field or path. Tommy Handley, who worked round there as a lad, puzzled London friends by saying: 'Tarrah well, see you in Hackins Hey'.

Tommy Handley filled one

This chap brought a want in. Tommy asked him was it a long one, and he was assured it was. It was also felt. So he filled it.

So many people came on and off in *Itma* and joined Tommy in a crazy dialogue, and we all laughed at it heartily, without any idea of analysis. But now, 30 years after, we can see that the great Liverpudlian Tommy Handley was a pioneer. From cat's whisker days, radio in this country had had its comedy element and we will not forget John Henry with Blossom, Stainless Stephen and others, but they were just voices on the air projecting traditional English music hall acts.

Another comic from Liverpool, Arthur Askey, who joined Stinker Murdoch on *Band Waggon* had initiated the zany element of humour which no other medium can do so well, and which turned its inability to show the characters into an advantage. Eventually it reached its zenith with *The Goon Show*. The inspired TV zanyism of Britain's *Monty Python* and the USA's *Laugh-In* stems from this pioneer work, as the best talking picture comedy has its roots in the silent days.

Tommy did, indeed, fill a longfelt want and helped radio comedy grow up. And yet, as with Chaplin's film comedy, his *Itma* and other BBC shows had its roots in English music hall. Most of us had seen in places like the Sods' Opera (The Palace), Poplar, the Liverpool Rotunda (or Roundy), Manchester Hippodrome, sketches in which various types come in and out and indulge in comic dialogue around a central character. And pretty lousy most of them were. In fact, Tommy toured with an Army sketch of that kind called the 'Disorderly Room' and that wasn't so hot either. Tommy was not at his best as a visual comic. But unseen, with a superb team and the talent verging on genius of Ted Kavanagh, he invented a new kind of humour just at a time when the people of this country needed it.

'*Hullo folks!*'

Coming over the air in 1939, a phrase which would drive me out of a theatre by its false joviality, made me and millions of others sit back for a sheer bath of pure verbal fun. The Thirties had been a bastard of an era. Though, after the hungry Twenties, most of us could at least afford a 'wireless set'. The last year of the Thirties, with war certain from the beginning and coming before it ended, was a misery. But on Thursdays, after listening to the latest caper of Hitler or some other piece of bad news, inanities from Chamberlain, platitudes from Roosevelt, the latest boring snippet about King Zog, we had our half hour. When the war came and, before very long, the bombs, we listened from under a table to that unmistakable, unashamedly Scouse voice, and the amazing oral tennis game following.

When Tommy died a few years after the war millions felt it as a personal loss. It did not seem unfitting that for a mere funny man a memorial service should be held at St Paul's. At the memorial service in Liverpool Cathedral we felt how fitting was the presiding clergyman's text: 'God hath made me to laugh so that all who hear will laugh with me.'

We did laugh *with* Tommy and his fellow-jesters. Once again their invisibility helped. If I see a farce in the theatre where the cast is obviously enjoying itself I don't enjoy myself. I feel they should be left to themselves. But we did not mind intruding on *Itma*. They surely enjoyed themselves; sometimes when Tommy was talking to Jack Train or Deryck Guyler, greatest of foils, he could hardly go on for laughing. Deryck's Scousey verbosity nearly always set him off. And I've seen that happen too.

I did not know Tommy very well at any time, and not at all before the war. He didn't get around much. Apart from his radio work he seldom left home, except to perform at private shows, such as Masonics, for which I am told he charged high fees. Like many comics from Liverpool he watched his money and lived quietly in private life. His fee from the BBC was always paltry, although he left a considerable sum.

But during the war it happened that I was in London about once a month. It was known that Tommy loved to hear from fellow Scousers. If in London on a Thursday, I would ring Tommy and quite often he would say 'Come on round.' I'd have a chat with him and Deryck Guyler and see the show. It was very funny. Not as good as on the air, of course.

Early in the war the BBC was evacuated to various parts – the variety to Bangor in North Wales, which is near Liverpool. I know many Liverpool people visiting their evacuated children thereabouts who found the *Itma* team's 'secret' studio and usually were heartily welcomed there by Tommy and the rest. From there comes a story told by Ted Kavanagh illustrating Tommy's humour off duty, when so many comics aren't comic. The hotel where they stayed had one of those slates on which residents indicated what time they wanted calling with what drink and newspaper. 'I know', said Ted, 'who to blame when I was called at four in the morning with a bottle of stout and the *Jewish Chronicle*.'

The man who is always funny can be tiresome in real life, but it was so essentially a part of Tommy – spontaneous, not studied – that everyone laughed with him. And that is what he got us to do on the air. It is often said that radio shows up the insincere. This may be so to some extent, but an actor's sincerity is like a politician's – just switched on for the moment. I am sure we have been as much imposed on by unseen phoneys on the air as by seen ones. But Tommy's sincerity, we felt sure, was not temporary.

In the Thirties, among established comics, I can only recall Billy Bennett – who when he spoke could hardly conceal it – saying he was from Liverpool. I do not say that comics from Liverpool, like Askey and Ted Ray, Bill Danvers, Harry Angers and others, concealed their origin. The broad ones called themselves North Country comics and the light comics, like Ray, adopted a *stage* accent used by so many, by no means Oxford or BBC, but not regional and as characteristic as parsons' English. But, of course, Ray and Askey could not hide the nasal touch any more than the most educated Liverpudlian. Tommy never tried to conceal the nasality. Gag after gag in the show meant more to Liverpudlians than to other listeners, and the names of characters were often based on real people in Liverpool. It is well known that he had as much to do with drafting the scripts as Ted Kavanagh, and in rehearsal he introduced new stuff. He also fostered Deryck Guyler's creation of a truly Scouse character, Frisby Dyke. Like Tommy, Deryck's family was reasonably well off (Guyler's are well known jewellers in the city) and both had good education. So they spoke well. But their speech was Liverpool through and through. Deryck has many voices, but he is at his best when he uses his native one. (Now, I am told, speech training schools are filled with aspiring actors trying to lose their Oxford accents and learn Scouse ones.)

Frisby Dyke was the name of a well known Liverpool draper. Peter Geekie, another *Itma* character, was a cotton broker whose name Tommy must often have seen as he moodied round Liverpool Exchange as an office boy. Poppy Poupart probably stemmed from Poupart, a well known fruit importer in Liverpool. 'Don't forget the diver' was one of the many catchphrases in *Itma* (no show before had so many, daily quoted, few since). Few Liverpudlians over 50 can have failed to see the one-legged man diving off New Brighton pier and later collecting pennies with 'Don't forget the diver, sir. Don't forget the diver.'

From boyhood, Tommy was what we in Liverpool call a Mark. You find them everywhere, but I reckon we have more of them in Liverpool. Indeed, when you find one outside Liverpool very, very often – in the army, say, or the navy – you find he is from Liverpool. They are not only the life and soul of the party, they turn every occasion into a party. We stodgy, dull, unsocial types despise them, and when they are bad they certainly can be very bad. But without good ones the world could be a very sad place.

So long as they know when to leave off. It is known that Tommy had a very serious side, almost a religious one, and he didn't overdo it. But he saw the funny side of things when others couldn't. Who else would have seen the name Peter Geekie and perceived its innate comicality and stored it in his head for years to delight others? And his humour, even at your expense, did not antagonise. Well, maybe one or two old ladies in the Liverpool 8 area did not join the laughter when Tommy was a boy. It was not a posh district – Tommy's birthplace, Threlfall Street, still exists. But it is now far down in the world, although it was not high up even then. There was a slight rural atmosphere. Plenty of bushes for Tommy to hide in and suddenly jump out in the guise of a weird old man growling fearsome threats. He was always dressing up.

He did not have much money. His mother was a widow in the days before widows had pensions. She wanted him to get educated beyond the elementary standard, and it wasn't easy when her husband, a dairy farmer, died young at the turn of the century when Tommy was still a baby. He spent any spare coppers on disguises; the only sweet he bought was a brand of sherbert with which a false moustache was given away. All his life Tommy had a thing about moustaches – he loved disguising himself. And he could, as a boy, put on the deep voice of a man without difficulty. Quite early he had a wide range of voices to go with varied make-ups.

The Good Ship Ebenezer

> She was so flippin' old
>   She knew Columbus as a boy, sir.
> Twas pump her bullies all night and day,
>   To help her git to Liverpool Bay.
>
> Scouse was our only grub, sir:
>   Brekfist, dinner, supper.
> Our bread was tough as a pawnbroker's brass
>   And the meat as salt as Lot's wife's ass.

Merseyry rhymes

Little Miss Muffet sat on a tuffet,
Whatever a tuffet may be.
So she wouldn't rough it,
A sailor said 'stuff it',
And made her sit down on his knee.

Murry had an Aussie white in a city lodge one day;
And ev'ry time that Murry sups, this sailor has to pay.
But when he follered up the street,
She made an awful fuss.
She kicked him in the cobblers
And caught a Dingle bus.

Hymie had a betting shop
He fleeced 'em white as snow;
And everywhere that Hymie went
He made a lot of dough.

What about the horses?

It is a fact not generally known that the number of horses used to
work a coach from London to Liverpool is nearly 200, and that
on an average these horses consume the produce of 700 acres of
land. A contemporary, after noting this fact, says: 'should railways,
at some future period, supersede stage-coaches entirely, what is to
become of this produce?' Now in the first railway experiment on
a large scale (as it might then be called) the Liverpool and
Manchester railway, much outcry was made as to the loss it
would cause, not only to the coach and horse proprietors but to
the agriculturist, as it was calculated there would be no more
work for fourteen horses on this line of road . . . and that conse-
quently the produce of as many acres of land as these horses had
consumed, would have no consumers. What is the fact? That the
horses now required in connection with the railway for drawing
omnibuses [sic], waggons etc. exceed all the coaches between
Liverpool and Manchester.

– *Chambers Journal*, April 30, 1836.

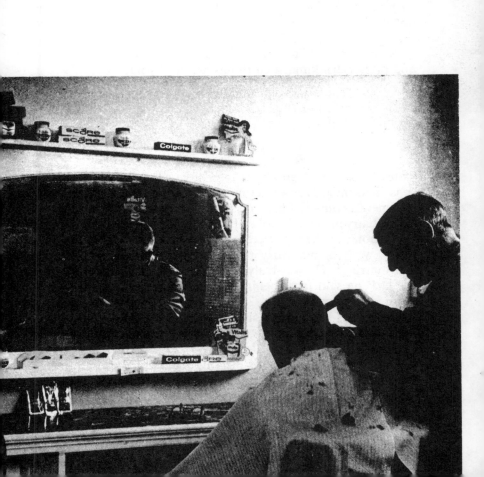

One of us

Doctor Abraham Clein, born in Cork, grandson of an Eastern European refugee from pogroms, graduate of Trinity College, had a beautiful, seductive, rainswept Irish accent. In every other respect he was a complete Jew. He gesticulated excessively, using every muscle from wrist to shoulder. He walked up and down with the lope of Groucho Marx. As a local politician he had some of the force and invective of Disraeli, with none of the wit. His nose was very hooked, and altogether he looked like the Ikey Mo of Victorian comics.

He supported Zionism with tongue and cheque-book – in fact was too apt to term any criticism of himself or another Jew or body of Jews, anti-Zionism. But he loved all the stale Yiddisher jokes and it is no accident that one of his best friends was Issy Bonn. Abie (nicknamed Scrooge, but I, though quite intimate with him, never called him anything but Doc.) was strictly orthodox. This was in the years I knew him well. I believe in later years there was a breach, but he was never a 'liberal'.

As with pious Catholics and jokes about nuns and confession and priests drinking, such things as my rhyme:

> There was a young fellow of Sydenham,
> Who lost his best pants with a quid in 'em;
> But strange to explain
> He found 'em again
> Down in Petticoat Lane with a Yid in 'em

amused the Doc. A good Jew is as sure he is right as a good Catholic is. This makes for a tolerance amounting almost to indifference.

I knew a couple of his wives and some of his children. When, in his obituary in 1966, I spoke of his being a truly Hebraic patriarchal figure none of them objected. He was well into his sixties when a young wife, in her early twenties, gave him his second son by that marriage. He was truly delighted. 'What d'you think of that, eh? eh!' he said from behind a broad grin. 'Eh, eh? D'you think I can do it again, eh, eh?' He was not abashed by the reply: 'What makes you think you did it the first time?'

His son by an earlier marriage had a practice in a small town in Ireland; he was the only Jew in town. When he married a local girl the priest gave them his blessing from the altar and asked the full church to pray for them. He settled down in the town and his wife learnt kosher cooking. It is said that the other husbands in the town are turning from bacon and cabbage with soda bread to noodle soup and bagels.

It was his early days in Ireland and as a young (and very able) GP in Liverpool, that amused me. He told me of a mature group of students at a dissection class in an upper theatre in the hospital. The examiner was passing round the leg of a recently carved cadaver. There was a loud gasp and 'Oh, my God', and the examiner looked up astonished. It was the window cleaner, who had been looking in through an open window. It took two of the students to stop him falling off his ladder.

The whisky bottle was always handy. He didn't drink such stuff. I rather liked the wine he had for Hebraic feasts. I called on him at midnight once during Yom Kippur, about which I had forgotten. He silently indicated the bottle and the glass. I thought at first he had put on the caftan for a laugh, like a jolly uncle with a paper hat, and kept giggling as I sipped. One way and the other, I knew a deal about Jewish customs and had mixed a lot with Jews. He was in so many ways – race, religion, education, comparative wealth – so very different from the very proletarian Scousers among whom he dwelt. He got on with them excellently and when he was coarse, as he could be, they chuckled heartily. He did not lack dignity – Scousers would dislike him if he did – but he had no side and did a good deal by stealth.

I went to him, of course, for medical advice but, like so many doctors, he was a hypochondriac. Most often we wandered on to so many topics (finally always politics), with me, no slouch at interrupting, trying to get a word in edgeways. He would be shooing me out to go for his lunch of boiled eggs when I'd say, 'Eh, I have to have a medical note for my job.' 'Yes, yes', heaving one from his pocket and putting it against the wall, pen poised, 'what's the matter with you?'

You could tell him leprosy or elephantiasis and he'd write it down, adding (now it can be told): 'When d'you want to go back? OK, double pneumonia, three days.'

Whatever of his early days, he took his duties lightly in my time. Doubtless he could still deal with serious cases, but how could he be sure he did not take lightly one not obviously serious when it was? It was so hard to get him to make a diagnosis. He didn't want to listen to your symptoms; he'd rather tell you his.

'Take this to the chemist right away, Frank', he once commanded. 'What is it, Doc?' 'It's not for you, it's for me.'

He had the job of passing some youths as fit to box at a sea

169

cadets tournament in Huyton one Saturday. I was in his little room with him when he said 'I've another appointment.' (He had an extensive private practice and also worked for an insurance company.) 'Here, take this stethoscope and you pass them, Frank.' 'But, but . . .' There were a number of bouts still to go. None of the boys dropped dead. During one third round I nearly did.

His growing interest in Catholicism led me to suggest he consult a Catholic doctor whom he knew well and I had known as a ship's doctor. Jerry D's scale of values placed his practice third to whisky-drinking and Church activities. Not for nothing was he called Doctor Hollowlegs. He frequently entered into Retreat to a Jesuit hall a few miles from Huyton in an effort, I suppose, to put Church work first in the list.

Jerry had been taught by the Js himself and I was familiar with the casuistry about drinking which Jesuit-educated drunks adduced. Drunkenness is a sin, you could say, and you cannot get a sin forgiven unless you were resolved not to do it again – that Firm Purpose of Amendment about which the thickest Catholic docker is aware. So you can't be forgiven, you can't get from the confessional box quick enough to sink another. Ah, to hell, a sin has to be wilful, hasn't it? Now it may be hard to commit adultery by accident or even murder a fellow in a fit of absent-mindedness but I declare to God I never wilfully got drunk in my life. I rest my case.

Anyhow, Jerry was a great one for a weekend Retreat and surely there was no better place to get a Catholic atmosphere. Non-Catholics are of course welcome, though it is not expected that they will take a full part in the ceremonies and they need not follow the general régime of modified austerity more than they wish. (The Js are extremists in nothing.) Nor need they pay any fee. Most do of course.

I heard from both of them after the weekend. Jerry drove Scrooge there. Scrooge said he felt a little awkward at first in chapel, which he insisted on attending. He was a bit conspicuous, in a pew separate from the rest. And with nothing on his head. I had often told him that our priests are ordained according to the order of Melchisidek, so he found much on the altar and garments reminiscent of the synagogue service.

He saw the people there for the weekend, mostly young, mostly ordinary Liverpudlians, as reaching towards God. He says he did that but he felt that Catholics were trying to do it at any time. He said they acted as if they'd come to spend a weekend with a mate.

The basis of a profound thesis between the God/Jahveh conception and Son/Brother innovation? (Yet the One God Jews are the greatest egalitarians, Trade Union brothers the most degree-conscious.)

After an excellent lunch with a couple of bottles of beer – 'He drank mine', said Abie – there was a little relaxation without Sunday papers. Football results from the day before, of more value to a Scouser than rubies or perhaps even a virtuous woman, were placed on the noticeboard. (When my father was in retreat there in the Twenties, he bore the then severer régime with fortitude, but he had to climb over the wall on Saturday evening to buy a *Football Echo* in the Ship Inn opposite.)

The *magnum silentium* which all members of the household and devout retreatants observe is complete from an early hour after lights out. This was irksome to such a tireless chatterbox as Abie. But Jerry shut him up before he was in clause 5 of the Beveridge Act. (They had adjoining cubicles.) Jerry said he could hear the Doc. tossing and turning all night thinking of a complete refutation of Bevin's policy in Palestine or five aces in a row. Roused by a brother next morning with 'Deo Gratias', he grumbled: 'Leave it on the mat.'

Then there was a football match in which residents, mainly Jesuit brothers, took part. (These brothers perhaps educationally inferior, or perhaps with more humility, choose to do the harder work and not take full vows. They look just the same as the priests.)

St Ignatius, the army officer who founded the Jesuits, had as a rule among the professed a Rule of Touch – that meant charging at football was forbidden. For the game, retreatants were not so confined. The brothers were pretty rough even then. And fitter than most of the retreatants. But one semi-pro footballer on retreat there turned out with them. They all had football gear of a rough and ready sort.

Dr Clein was picked as ref. He doubtless saw soccer played at Trinity. He played no games. From his youth in Cork he knew only Gaelic football, which though played with a soccer ball and goalposts was closer to the Massacre of the Huguenots than to the Wembley Cup Final.

He had very bad eyesight anyhow. He showed no favouritism. His decisions as far as both sides were concerned were almost always wrong.

With the wisdom of Solomon, when the score stood at five –

four for the residents Abie gave the retreatants an offside goal and all went off happily to the ablutions.

At recreation Abie had spoken of how close much that he had seen and heard of the ceremonies fitted in with his own religious experience. When, in a brief talk during Benediction and the recital of the Office, the priest had spoken in favour of chastity, Abie nodded agreement. When the priest denounced trades-people and others who dealt unfairly with their fellow-men, Abie nodded even more vigorously. When J. mouthed the names of a solicitor in Liverpool, a chemist and a hotelier who hadn't a fore-skin between them (J's phrase) Abie mouthed the name of a council official doing two years for fraud.

Referring to Moses, Abie remarked how he had led the Jews into the Promised Land from the dried up Red Sea. 'Yis', said J, 'but he shouldn't have turned lift, then you'd have had the oil wells.'

Driving back towards Prescot for Huyton, leaving behind the stink of St Helens and the grace, peace and quietness of the retreat house, there was silence for some time. They must both have felt how much they were leaving. You can buy silence from juke boxes in New York for ten cents. It is worth thousands. Then Abie had to break it. 'Well', he said 'they didn't make me a Christian.' Letting out a string of oaths at some tardy pedestrians opposite the Hillside, Jerry countered: 'They didn't make me one eether.'

Fur's fur

Teacher (in small Catholic school, beginners' class): Boys, a little Jewish boy is going to be with us for a little while. I want you to treat him as one of ourselves. There must be no discrimination in any way, he is just one of ourselves. Welcome to the class, Isaac. Boys--!

Boys: Welcome, Isaac.

Teacher: We are going to have simple spelling. Just boys' names. I'll pick them out of the TV programme in the newspaper. (To Welsh boy) TOM Jones. That's correct but it's TOM not TAM. Now, Robert. Bob Hope. Bob Hope, with a aitch. Good, good. Now, Isaac – Engelbert Humperdinck.

Orange and Green

(Music Trad. *Wearing of the Green*)

Now my father was an Ulsterman, proud Protestant was he,
My mother was a Catholic girl from County Cork was she.
They were married in two churches, Lived happily enough
Until the day when I was born, then things got rather tough.

Chorus: For it's the greatest mix-up that you have ever seen
My father he was Orange but my mother she was Green.

Baptised by Father Riley, then rushed away by car
To be made a little Orangeman – my father's Shining Star.
I was christened David Anthony and yet in spite of that
To me father I was William, while my mother called me Pat.

Chorus

With mother every Sunday to Mass I'd proudly stroll
and later on the Orange Lodge would try to save my soul.
For both sides tried to claim me, but I was smart because
I'd play my flute or I'd play my harp, depending where I was.

Chorus

When I'd sing those rebel songs much to my mother's joy
My father would jump up and shout, 'Look here William my boy,
You've sung enough of that lot', he'd then toss me a coin,
He made me sing The Orange Flute and the Heroes of the Boyne.

Chorus

One day my Mam's relations they came to visit me,
By chance my father's kinsfolk were just sitting down to tea.
Well we tried to smooth things over, but they all began to fight.
And, being strictly neutral, I bashed everyone in sight.

Chorus

Now my parents never could agree about my type of school,
My learning was all done at home, no wonder I'm a fool.
They've both passed on, God bless them, but I am caught between
That awful colour problem – of the Orange and the Green.

– Tony Murphy, Huyton, 1965.

173

Lollipop man

'I was born somewhere in Liverpool. My father was no good. Like Judas he has gone to his own place. Of him I will say no more. My mother was just the opposite, so very good. This too is all I must say of her.'

It was on Lime Street Station where I met him in 1969 on his return to Liverpool after nearly 60 years away. As a lad of 12 he earned his first coppers here, and behind, in the warren of shabby streets he wandered round as a barefoot boy. Nearby is the crossing he now guards as a lollipop man. Aged 73 he is a retired parson, and lives alone in a small house in an Everton Street which, if not exactly a slum, is shabby, indifferent and without grace. The police station from which he was issued with his uniform and the lollipop is the same one where in 1910 he was given a good hiding from a bobby, an event he recalls with gratitude. It is little changed from what it was all those years ago, a gloomy, damp-souled place: it is in a down-at-heel cobbled street near my own old home which at one time may have justified the name Rose Hill. Now it's just a sour irony. The police station has always had a name for being tough; an old police superintendent who started there told me he had an inspector who used to say: 'Put the poker in the fire and we'll get a voluntary statement.'

Few other relics of his boyhood remain. Gone is the tin school, in those times called a ragged school, the lodging houses, where the barefoot lad slept with lascars, the pubs behind the market where he touted men for prostitutes, the market itself, the music hall outside which he and his barefoot pal Jimmy begged pence from stars of the day like George Robey. In Lime Street a few years before the First World War he, with Jimmy, was recruited into the Army, to get the first full suit of new clothes he had had up to then. When I met him he was an Anglican clergyman, though he did not look like one; he looked more like an old lag.

Not tall, he had the stiff firm stance of an old soldier, and a battered, narrow-eyed, tough-looking face, so that I was not surprised to learn he had been a useful boxer. He still had a wiry frame and the neat, swift movements of the trained pug. His clothes were not shabby but they were not smart and he wore a clean coloured soft collar with a shirt of a different colour and a nondescript woollen tie. No wonder I did not recognise him at first. I knew from correspondence that he was an ordained clergyman. I know few Anglican ministers, but he did not look like any

174

I had ever met. He did not talk like one either. His voice was pleasant, slightly musical, and his accent was a medley, as I have often found with old soldiers and sailors, not readily associated with any particular place. The slang he recalled from his boyhood was unlike any slang I had ever heard, owing something to parly-arlie and thieves' lingo picked up, I suppose, from villains, itiner-ants, drunken sailors and whores, and used almost as a secret language by Andy and his fellow ragamuffins.

Andy Clerk is what he calls himself, but I know his real name, and I have been able to verify what he had to tell me of his life after he left Liverpool's mean streets when he was 14. I have even seen a letter signed Cantuar. What he recalls of his years in Liver-pool before that has the hallmark of utter truth: a pitiful, never self-pitying tale of endured poverty and neglect when the great Empire for which he was to fight and its great seaport on the Mersey were at the peak of prosperity and the Church for which he was to work at its most influential. He has outlived all his old associates. His tale is unique, mostly because he has such a good memory, but one has heard of enough like it to accept it. Andy is always so cheerful about it – like a leper in a clown's hat, a grinning skull.

When in the railway refreshment room, after we had somehow become acquainted, I bought him a roll and coffee and assumed the self-mocking role of the unregenerate which I tend to do with ordained persons. 'I usually meet people in a pub', I said. He said: 'Let's go.' And it was in Dan English's pub in Commutation Row, across from the station, that I heard the first of his amazing story, which was to lead to my spending much of one year scrabbling through a vast pile of ill-written text on thin sheets which opened with the words of this little sketch.

My eldest child Mary has spent a deal of time in hospitals where she reads a large number of newspapers supplied by her husband, who works for a wholesale distributor of periodicals. When Mary reads a paper she reads it. When therefore she saw, in an obscure provincial newspaper, an advertisement for a writer to help some-one write his life story, she at once thought of me. My big desire at the time was to complete writing my own life story, and to live a bit more life.

Anyway, I took a risk and wrote to the box number. The reply told me that the book the advertiser wanted writing was indeed his life story, that he had already assembled much material, the fee would be fair and a free hand given to the suitable applicant.

175

The advertiser was a retired parson, at the moment in a provincial town. His story opened in Liverpool where, on his pension from the Church, he intended shortly to retire. The Liverpool connection clinched it, hence this meeting. The fee was indeed fair, though, in fact, it all went in expenses, typists' fees and so on. By the time it was clear as a moneymaker it was a dead loss, especially as it kept me from doing my own writing. It wasn't easy to shape. Long stretches had to be thrown out – very often the expressed opinions and prejudices of an old man. He had no plan, no values. Excellently recorded events in his life would be mixed in with trivia. A promising line would suddenly stop abruptly. There were few living people besides himself, especially in the Army section. For me, thinking of the post-Kipling British Army, it had the makings of a good story. I rubbed my hands when he was posted to India. Almost at once he was on the troopship coming back. He had a few good yarns about life on a troopship *circa* spring 1914, but he didn't, there or in other places, give me a picture. There was little direct speech, there was no sound or smell. He just recorded what happened with irrelevancies – about, say, the merits of corporal punishment or the selfishness of the higher clergy. I had to make a picture and invent evocative touches.

Of others in his story I could make something only of his slummy mate Jimmy who joined the Army with him and was killed in 1915. Girls he knew as a boy, ragged as himself, I perhaps should have blown up and maybe there was the makings in the master of his ragged school. Even as a parson his had not been a happy life – though it was not clear what went wrong at that stage of his life – but his cheerfulness and acceptance were most attractive qualities, and if I had had more material could have brought him readers if the eventual book had been published. I was not the man, that's all about it. I can say only that I did my best, which is a sad half-hearted thing to say of oneself: there are so many other things one would rather say.

It was a long time before there was a book to send to a publisher. I suppose I typed from Andy's material, with much scrapping of his stuff and additions of my own, about 100,000 words. I brought this down to about 60,000 in three roughly equal parts. The first part, Liverpool slum boyhood, I called 'Rags'. The second 'Khaki', led to the third with: 'It was the Recruiting Sergeant who told me I was a member of the Church of England', and a kindly word of advice from the Army chaplain at the end.

I had found a literary agent whose chief adviser was very

interested in the book. When the book was finally typed, I bunged it off. Then I took a holiday. When I returned I found the book had also. The adviser who had liked the idea had left the firm and the new adviser was against real-life material. (Andy, who had always wanted me to turn his narrative into fiction, which I strongly opposed, now felt justified. But it was a very bad idea. Any success would come from the authenticity of the story.)

There was no comment on the quality of the book. Typists' fees, postage and other things had skimmed most of the cream off the generous reward Andy had given me for the job. Unhappily, therefore, determined to keep a promise to do my utmost to see the book into print, I faced the prospect of using up more time and money sending the book the round of the publishers, some of whom have been known to keep a book six months before rejection.

Andy would not wait. I had had some (unprofitable) association with publishing and had good printer friends. Andy offered me a considerable sum – or rather, through him, his backers, of whom I know nothing, did – and I could easily have taken him, them, for the lot, for the printing of a few hundred. I suggested that it could make a small paper-back based on a dozen or so of the drawings and had an estimate for this and for some prose matter from the 'Rags' section of the book, rewritten in places. Two thousand of these, at a fair book token sort of price, with those very fetching drawings, properly circulated, would pay the printer and give him a few bob over. It meant a lot of work for me, but I was ready.

Andy was impatient. It would take a few months. He found someone else to devise a text, based on mine, choose a selection of drawings and found a printer of his own. The result, though very expensive, was a good piece of work. But he proceeded to give the book away in handfuls. A good friend of us both, with experience of the bookselling world, took what was left of them and placed them in local shops where, after some publicity, they sold reasonably well and a complete financial loss was avoided. Andy is still a lollipop man. It is just barely possible a publisher missed a potential best seller.

The only one I could ever bring myself to cheat would be a rogue. Rogues can be cheated, I am told, but I'm not clever enough. Andy, eating his sausage from a grocer's box while reading *Boxing*, smiling at the kids on the crossing, not one of whom fails to greet him as a friend, and walking round the streets he first knew 70 years ago, is a simple soul who somehow has emerged unsoiled by the squalor of his youth – good hidings, bloodshed, clerical snobbery, lack of education, hunger, smells, disappointments – with no bitterness or resentment or jealousy (or success) to spoil his last years. Who said 'Suffer little street arabs to come unto me'?

PART SIX Liverpool Judies

PART SIX

Liverpool
Judies

Liverpool Judies

Baroness Gaitskell, opposing the Bill as it stood, spoke of strong
young women openly flaunting six – *Liverpool Echo*, 1969.

A smart Yankee packet
lies out in the bay
A-waitin' a fair wind to get under way
With all of her sailors so sick and so sore,
They've drunk all their whisky and can't get no more
Singing roo-o -o-ol, roll bullies roll,
Them Liverpool judies have got us in tow!
> – Stan Hugill, *Shanties from the Seven Seas*

. . . Liverpool town where I was born,
Where there's lots of girls, With peroxide curls
And the black-an'-tans flow free –
We're six in a bed At the old Pier Head –
An' it's Liverpool town for me.
> – Stan Kelly, *I Wish I was Back*

Mon amour she said – her last lover had been French –
composing those truly gorgeous limbs for a carefully
organised orgy . . . I felt like the male spider . . . *mon amour*
I was only from Liverpool.
> – Nicholas Monsarrat, *Life is a Four-Letter Word*.

Maggie May

(The Liverpool anthem)

Come all ye sailors bold
And when my tale is told
I'm sure you'll all have cause to pity me.
For I was a goddam fool
In the port of Liverpool
When I met up with a girl called Maggie May[1]

Oooh, dirty Maggie May
They have taken you away
And you'll never walk down Lime Street[2] any more, any more,
For you robbed full many a sailor
And also a couple of whalers[3]
And now you're doing time in Bot'ny Bay[4], oooh!

I paid off at the Home[5]

---

1. Nobody challenging my version can deny the traditional opening, though some dastards have tried to shift Liverpool to Hartlepool and other pools. But Nellie·Ray, as a variant of the lady's name, cannot be ignored. Maggie May is so typically Irish though. And the judies were so often Irish. How old is Maggie? An oral tradition before a written one is almost certain, though, like other sailor songs, it could be based on a music-hall or free-and-easy song, maybe of different subject. Glyn Hughes is of this opinion. Woman-like she is coy. Extracts from a sailor's diary in magazine *Blue Peter* in 1930, the diary being for 1830 (Charles Picknell) place her on a ship to Van Diemen's Land in that year. Points made in the notes led to from the transcript give a clue – but never forget, there are many versions. Must be with this sort of song, remembered by drunken sailors, sailing from various ports, adapted to their own circumstances. Where certain lines recur the first version can be conjectured.

2. In early versions it certainly is not Lime Street, that thoroughfare not having gained the reputation it had in the Thirties and now, alas maybe, no longer merits. It was probably Paradise Street, frequently found in other Liverpool-based sea songs, cleaned up completely about 1850. Let us have no truck with streets outside Liverpool, like Peter Street and Wind Street.

3. The bad hearing of the drunken sailor in some versions has ridiculously 'tailors' for 'whalers'. Whalers have a part in deciding her age. Few here before 1850.

4. Tune is the same as a music hall song called *Botany Bay*, I'm told of the Fifties again. But many versions give Van Diemen's Land, making her older. On this and other points the Liverpool magazine devoted to old shipping matters had violent correspondence from old master mariners who discussed the whole subject as if it was a first Folio or the Dead Sea Scrolls, round 1953. One amazing version had the sailor pack up the sea and become a singer outside The Clock – a once notorious Liverpool pub.

5. The Home settles it, not the date, place. There are many Sailors' Homes but only

From a voyage to Sierra Leone
And two pound ten a month was all my pay[6].
When I drew the cash I grinned,
But very soon got skinned
By a dirty robbing bitch called Maggie May.

Chorus: Oooh, etc.

In the morning when I woke
I found that I was broke
No shoes, no shirt, no trousers could I find.
When I asked her where they were
She said, 'Oh, my dear sir,
'They're down in Lewis's pawnshop, Number Nine[7].

Up to Lewis's I did wind,
But no trousers could I find,
So the policeman took that wicked girl away, girl away.
And the judge he guilty found her
Of robbing a homeward bounder,
And now she's doing time in Bot'ny Bay.

Oh, I'll not forget the day
When I first met Maggie May,
She was strolling up and down old Canning Place
In a full-sized crinoline
Like a frigate of the line[8],
As she saw I was a sailor I gave chase.

Chorus: Oooh, etc.

---

one Home – Liverpool's. Not there before 1850, talking of age. Probably another Home existed earlier. Canning Place where she 'cruised', near the main docks for foreign ships, is site of the Home.

6. Two pounds ten suggests 1850, but pay may have, in earlier version, been lower. In later version it is three pounds ten.

7. If we only now knew where Lewis's pawnshop was we could finally fix date and place, for this is constant. On the whole it is likely to have been in Liverpool where pawnshops had Welsh names and the date 1840-1850. There were policemen you note, and Botany Bay is the most frequent penal settlement found in the main versions. Little Maggie or the goddam fool now care! But this is a true Liverpool cameo, showing just what we came from, in post slave trade times.

8. A 'frigate of the line' describing Maggie's promenade tells us nothing, for crinolines lasted so long in the last century, even for lower classes. But what a lovely picture!

This version, the one I render when persuaded to, and just try and stop me, is as I was taught it by my guru the Whackerishi. It does not precisely mark any version in print and I'm sure an early verse has slipped into the end but – The Law, the Law.

Sad then that when Alun Owen's musical *Maggie May*, with music by Lionel Bart, had its first provincial run it opened, of all places, in Manchester – and this despite its theme, Owen's Liverpool origin and the suitability, to my mind, of our biggest theatre (scene designer Sean Kenny is thought to have said no to this). I wrote a protest song as soon as I heard and, on the show's first night in Manchester, the Liverpool group The Spinners rendered this, to the traditional tune at the Royal Philharmonic Hall, Liverpool. There was frantic applause from the dinner-suited audience. (I had to take a bow. From a box.) I may quote a little:

*Oh come back Maggie May**

> Say tarrah and run away
> Back to Park Street and the bevvy will flow free.
> Oh, Maggie Maggie May,
> They have taken you away,
> This is something that we find hard to forgive,
> Fir they've shipped our dear old gal
> Up the Manchester Canal
> And in Coronation Street she'll have to live.
> It is sad our famous filly
> Must parade down Piccadilly
> When down Lime Street is the place she ought to be.
> Every whacker's heart feels moody
> When the seafront's best-known judy
> Is an exile, and so far off from the sea.

*An extended version of this song is given on p.66.

Courting

'And where did this incident take place?'
    'Between two waggins, sir.'
    '– Two waggins?'
    '– Yis, the wagging of his an' the wagging of mine.'
Silence in Court.
    The Police Court in Dale Street – I know it shouldn't be called

that but that's what it is to all of us – was the place for a giggle when the Maggie Mays paraded. They were usually with the drunks in Number Two Court. But sometimes they were in Number One, the Stipendiary's. Before Stewart Deacon, a wise man, who knew his law but was deaf and sometimes pretended to be deafer. He relished a little salt. I'm sure he chuckled later over the waggin reply.

I wouldn't be sure about the reply in a maternity charge when he asked where the alleged incident took place – 'In a doorway, standin up, and you know as well as I do, me lord, you can't do much that way.'

One told him, in short and simple terms, just what had been done to her.

'I don't understand you, madam. Your terminology puzzles me.'

'Aw, g'wan,' she said, 'cod on you don't know!'

'And what were you doing at the time, madam?'

'I was having a Jimmy Riddle, sir.'

'What was that? Speak up!'

'Having a Jimmy Riddle, sir.'

'Is Mr Riddle in the court?'

Bigamy Liz

I'm Bigamy Liz, Bigamy Liz,
If I'm not married then nobody is.
I've husbands in the Argentine, husbands in Japan,
Three or four on the Castiron Shore*
And two in the Legs o' Man.
You've heard of the woman who. lived in a shoe,
Had so many kids she didn't know what to do?
I've as many husbands as there's monkeys in the zoo!
Bigamy Liz, that's me.

James Laver, Liverpool writer who recalls it says Dublin actress, Maire O'Neill, favoured for line three 'Six or seven in Armenteers, four in the Sudan' and 'Isle of Man' to 'Legs o' Man' which is a well known pub near Lime Street Station.

---

* A scruffy bit of sand and rock at the North End of the Mersey which delighted children years ago; now part of Otterspool Promenade. On the site of a former castiron manufactory.

187

Arsenic in Aigburth, or Three Nights

Oh naughty Mrs Maybrick what have you been and gone and done?
Your goings on are bad, I must confess.
To get mashed on Mr Brierley was very wrong entirely,
So you get yourself in such a blooming mess.

When this song was published, to the tune of *Maggie May*, in 1889, the lady was in Walton Gaol awaiting trial for the murder of her husband. As the song, actually labelled 'comic', quite unpublishable nowadays of course, gleefully states,

Mr Maybrick has been poisoned
And the charming Mrs M
Is a well-attended guest in Walton Gaol . . .

Maybrick had been poisoned, that is sure. Who poisoned him, although Mrs M was sentenced to death, black cap and all, at Liverpool assizes, by Judge Stephens, is uncertain. Maybe Maybrick himself.

What she, an American girl of 25, had gone and done was marry a rich Liverpool merchant, twenty-four years older than herself. He was a womanising drug-addict, and she allowed herself to be picked up by a young rakehell named Brierley. She paid a visit to a sick aunt. As have so many provincial wives in similar circumstances.

'I was guilty of intimacy with Mr Brierley,' she told the judge, 'I am not guilty of this crime.'

I have stayed at the London hotel near Villiers Street where a few months before the song was published she spent three nights with Mr Brierley, the masher. Even then it can hardly have been a very Sardanapalian place in which to sin. For this 'sin' she was to spend fifteen years in English prison cells, one of them the condemned cell.

She went to the Grand National at Aintree, Liverpool, with her husband the day she came back from London. Brierley was there; the three chatted. He and Maybrick moved in the same Liverpool social circle. But Maybrick was well up in the seduction game himself and, if he had accepted the aunt story, he was not deceived by Brierley's apparently casual manner to his wife. Back in their Gothic-named home, Battlecrease House, Aigburth, Maybrick gave her a black eye.

A black eye in Aigburth! As if she were a working-class wife, in, say, Christian Street. Even now it has a faded gentility. Then it was one of the most genteel parts of Liverpool, facing the Mersey at its best point, south of the busy docks, flowing towards its sources. Solid houses set in greenery, on the slope of the city's second highest hill of its seven. Already the wealthy and cultivated gentry of the early part of the century, who built the modern city, had moved elsewhere. But Maybrick and his neighbours, especially in Riversdale Road, still not without an air of unostentatious prosperity, a good address for a trade union leader, a BOAC pilot or a director at ICI, were well-off enough.

Before long there was, as it might be in Scotty Road, a police car – 'the hurry up van' – in Riversdale Road. The little lock-up to which it took Mrs Maybrick on May 14, 1889 in Lark Lane I visited recently. Little changed I'd say. They had been married eight years and she had two young children with whom, no doubt, she had as little to do as other merchants' wives in those days. She never saw them, a boy and a girl, again. James Chandler Maybrick, aged 8 at the time, died at 29 in British Columbia and was known as Bobo. His name was mentioned when his mother was tried. The chief witness against Florence, a maid called Yapp, said she gave him a letter from his mother to post as he went to the pillar-box. He dropped it in the mud. Opening the envelope to put the letter in a clean one she, well, she read the letter. Sir Charles Russell, for Mrs Maybrick's defence, cross questioned the maid closely on this evidence, but did not break her. He firmly believed in his client's innocence. Later, as Lord Chief Justice, he firmly announced his belief. So did another barrister, Alexander McDougall, who dedicated a very able book on the subject, *The Maybrick Case*, to the two children using these words:

'With the sincere hope that it will enable them to feel during their lives that the word "mother" is not a sound "unfit to be heard or muttered" by them and that when they are able enough to understand this record of facts and circumstances . . . they may have throughout their lives the comfort of feeling that their mother was not proved to be guilty of the murder of their father.'

The other child, Gladys, was 3 (McDougall says wrongly 4) and I cannot trace anything of her subsequent life.

The letter referred to was to Brierley and it read:

'He is sick unto death. The doctors held a consultation yesterday, and now all depends upon how long his strength will hold out . . . We are terribly anxious. I cannot answer your letter fully today, my darling, but relieve your mind of all fear of discovery now or for the future.'

One thinks of Oscar Wilde's children, of Mrs Thompson's foolish letters to the murderer of her husband, of justice, of mercy.

Maybrick had met her in Alabama, where he was on business and, though they married in London a few months after meeting, they lived some years in Norfolk, Virginia. Probably business brought him back with her to Liverpool.

Though he rode and went to races, he gave much of his time to business and, with little to do, she must have spent lonely hours every day in that big house in Aigburth. Did she ever dream of the cotton-fields while he was dealing in cotton shares in Liverpool Exchange, a long carriage-drive away? He was away a deal at night too. There would be occasional mixed social occasions, amid the plush furnishings and gilded valances, under the glittering chandeliers, but the other wives must have seemed very strange to the young American girl, and the other men who were much like James Maybrick himself.

Except, maybe, Brierley. Drawings, allegedly from life, on top of the song-sheet showed him as the conventional moustachioed drawing-room lady's man of the Victorian *Punch*. She is insipid-looking and pretty as a du Maurier lady. Maybrick looks the born-to-be-murdered type he certainly was. He kept a large number of servants, leaving her, like any other Victorian lady, with little to do.

He died of poison on May 11. Much arsenic was found in the house. His wife was arrested three days after. But she was suspected long before his death.

If Florence Maybrick's situation at times reminds us slightly of Henry James, what the murder in Battlecrease House lacked for solution was Agatha Christie. I am sure her spinster sleuth would have found someone other than the obvious Florence on whom to pin the crime. Maybe the well-named Alice Yapp. Maybrick, as his wife had known for some time, took loads of drugs, including arsenic. It was quite a drug-taking age, the Victorian one. Drugs were easy to get and drug taking did not carry the obloquy (and glamour) it does today. Mothers gave children opium to quieten them.

Readers were not shocked by Sherlock Holmes's cocaine. Men took hard drugs under stress of work, as we might take an aspirin. They took them to reinforce waning sexual powers. Maybe Maybrick, aged 50, did. Men took arsenic to obtain the fashionable pale complexion. Maybrick was a vain man. Plenty of arsenic was found in his effects after his death. But there was arsenic among Florence's effects too. And in medicines – possibly put there by her. Until a few days before his death she was in charge of the sick-chamber. Then, already suspected, she was barred from it.

At the trial the Home Office expert said Maybrick had certainly died of arsenic poisoning. Another expert – it so often happens – flatly contradicted him. Arsenic had nothing to do with the death. And, if it did, he could have given it to himself. At the trial there was much evidence of his constantly taking large amounts of drugs. One said he wouldn't be surprised at anything found in Maybrick's inside: a druggist's waste-pipe he called it.

If only on the night he hit her she had carried out her threat to leave him! But she was penniless; indeed heavily in debt for those times. She owed £1,200. A family doctor, consulted about divorce procedure, then most rare in such English circles, advised against it and saw Maybrick on her behalf. He paid her debts and there were mutual expressions of contrition and a firm purpose of amendment.

Then Florrie bought some arsenic. And sent a letter, clearly addressed 'A. Brierley Esq.' Poor innocent, she gave it to Yapp to post.

Maybrick, a hypochondriac, had been in and out of sick-bed a good deal in the past few weeks, and at this point was in real pain. When Yapp read the letter she took it straight to Brierley's brother Michael, to whom she had already expressed suspicion of Florence. She said she had found a package marked 'Arsenic' in Mrs Maybrick's box which, of course, she had searched. She told him too she had seen Florence 'tampering' with her husband's medicine bottles. Whatever of the package marked 'Arsenic' which, with the tale of tampering, would have interested Agatha Christie, Florence *had* bought arsenic. She had bought fly-papers which, in those times, contained arsenic. There was, servants attested, no particular fly trouble in Battlecrease House.

Servants also attested, later, that they had found fly-papers soaking in basins in Florrie's room. Florrie, in a statement to the judge, said she used the arsenic thus obtained as a face lotion, as did other women. (In those days the defendant could not give evidence.)

The message to Brierley read by Michael ('He is sick unto death') – at a time when Maybrick was having a good spell – Yapp's statements and the fact that Maybrick had taken a turn for

191

the worse after eating invalid food prepared for him in a jug supplied by Mrs Maybrick (arsenic being later found in the jug). That was about all the evidence.

Anyhow, the prejudiced and sick judge, Mr Justice Stephens, and a middle class Liverpool jury in 1889, never thought for a moment that James Maybrick could have poisoned himself, or that Michael could have poisoned him, or someone else in the house could have done it. The adulteress was sentenced to death.

After some public agitation, and a plea by Cardinal Gibbons of USA, she was reprieved and went back to America, when she was released in 1904. She died, aged 80, in America. Penniless, alone, in squalor. But she had been back to Liverpool once. To the Grand National.

Alfred John Reynolds, who had a waxworks show in Lime Street in what had been a Freemasons Hall and was later to become BBC Liverpool, tried to get pictures of Mrs Maybrick during the trial to make a model for his Chamber of Horrors. But the Maybrick family foiled him. He went to the trial and secretly sketched her. Maybrick's family tried hard to buy the model but to no avail. It was, however, melted down in 1922.

At the Wash'ouse*
Two Shawlies talk while mangling

She's gorra lovelee home; muriels on the wall.

I wuz thinkin of goin in fer dat radio infusion.

Luvlee place, all this contemptuous furniture.

When I emptied the refuge in the dust-bin.

He's incapacitated in Walton Gaol (could be).

Tubercular steel chairs.

She's gorra lip on her like a roll a lino (or, like a Prodessan poor box).

---

*The wash-house is, even if modernised and now called a 'laundry-ette', the working class woman's club. When I took a BBC producer to a Liverpool one to get a glimpse of true city life I marvelled at the amount of washing a skinny little old girl could carry on her head. Grinning she said, 'It's the on'y at that suits me'. At first, though, she didn't want to go in this particular wash-house. It's a Prodessan one, she explained.

Of course she's gorra minx coat.

They charge contortionate prices in dat shop.

Luverlee kitchen; one of them persian heaters.

Yer don't wanna get embodied wid iggerent people like dat.

He comes of a good famlee, I've seen his gynaecological tree.

He's absolutely under her denomination.

Has a chiffonier to drive the car a course.

Me grandkids concocted together to buy me a birthday present, God luv em.

She puts massacre on her eyes.

He strongly dissembles her mother.

I hate going up dem osculators in Lewis's.

But his brother is so self-scented (could be).

I says I am unable to recuperate yer hospitality, like.

There was all sorts of miraculous (miscellaneous?) goods on sale.

Got a clock wid Axminster chimes.

Such a good son to me, if I dhrop anyting he kicks it towards me to pick up.

She give us lovely chateaus for tea.

On the China boats, says he'll bring her back a kimona, hope it doesn't frighten the kids.

On'y ting, the pudding didn't have the right constituents.

A round table monologue

So easy to start a dust up, in'it? The doctor asked her to bring a sample and she's carrying it down the street when the ould one asses her, 'What might ye have in the bottle, Mrs Rafferty.' And Mrs Rafferty tells her. Well I've never laffed so much sence the missus caught her nose in the mangle.

Then there's a shawlie lookin in C & A's – what does C & A

mean? Coats an ats a course. And she simply says that's the one I'd get. How was she to know the woman next to her had on'y one eye? Then she asks a hump-back to lend her a shilling till she gets straight. Mind you she doesn't arf look after him – she irons his bootlaces.

Eh, dis bus conductor, he cudden drive a bargain. Anyhow, she starts to take exercises and she's stripped off with her back to the bedroom door touching her toes when he looks in. 'F' evvins sake, Maggie,' he says, 'comb yer air and put yer teeth in.' Laff!

She went to see the boxing at the Stadium and fainted at the sight of blood. Took four fellers to carry her out – two a breast. Then he gets the idea of slimming. Passes a place advertising a course of three lessons for three guineas. There's another three lessons six guineas. He puts down the three guineas and goes into a cuticle to take his clothes off. In comes a smashing blonde judy, in her bare pelt, bare as a badger's. 'Come to massage me, ducks', he asses. 'No,' she says, 'you gorra chase me round this little room. Everytime you ketch me you can tear a slice off.' She wasn't so fast. Next morning in the bathroom finds he's lost half a stone.

He's round there again soon as the place is open. 'Gimme the six guinea course.' Into cuticle, bollock naked in a minute. In comes a huge bare Negro grinning all over his face. Me laddo says, 'OK, bring in that blonde again.'

'No,' says Happy Harry, grinning away, 'you're taking the six-guinea course. In that course I chase you. On your mark –!'

Mirabel and the Grand National

'The Grand National Sweepstake is something England gave to the world, something for which the world is grateful and of which all Englishmen have reason to be proud.'
– *Sunday Telegraph*, July 5, 1964.

Mirabel Topham is the Grand National, the Grand National is Mirabel Topham. Is or was? There have been as many last Grand Nationals in the past ten years or so as Harry Lauder had farewell tours. As I write the 1971 Grand National may in verity be the last one.

The 1971 race was the 125th. The race started in 1839 (Lottery won) but on seven years, in the two world wars, no race was run. This was at Aintree, a steeplechase, but yet handicapped. For two years before that the Liverpool Steeplechase had been run at Maghull, near Aintree, the sponsor being a John Formby.

William Lynn was a Liverpool innkeeper, his pub being the Waterloo Hotel in Ranelagh Street, not far from the statue by Epstein and very near the city's old haunt of culture The Lyceum, about to be improved out of existence as I write. (Town planners use the word 'improve' much as occupying troops use the word 'liberate' or Communists 'liquidate'.) Lynn's grave is one of the many interesting ones to be found in the old cemetery behind the Anglican cathedral if you have a day or so to spare and a good team of beaters. The coursing classic, the Waterloo Cup, had its name from his pub, not from the place near Liverpool called Waterloo, named, like the pub, after the battle.

Lynn was associated with some noble gentlemen with local associations, such as my Lords Derby and Sefton, and Lord George Bentinck, who formed a syndicate. Formby may well have, as we racing types would term it, been done a thick 'un. He would not be the last one to think the word 'syndicate' like 'combine' or 'take-over' was a synonym for conspiracy if nothing worse. He fathered a nasty pamphlet on the subject.

Yet the Grand National was a gear name, I like especially the typically Liverpudlian Grand (which, as a spectacle, it has never been) and it would not have become international as the Liverpool Steeplechase. Promoters of older races like the Derby may have sniffed at the name National, and for a steeplechase at that. Even so it would never have been grand but for an ancestor of Mrs Topham's husband, Edward William Topham, a handicapper of genius content with the more modest description The Wizard. Topham, a Yorkshire man settled in Cheshire with some land in Aintree, at Warbreck Moor, was certainly to take the science of handicapping seriously. He started at Chester Racecourse, a much better course, by the way, than Aintree.

One might think that if Topham had turned to more serious pursuits than handicapping, if there are any (diplomacy for instance), he might have been a world benefactor. He is described in a contemporary magazine as having introduced the flattering system by which every animal appears to have a chance. He pleased everybody or almost everybody (how I envy him) while getting his own way. 'Everyone was pleased with the way in which his horse was treated and the public always made up their minds that the handicap was made for one alone.' Handicapped Grand Nationals started in 1843, Lord Chesterfield's Vanguard winning.

Interest had almost waned when the National was revived after the war in 1946 and Lovely Cottage won. For years thousands poured into Liverpool, especially from Ireland and the USA, for the famous race. The city was a lively place in the morning, quiet by afternoon when all the visitors were at Aintree and many of the citizens, at home or work, crouched over radios. The town was lively again in the evening, especially, until the early hours of the following morning, at the Adelphi Hotel (opposite Epstein's statue). But the Adelphi is for the rich and few Scousers are rich.

There are some Liverpudlians in there, as we have some rich and others nimble at getting into places uninvited. It would be difficult to check up on everyone at the huge do customarily put up by the winning owner, especially after the champagne has flowed a while (into the waiters as well as the guests from what I know of such things). I remember having wine in a less elegant hostelry near the Adelphi on the big night with Charleston Charlie, a good-looking, well spoken man about town, a squire of dames when they were in the money, never in it himself. We were in Yates Wine Lodge, the drink was Australian Vin Blanc, rather a good year.

'Sorry I can't get you no plonk back, old top,' said Charlie, 'tell you true damned awkward sence they shifted the race to Friday from Wensdy. I drew my dole of a Wensdy. Haven't a bean. I wonder could you . . . No, you wouldn't have.' I was already vigorously shaking my head. Not for nothing was the dancing man known in some circles as The Plumber because he's always on the tap.

'Frank,' more in sorrow than, 'I don' wanna tap you. I just wonder, you know anyone could lend us a dinner suit?' I, a bit of a pedant at times, was about to say I didn't want to share a dinner suit with him. 'What d'you want a dinner suit for, Charleston?' 'Get in the Delly. In a dinner thingy I can just moody in, fill up with the best scoff, caviare butties, the lot, bevvy galore and bag off with some judy in a tarara for a night's kip.'

I couldn't think of anybody with ready access to a dinner-suit in Lime Street at that time of the evening, though there were quite a few who'd get you one or anything else within reason with reasonable notice.

Go to the race – we don't. Not nowadays. In my first year at college, the year Poethlyn won, prefects were sent to the race to see if any of the boys were there. They found no boys but three teachers, all straight out of sick beds. (While I'm really digressing

I must mention a boy at that school who 'sagged' for many weeks spending his dinner money on the ferry to New Brighton to laze on the sands during a very warm summer. He sent notes under his father's signature. Finally he decided to stop away altogether and sent a note saying he was dead. The head immediately sent a master to the boy's house with a message of sympathy. The boy opened the door.)

Even if you could afford the best seats you will not see the race; elsewhere you see the coloured blouse of a jockey and a few yards of horseflesh. In every other way the amenities are not good. I went with two Irish friends the year Sheila's Cottage won. Up to the race, or up to the entrance to the course, reached after a long walk and much pushing and jostling, since the car must be parked a few miles back, we had had a pleasant time. And after. I had met them on the boat early that morning. My old friend Joe Liggett, purser steward, had fixed them up with a good berth cabin where I soon found them. With six others. The boat was packed (nowadays more fly in chartered planes) and there were squatters in every cabin. The six were lying in all shapes on the floor. My two mates had been unable to shift them. I used my authority and got them out. And in their haste they left behind a bottle of whiskey. The Customs usually let the crowd for the Nash have a bottle each but they had theirs already. We must either, I told my mates, find the owners – they looked completely shocked – or consume it right now. On the way to their cabin I'd asked the night steward for two teas for them and bacon sandwiches. (There was a Papal dispensation on Grand National Day.) John, the man with the hollowest legs in County Wexford, tipped the tea into the sink just as Aidan, the other, was soaping himself for a shave. The Liver clock struck seven.

A passing stewardess gasped when she saw through the port Aidan shaving with one hand and drinking a staggering measure of whiskey from a tooth-glass held in the other, while John and I genteely sipped what she would think was tea. The rest of the day had been like that.

We couldn't afford the best stand, and the two boyos, used to the magnificent courses in Ireland, were a bit disappointed. However, we eventually saw the whole race from start to finish. We found a fellow in a caravan watching it on a large TV screen and he kindly moved to let us look through his open door.

Actually we backed the winner, and they decided to stay a few more days in Liverpool. They stayed at my sister's South End home near a quiet pub. They were in there at opening time, which in Liverpool is 11.30, rather late in the day by Irish standards. In the four days they were at my sister's they rarely went beyond this pub.

Those were the days, just after the war, when Guinness was in short supply. On the third day, the publican, who came from the same part of Ireland, asked when they were going back: 'My other customers are complainin; haven't they dhrunk evry drop of porter in the place?'

The next day Aidan, who was the local undertaker back home, received a telegram saying a dead man was awaiting his services. John went with him; he was the local publican but he had not worried about his services being needed, his customers could 'furridge' for thimselfs. They haven't been to the National since. Nor have I. Nor will I ever go if there is another. They've our TV over in their part of Ireland too. Watching it on the screen in comfort and entirety one misses a good deal. But they can see racing in fair comfort quite cheaply in Ireland without the hazards of a Channel crossing. ('God I could never fly, yiz'll never get me up in one of them yokes.') And the loop men with the twisted belt and the three cards, the tipsters and tic tac men and the like are as plentiful, all the joyous adjuncts to going racing, and more amusing. And the booze, slightly dearer, is better.

Mrs Topham will not miss my custom nor that of other locals. She has done wonders – the place has improved immensely, the jumps are less cruel to men and beasts, especially Becher's (where a Captain Becher fell after remounting in the first National) and Valentine's (named after a horse in an early race).

Valentine's was the scene of one of the most mysterious happenings in modern racing history. In 1935 Golden Miller, Miss Dorothy Paget's wonder horse, who stood to part the bookies from over £2 million, simply refused to jump and threw the jockey over its head.

Many still ask why. He was not a lazy horse but he was said to be a rather bolshy one. Miss Paget was said to have been very cross with trainer Basil Briscoe who, therefore, asked her to remove all her horses from his care. On the day after the National, Golden Miller stopped at the first fence and threw Wilson again. It wasn't a grudge against Wilson nor indeed against Briscoe, for with a different jockey and a different trainer he repeated the act in the next two years – at Valentine's.

The National tends to be soft going; Briscoe may have overtrained him on the hard Newmarket ground. Maybe he didn't like the Very Important People in Lord Sefton's box by the jump: they included the then Prince of Wales and could have been noisy. (The presence of the King in 1937 was taken by Liverpool punters as a good reason to back Royal Mail, which won.) Valentine's must have had some association, but he went over it to win well enough in 1934. Did he feel resentful? Did he say: 'To hell with it, I'm not starting off in that routine again.' Perhaps a bookie once did him a kindness. He was put to stud in 1939 and lived to the good old age of 30. How much better good horses are treated than good workingmen at the end of their toil.

Something unusual happens any year half justifying the name 'Grand'. What about the Queen Mother's horse, Devon Loch, jumping over an imaginary obstacle a few yards from the winning post, well ahead of the others, and stopping dead? Easter Hero pausing at the Canal turn (this, by the way, was the very best place to see the whole race until a few years ago and was free to the public) making 21 others fall? Gregalach at 100 to 1 won that year, 1929. Of 36 starters 11 fell in 1951, 11 year-old Nickel Coin winning.

A horse to win two years in succession was well before my time. It was called The Colonel and won in 1869 and 1870. It put up a good show again in 1871, but was beaten by a quiet little horse called The Lamb which had already won in 1868. This horse was the pet of a small boy who died. A Dublin vet. bought it for £25 and leased it to Lord Poulett. On both occasions it was ridden by a 'gentleman rider'.

You know about the chap who was having a chat with a horse who had said good morning to him as he was passing? It was pulling a coal-cart and when the coalman noticed what was going on he said to the chap suspiciously: 'This 'orse bin telling you things? As a matter of fact – did he tell you e'd won the Grand Nashnl? Well, as a mat – He's a blurry liar, e was only second.' A winner did once finish up as a cart horse.

The mother of Abd el Kader, who won in 1850 and 1851, once pulled a stage coach, an occupation more associated with dignity than speed.

The 1901 winner, Grudon, ran in a blinding snow storm with butter spread on his hoofs to prevent slipping.

You can win many a bet with little snippets of horse-lore. I was asking a bloke in a 'Pool pub the other day winners' names for many years back: Father O'Flynn 1892, H R H The Prince of Wales's Ambush II (Anthony up), Troytown 1920, 1930 Shaun

Goilin. He was a proper Leslie Welch till I asked him what won last year. Like when Houdini couldn't get out of a cell in Walton Gaol because it wasn't locked.

A couple of years ago I went to a race meeting in the South West of Ireland, at a very small town called Listowel (so small that when I asked the policeman the way, he said: 'I'm a stranger here myself.') It was a much smaller course than Aintree but much more fun. It was (as I had found grander tracks like Dundalk and Punchestown) a gay social occasion. I lost a few pounds, but that does not matter. I am not really interested in backing. I back to win, of course, and I have none of the real punter's subconscious death wish, the desire to lose. I'm annoyed when I lose but the good time I had, hardly ever looking at a race, made it all worth while. Yet I came away a little upset. For on the race card I saw that Listowel races, only about 150 years old, was the oldest regular race meeting in the Isles. (They mean the British Isles but they would no more use that term than a Frenchman would speak of the English Channel.) What piffle . . .

Extract from Liverpool Town Records for 1577: 'This year on the holy day of the Ascension, there was a running of horses at Liverpool for a silver bell given by Mr Ed Torbock, to be run for every year under the patronage of the Mayor.'

I have seen, but never spoken to Mrs Topham. She is handsome, in a heroic mode. Before she married she was an actress. I don't know if she played in the legitimate theatre but she would be ideally fitted for the role of Lady Bracknell. I have met Colonel Topham who looked a gift to the casting office as a typical English Army officer.

Perhaps she could not have done it without him. But she is the one who kept the race going, moribund when the war ended and almost forgotten, and, despite many threats to put the shutters up (not entirely seriously in every case), has kept the business going and won every fight. (Her brother-in-law, by the way, Arthur Ronald Topham, as 'typical' looking as his elder brother, seen in impeccable morning dress with grey topper, buttonhole, wing collar and grey tie, could at once have got his start in the Ascot scene in *My Fair Lady*.)

A man who works for her told me she is a holy terror. (The people I meet!) But it must be remembered that she has worked hard and doubtless expects others to. She has had a lot to do and I believe she has done it all almost single-handed. Hungry for land or houses and other purposes, Liverpool Corporation very rightly has always had an eye on Aintree. The Corporation has built all round this part of the south-eastern part of the city, including the first Mr Topham's Warbreck, and at the northern end of the city has little further room for expansion. Maybe it could expand and the Grand National could survive somewhere else round Liverpool. It has never been properly used. Could not this great sporting city have a huge sporting arena, capable of housing World Cup games, the Liverpool Show, various activities a home for both big football teams, who now occupy even more suitable land for house-building?

Anyhow Liverpool wanted to buy it, sentiment cast aside, in the usual way. Couldn't the Grand National be on the Cheshire side, at the Southport end, on the former US air-base at Burton-wood, near Manchester Airport? What's magical about Aintree?

Mrs Topham was willing to sell. And did not fight the Corpy. The fight was over how much. From 1966 to mid 1970 the argument went on. Liverpool would be backed by Government money and racing interests take the National over and build on adjoining land. She wanted too much. Liverpool offered £1¼ million.

'Not enough', said Topham's chairman and managing director, Mrs Mirabel Dorothy Topham.

She has squabbled with bookies and about cinema, TV, broadcasting rights. Few who heard them will forget the terrible lash-up caused when she employed her own commentators for the broadcast. At last we realised just how expert the B B C commentators were.

Another thing separating this powerful lady from Liverpool and its citizens was the ending of the traditional Jump Sundays. This was, for many years, an annual ceremony, of a purely secular inconsequential kind, by which, on a Sunday, whole families walked round the whole course 'inspecting' the jumps, all in a world's fair atmosphere with the tipsters, dressed as jockeys, often claiming close personal association with Lord Derby – Only last night up at Now-sley he says to me "Alf"' – it was Frith's Derby Day with a Scouse accent. It was a job, as Scousers are probably the worst section of the untidiest race in Europe; she scrapped it.

In September 1939 – a year when authority went to the heads of quite a few leading military types – the course was occupied by HM Forces. Mirabel had them out within a year, and her interviews with the blimps must have been worth witnessing. A National was actually run in 1940, and Lord Derby congratulated her for 'giving the country a tonic in its hour of need'. With the fall of France the racecourse was again occupied by troops and gear of many nationalities. She and her family lived in a lodge on the grounds throughout the war.

Two months after she had speedily dislodged the occupying forces she staged the first postwar National. It was Lord Rosebery who now offered, for the racing authorities, congratulations. Arthur was clerk of the course, his son handicapper. In 1949 she purchased the land from Lord Sefton. She brought International Motor Racing to Merseyside, and in 1957 the Grand Prix d'Europe. The use of the motor-track by the BBC, who had the TV contract, made more of us satisfied to sit at home to see the race. The Irish Sweepstakes between 1958-1963 gave Tophams Ltd, now, with Arthur dead, controlled by her, £30,000.

For the first race in 1827, Liverpool Corporation provided a purse of 120 guineas for first, 30 guineas for second. They have given nothing since. I am no punter – my father did enough of that – but I don't think I have failed to back a horse in the National since I left school. Nobody in Liverpool, of any degree, fails to. I have even won. Looking down the winners since Poethlyn brings me memories of easy money as easily dissipated, up to 1970 when I picked the first three out of only five that finished.

Twice has only one horse finished – Glenside in 1911, owned by Liverpool shipowner Bibby, was the last of a field of 32 and only just made it to the winning post. When Tipperary Tim won on its own in 1928 I had backed it. It's often a horse with an Irish name, almost always an Irish horse. The day the very old horse Sergeant Murphy won, Tom Webster had a sketch on the *Daily Mail* sports page showing a horse with a sergeant's stripes on its fetlock. The year before, his cartoon had hinted at the eventual winner. He said he couldn't do it again, but he'd show a certain loser. Sergeant, ridden by 11 stone 3 Captain Bennett not only won, it won in record time – and died shortly after. I had Battleship (1938) and Major Furlong's Reynoldstown (1935). I couldn't believe it would win again the next year but it did.

I was present when Joe Griffin, the tinned meat man from Dublin, gave his Early Mist to a Dublin boat steward and a fiver to put on it. I'd a couple of bob. Next year when Griffin won with Royal Tan and I witnessed a similar scene I didn't bet. Griffin gave a thousand pound party that night at the Delly. Shortly after he was in gaol but, on one occasion, the gaol being in Ireland, he was let out to attend a race meeting.

I did not back Russian Hero in 1949. Even my Communist mates didn't, though the *Daily Worker* was the only one to tip it; it came in at a fantastic price. It was very foggy that year and many swear it only went round the course once, hiding under some trees, until the field was coming round second time. This sounds Russian, if not heroic. When real Russian horses ran, at Mrs Topham's invitation, they were no good. Airborne won at a good price. I was on it. Many round Liverpool's waterfront were. A Dublin newspaper appeared round there with Airborne written in its stop press. This issue had been flown into Speke Airport and marked 'airborne', in the office to distinguish it and its fellows from the other seaborne issues. We thought it was a last-minute tip.

Make yer name Walker!

Liverpool is a tough place. It was tougher when I was a lad, 50 years ago. Our street in Everton, Liverpool, near the docks, was very tough, though it had two churches, Anglican and Roman Catholic. (It had a synagogue, too, but that has nothing to do with my story.) And two schools, Anglican and Roman Catholic.

The street became tougher the farther down you went. We lived at the bottom. At the top, where the two churches were, bobbies walked along in twos; at our end they ran down in fours. Husky dockers and Cunard bo'suns were chary about going round these parts after dark. One tiny woman, however, could walk around it unharmed at any time – and very briskly.

Her name was Crosbie. She was a spinster and I never knew of anyone calling her anything but Miss Crosbie. I was one of the few who knew her first name was Jessie. She was headmistress of St Augustine's School opposite to my home.

I first saw her in 1918, when I was off school with the distressing ailment called mumps. I was alone in the house, as my mother was helping my father in his butcher's shop on the corner a few yards away. It was pleasant, even with the mumps, to be in a warm bed, reading comics, books, chewing stickalice, drinking lemonade, while other kids toiled in dreary cold classrooms. But not on this day, November 11, when, at the eleventh hour, the school bells and church bells, factory hooters and ships' sirens rent the air, proclaiming that war had ended. I rushed to the window.

Out of the school opposite, in an orderly procession, and at a quick pace, marched some hundreds of children behind a shabbily

dressed woman of formidable aspect. She walked quicker tha
any of her followers and was smaller than many. This was Mis
Crosbie. I thought her old, of course, but I know now she wa
about 28. In the mid-Sixties she told me she was 75.

I wrapped a thick scarf of my father's round the mumps an
put my brother's overcoat over my nightshirt; he was at the Fron
and twice my size. Tripping every yard I ran across the cobble
street and tagged on to the procession.

Its good order was the more remarkable, as all over the rest c
the street grinning and shouting kids and adults were millin
about aimlessly and, because of the Liverpudlians' tendency t
break windows when feeling exuberant, pub owners and shop
keepers were closing to join the shifting mob more or less heade
towards the city centre.

The procession was remarkable too, because Miss Crosbie wa
carrying a large Union Jack and nobody lived in our part of th
long street but Irish Catholics. St Augustine's was the Protestan
school.

My mother, who had been helping my father put up his shutters
ran across and dragged me, tripping at every step, into our hous
where she cuffed me and cursed me.

'Bad luck to ye,' she said as I yelled, 'for goin' among 'em!'

The next time I saw Miss Crosbie she was drinking tea with m
mother, under a picture of the Pope, behind the lace curtains i
our parlour, by the bamboo table holding the huge spreadin
aspidistra plant.

She was a hardshell Protestant, I came to find out, and she wa
quoting the Old Testament to my mother. She might just as wel
have been reciting Einstein's Theory of Relativity – about whicl
Miss Crosbie probably knew nothing either. She followed a des
cription of the Lord feeding the Jews manna with the New Testa
ment story of the feeding of the five hundred.

It was the hungry Twenties, when thousands were unemployed
in Liverpool. Miss Crosbie, ahead of her times in so many things
found it was no good trying to teach children with no food in thei
bellies. Nowadays, and for many years, every school child in
Great Britain, rich or poor, can have a cooked meal. It was no
so then. Certainly not out of public funds.

But Miss Crosbie, who had nothing but her own salary – and
teachers in England have never been well-paid – was going to se
her children had meals. And she was going to see that local shop
keepers, Catholic or Protestant for the nonce, supplied the food

And she knew their wives were the ones who could tell the shop-keepers to do this. And as soon as Miss Crosbie had bustled across to ring the school bell, my mother, who thought the main subject taught in that school was how to blow up the Vatican, was away, almost as briskly, to Dad's shop to tell him to do it.

Often in the coming years Miss Crosbie joined my mother in a cup of tea but remained convinced, no doubt to the end, that my mother paid the priest to forgive her sins and that my kindly dad, as a Knight of St Columba, had taken an oath to destroy Protestant babies.

Yet the third time I saw her she was entering the priest's house, near our school, at the top of the street. As the rector was not only a priest but a Jesuit, it must have taken considerable courage; no doubt she had contemplated the extreme likelihood of being incarcerated in a nunnery, probably walled up.

The outcome of this strange encounter between the cultivated, elegant clergyman and the bustling, ill-clad woman with the rasping nasal accent initiated one of the strangest examples of practical church unity, a voluntary movement, led by two strong characters, unique in the history of Liverpool slums.

Even well-fed children couldn't learn – and both Father Dukes of Saint Francis Xavier's and Miss Crosbie were devoted to learning, though she had little – if they were tired. And since we kids roamed the streets till all hours we did not get enough sleep. The streets were not good places for roaming kids after dark, in any case.

Teachers were obeyed by children in those days and, for Catholics, the priest certainly was. Adults were not consulted. Most of them did not care what the kids did or didn't.

Every evening Catholic schoolchildren, by order, attended Benediction at their church. Every evening from five o'clock Miss Crosbie conducted a 'play centre' at her school which every pupil was to attend. At eight o'clock she led all her children out into our street and Father Dukes led the others out of the church and, helped by teachers from both schools, each child was led home, the odd truant, if spotted, being pressed into the ranks en route.

Then vigilantes from among the respectable parents patrolled the streets to see no kids emerged again, until, at least, the pubs were closed. They acted voluntarily too. She and the priest maintained this 'curfew' till he moved to higher office and Miss Crosbie, when the city took over her school and it became non-denominational, moved to another Anglican headmistress-ship.

The play centre at her school was, like the school-meals service, the first in the country, but it was officially adopted and became nationwide in the Thirties, and nowadays special clubs exist for the same purpose. Quite simply, for a few hours in the evening, the classrooms used by day for study were used for games and hobbies; you could read, play ludo or dominoes or indoor football or skip, you could make toys, paint, do what you wished, under discreet supervision.

I could record many other innovations the little woman made, many of which became official. I'll cite one more. She somehow persuaded the local council and philanthropists, once more waiving religious discriminations for the nonce, to install baths in her school. None of us had bathrooms in our homes and many of us didn't feel deprived.

Persuading the children to have baths in the school was no easy thing. But then she invited the mothers to bring the younger children and bath them. Then, while she and others taught the youngsters simple subjects, she let the mothers have baths themselves and even do their washing. She and others would talk over various things as they scrubbed the clothes.

So St Augustine's had the first nursery school in the country and the first parent-teacher organisation.

As a boy, my last encounter with her was when I was playing cricket outside my home using a lamp-post as a wicket. I hit the ball over the school wall and shinned over the wall after it. As I dropped into the school-yard I heard girlish screams and I saw a row of girls who had, under Miss Crosbie's guidance, been performing physical exercises, with their thick blue bloomers pulled over their skirts. But it was not my masculinity which made her lead me by the ear and push me through the door. 'No Catholics here', she said. 'Make yer name Walker!' This Liverpool expression means 'beat it'.

I know nothing of Miss Crosbie before she came to St Augustine's (she was clearly of working-class origin) and until a few years ago, I knew nothing of her after she left the school. But it is on record that no pupil at the school, before she came, had ever won a public scholarship towards higher education; during her years they held the record for such scholarships in the city; after she went there was a decided slump.

She never married, though she had a delicate rosy complexion, a pleasant smile, rarely seen, bright blue eyes and a trim figure. The school janitor once told me she was courted by a good-looking doctor but 'he wanted her to pack up the teaching so she told him to make his name . . .'. I finished the sentence for him.

When I spoke to her, over, of course, a cup of tea, in her little room in a decaying Liverpool suburb, I delicately touched on the subject.

'I suppose,' she said, 'I'd have liked to have been a mother like your mum. But, Councillor, didn't I have hundreds of children? I'm honorary grandmother to a few dozen. My old pupils come to see me, y'know, some of them real grandmothers now.'

On the mantelpiece were dozens of letters from old pupils and photographs of them and their children. Over it was a picture of her leaving Buckingham Palace after getting the Order of the British Empire.

I had met her for the first time since my boyhood that evening. As a member of the local council I was a 'governor' of a school controlled by this local government authority. One of my duties was to attend, with other governors, talks on modern teaching methods and the like, by professors and the like. And pretty boring they could be.

But this evening the lecturer was Miss Jessie Crosbie. (I knew her Christian name at last.) She had no letters after her name suggesting pedagogic distinction, only O B E, indicating a royal honour but not a very high one. She spoke forthrightly, moving at the old pace backwards and forwards on the dais, in the same dear old accent, and I have never heard a more intelligent and practical discourse on education, though she lacked all oratorical flourish.

She was doing a deal of this lecturing now, I learnt, and writing for educational periodicals. She was still ahead of her times. Indeed the Director of Education for the city had quietly told her to tone down her rather revolutionary ideas a bit. She took no notice of him. She probably told him to make his name Walker.

She died the year after, following an accident in the street. Her eyesight was failing and, moving briskly as ever, she walked in front of a fast-moving automobile.

Slum clearance in Liverpool, started by German bombers in the early Forties, and carried on by the city council in the late Forties, had led to many people being rehoused in sky-scraping blocks of flats. These tend to be called after distinguished politicians.

Not a brick was left standing in the street I was brought up in. Where my father's shop was is a towering monstrosity called after Lord Salisbury, one-time Prime Minister, who was landlord of the street originally. (It was his policy to mingle Catholics and Protestants – and even Jews – together, which is not usual in other parts of the seaport.) Next to the old school in Salisbury Street a tower was erected on one of the cleared sights. It was doomed to bear the usual name of a nonentity.

But a body of ageing citizens, distinguished in the professions and arts, thought otherwise – and acted. They were ex-pupils. The tower was called Crosbie Heights. 'I taught them the four "Rs",' I heard her say, 'the fourth was "Respect".' The odd thing is that now she couldn't get a job as a teacher. She never had a certificate.

*　　　*　　　*

Miss -----, teacher in a Bootle school, can see nothing strange in teaching a class in the nude.

– Liverpool Echo, 1956.

Children trading in the street
'I wonder what it feels like to be poor'

Regulations made by Mayor, Aldermen and others under etc.

December 3, 1902.

1. No licence to be granted to any child under 11 years of age.
2. All children over that age, being boys and girls under 16, shall be entitled to licences, provided the Corporation are satisfied:
    (*a*) that they intend to trade in the streets of the city;
    (*b*) that they are not unfit to trade through being sickly, blind, deaf, dumb, deformed, or mentally deficient;
    (*c*) that they have the consent to their being licensed of the persons purporting to have their custody, charge, or care of them, if such persons are fit persons and have fit homes.
    If the person having the custody, charge or care of any child is not a fit person, the consent of such person shall not be necessary to the child's being licensed.
    In the case of a child having no home or no proper home, the Corporation shall be empowered to require, as a condition

210

of a licence to trade being granted, that he or she shall be required to live in lodgings, provided always that no child shall be required to live in lodgings which are not under the control of a person of the same religious belief as the child. In case of a dispute as to the religious belief of the child, the same shall be determined by the Stipendiary Magistrate, whose decision shall be final.

3. A licence is issued annually.

4. Every licence-holder shall have a badge. These badges shall be of two sorts, distinguishing children exempt and not exempt from school attendance.

5. No charge shall be made either for the licence or the badge. A deposit of 6d shall be left on the issue of the badge, etc.

Food and Betterment Association

Chief objects: To supply halfpenny and free meals to school children and others in the poor districts of Liverpool, Bootle and Birkenhead.

Second object: To supply the young and adult sick poor of Liverpool and Bootle with specially prepared invalid food – in each case irrespective of creed.

– Liverpool School Board Official Manual for 1903.

Liverpool Police aided Association

Objects:

1. With the aid of the Police, to clothe the ragged and suffering children, who are compelled, through the poverty of their parents, to run about our streets half naked or in rags, many of whom are thus prevented from attending school or obtaining employment.

2. Where such poverty is the result of crime or profligacy on the part of the parents, to bring them under the notice of the Society for the Prevention of Cruelty to Children.

Children's Aid Society

Objects and Methods:

The Society is unsectarian; its main object is to mitigate some of the hardships unavoidably entailed upon poor people in the due administration of the Compulsory Education Acts. The chief difficulty with which poor parents have to contend are:

1. Clothing and boots for the children.
2. Suitable guardianship for their infant children while the mother is absent at work.

In the first case, the Society supplies, in properly recommended cases, clothing and boots to be paid for by instalments proportioned to the parents' needs and collected weekly by the Society's visitors.

In the second case the children under school age are received at Day Nurseries from 7 a.m. to 7 p.m. and fed, warmed, and tended at a charge of 2d per day for each child. The committee also supplies clothing to the four day Industrial Schools of the Liverpool School Board, according to funds at their disposal. No payment is required from the parents in these cases.

Provisions with reference to the attendance of children at school

Under the operation of the Elementary Education Act, 1876.

1. All children over the age of 5 years of age and under 12, are to attend school full time . . .
2. Partial exemption for fully employed can be approved by H M Inspector and a school headmaster.
3. Children over 12 but under 14, not employed in any Industry regulated by the Factory Acts, are entitled to full time exemption.

The Bellbottom song

Once I was a serving-girl down in Scotty Road,
And I used to love the mistress and the master too.
One day there came a sailor, a sailor home from sea,

And he was the cause of all my miseree.
He asked me for a candle to light him up to bed,
He asked me for a pillow for to rest his weary head.
Me being very young and innocent of harm
Jumped into bed just to keep the sailor warm.
And next morning when he woke
He handed me a five pound note (!)
Take this, my dear, for the damage I have done,
It may be a daughter, it may be a son.
If it be a daughter, bounce her on your knee.
If it be a son, send the bastard off to sea,
In bellbottom trousers and a suit of navy blue,
And make him climb the rigging as his old fellow climbed up you.

– Glyn Hughes, who remembers it, says it is customary to add:

Never trust a sailor
An inch above your knee
I did and he left me
With a banjo on my knee.

It is always called *The Bellbottom Song* but there are other versions (e.g. in Hugill) but 'Scotty Road' is constant. An old sailor, Jimmy Johnson, retired to the Lake District, told me that as a lad he was put ashore on a small Pacific Island to buy some stores. As he approached he could hear a whiskeyish voice bawling the tune out, and 'I knew I was going to meet a townie'.

Don't send my boy to sea
A Liverpool lady dies

6th June 1673 – As you wel knowe I have taken partie withy as a loyall wife ought to doe. Therefore these are the desyres of a poor dying wife; that you would be pleased never to forsake these poore children I have left behind mee; you have no reason but to marry; but for Jeasus sake be not harsh with them. But bee-stow your doughter as soon as you can be-cause you know the bad sukeses the doughters have had formerly of this fammilee for if you keepe her at home in your fammilee there can be mouch danger . . . and my desire is that you will give her my child ben linnings the quillet boxe; and a tronke of your best linnings . . . I have Church stoffe

213

I wold have you give it to the Church that my soule may be praud fir, and if you will give it my doughter will tell you whoe it must be given too for Leagsiz or any such other thinge I beg none but too that is Boden and Jonathan for they have taken a true part with me and you Deare. One thing more I beg of you that you will not think of leting Cleave go beyond sea but that he may be a good honest conteri gentleman . . . Theze are all the desyres of a poor dying wife Dorothy Moore.

– Moore Rentals 1683.

Liverpool Lorelei

It was on my way to Liverpool that I had the first of my queer fits of unconsciousness, when I would fall like a log . . . These periodic visits to Liverpool remain among the happiest of my life . . . I lived in an atmosphere of complete freedom as far as sex was concerned . . . Perhaps they were proletarians, these wonderful Liverpool girls. Perhaps they were what all our women-folk will become in a few hundred years . . . One girl, the daughter of a seafaring family, had limbs so slippery-smooth as to be hardly human.

– J. C. Powys, Autobiography.

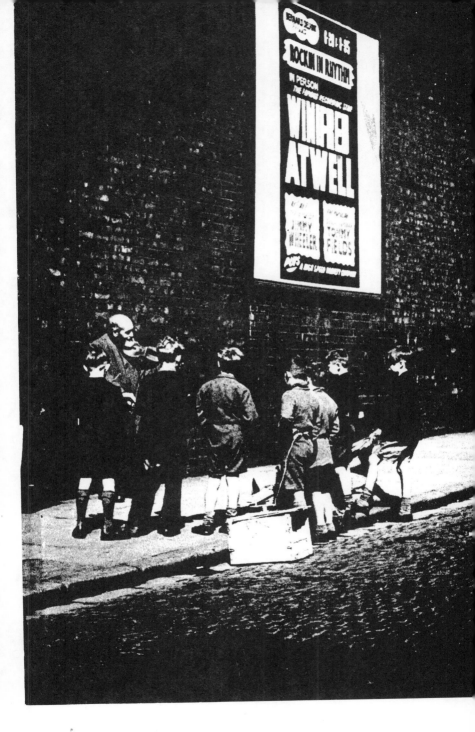

PART SEVEN **The
Talking
Streets**

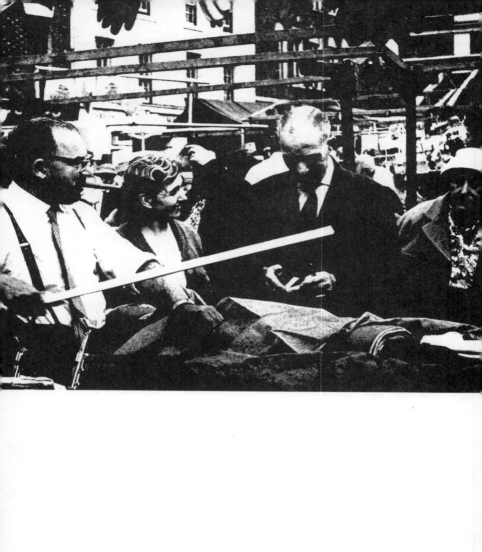

PART SEVEN

The
Talking
Streets*

People talking

The Talking Streets, first broadcast on October 27, 1958, was the genesis of the BBC TV documentary *Morning in the Streets*, which added to Denis Mitchell's growing status and gained some repute for the other two members of the original team and the TV cameraman Roy Harris. (All four are Merseysiders, Stan and Roy's associations being close.)

The team was given a luncheon in 1959 – a luncheon, nothing more – in Manchester at the BBC place in Peyer House for winning, with *Morning in the Streets*, the international Italia Prize, estimated to be worth £500. (I received the news while I was in Paris, a good place to celebrate.)

It was, like the Battle of Waterloo, a damned near thing. Expediency played a large part along with an exigent exchequer which made Denis just do his best with the materials available – including me – in the time allotted. Practically all of the visual work on the film was done single-handed with a small hand-camera.

Most of the human sounds used in *Morning* and such effects as the dripping tap, almost a sign manual of Mitchell's work, were already in *The Talking Streets*. And the making of that, by two men and a tape recorder, one of them knowing nothing whatever

---

The Talking Streets was a documentary broadcast impression of life and opinions in the back streets of a Northern city in the morning. Research was by Frank Shaw, the singer was Stan Kelly. The programme was arranged and produced by Denis Mitchell.

about the business, the other working from no set plan, was eve
more hit and miss, opportunist, unplanned, impromptu.

When he was with the BBC Northern Film Unit and was chose
to direct a film on Strangeways Gaol, Denis Mitchell went t
prison. When he came to Liverpool to make a film about life in
Liverpool slum street he went into lodgings in a Liverpool slur
street. It was a very nice house kept by a very nice woman whos
son was the unpaid editor of a small Labour paper I had writte
for (unpaid). Her name, Murphy, commended her. She was
widow left with three children, the unpaid editor became a docto
and a magistrate, she had a girl (a teacher) and a son (ditto). Bu
their house was in a slum, the Lambeth Road area, near the Nort
Docks, in the area you run into as you pass from Scotland Roa
into the roads leading to North Lancashire.

There I would meet him every morning for a fortnight and i
would be getting dark when we got back. We had already met
few times in Manchester and Liverpool, made rough plans
mostly ignored later, met a few people, most of them of no use t
the project, walked round the town a bit. I could only give him th
odd hour from my own work. Now I was on annual leave.

On the corner of Lambeth Road, waiting for a taxi (we use
taxis throughout – getting them and directing them and assessing
time for return was part of my job – a car and a driver would hav
made a great difference but such was not budgeted for) Deni
spoke, and what he said established me as his ally from the outset
First, showing the economic realist inside the good artist, whicl
is how I like my artists, he said: 'How much do you think yo
should get?' Hitherto, I'd been getting odd quids and fivers fo
preliminary research (a word I was new to then and still fin
equivocal, though I could not agree with the jealous friend wh
defined it as 'going on the piss with Denis Mitchell').

I named a figure – after all I was giving up my leave (at the las
moment I deleted the adjective well-earned before leave). 'Non
sense,' said Denis. 'OK,' I said resignedly, 'what do you think?
He named a figure five times as much, with expenses.

Have you had much to do with producers? On my desk at th
moment is a file labelled 'Editors, Producers, Publishers and othe
Bastards.' Denis Mitchell – and the publisher of this book – ar
excluded.

Second question: What do you think of this job?

Frank Shaw: I'm new to it. I'll do my best. I hope you'll ge
something good.

DM: Frank, this is going to be a masterpiece or nothing.
I tell you, I'd work for nothing for Denis. Mind you there were
times in 1969, making another documentary with him in Liverpool
and living with him and his charming wife Linda at their Chelsea
flat during the later cutting period, when he nearly went in that
file . . .

He lugged the heavy recorder himself. I filled the big pockets of
my overcoat with tapes. I took him to people – in pubs, shops,
pensioners' clubs, youth clubs, council offices, round the docks,
up back streets, to churches, police stations, drinking clubs, parks,
garden suburbs, wash houses, on the docks, bobbies, priests,
publicans, do-gooders, criminals, boxers, dockers, comic turns,
cinema managers, shopkeepers, celebrities, bookie's runners, sailors,
Bessie Braddock's waiting room.

I shall not weary you with the technique of research which I
was learning, with little guidance and much tut-tutting, by trial
and error. One contact led to another, but you can guess what it
involved in door knocking and hanging about, telephoning and
writing, facing insults and ignorance and sudden moments of
absolute success.

Writing must, for long, be king but, for some purposes, the mike
serves better. I am sure that many great writers of the past would
have been as great on TV. For Defoe the mike would have been
the thing. How much better Mayhew would have been with a
tape recorder! Yet what a wasteful, harsh medium it is! All art is
selection, but this is murder. We worked a ten hour day, drinking
while we worked, snatching meals anyhow – in taxis until the
drivers objected to the smell of chips.

That meant half-a-dozen or so tapes a day, each taking an hour.
He did cutting at night time. Mrs Murphy wondered when he slept.
If, of each hour, one minute remained, it was surprising. The hour
or so left when Denis went back to Manchester was cut to half an
hour. With film, in *Morning*, and new sound (children at a Catholic
school, Vera and the budgie story) about ten minutes was used.
There are sixty full seconds to a minute with Denis Mitchell.

Here are some of the things said to Denis by my contacts and
recorded during that fortnight.

*   *   *

And me dad used to go away to sea, like, and he was never very
kind to her, he used to give her beatings for nothing, and she was

221

a good worker, and when he come home from sea all the mone
would go over the counter. And then of course my mother die
on Christmas Eve, and she left me 14, the little baby 12 months ol
and another one 4. Me dad stayed with us 8 weeks, and then h
got a ship and went away and left us.

He left me £2 2s 6d a fortnight to live on, like to keep the chil
ren on, and I was hopeless, I didn't know how much anythin
was. And we never heard no more about him you know. And
was 32 years after when he sent to the parish priest in St Anthony
to ask the whereabouts of us.

So, anyhow, Mrs Teeny and I went over to Manchester like t
see him, and when he opened the door I said, 'Hello', and so h
said (he'd gone white, you know), so he said 'Who are you?'
said 'I'm Bessie.' He said, 'Who did you say you were?' I sai
'Bessie'. So he said 'Oh you were *that* big when I went away.' S
of course he died after, then I had more trouble on my plat
My husband never ever got much work, and I've had to work a
my life, but thank God, God's been very good to me, and H
Holy Mother.

*   *   *

On a Christmas morning there was a van used to come roun
we used to call it Father Christmas. I don't know whether it wa
the Methodists or the Wesleyans. I can't tell you which; it belonge
to Central Hall. I think they were Quakers or something and the
used to come round on Christmas morning with a van, and they'
give each little child a little underwear and a doll and that's a
the children ever got. There was no Santa Claus and no stocking

*   *   *

Why should a man work when he has the health and strength t
lie in bed?

*   *   *

We went to Shrewsbury yesterday with the Bootle Evenin
Townswomen's Guild, and oh the countryside was magnificent
There was every shade of green, I didn't know there were so man
shades of green. And the little lambs . . .

*   *   *

I've got a nice bed, a feather bed, with sheets and blankets a
clean. Well, what more does a man want?

If God was to take me I'm quite happy, I've done no harm to anyone, the only harm I do is I get a couple of Guinness of a night. I'm all right. My eyesight's gone funny, you know, oh ay . . . I hope I'm not found dead, here . . . Sit here for hours talking to myself . . . All I'm praying for is my soul. I've done no harm to anyone . . .

*   *   *

And the flies! There's a fruit-shop downstairs and the smell from that fruit shop is wicked. And there's bugs and there's fleas and there's rats in the lavatory downstairs. You can hear them running down the stairs of a night – you'd think they had clogs on. It's true! I've got cats here, I have two cats, a big one and a kitten, and the big one ran out with fright and left me with the little one. The big one won't stay, it goes out. And that's no good. Even the cats is afraid to stay in the bloody house, and yet we've got to stay here.

*   *   *

As sure as day, this dream will come back – I'm always going somewhere, enquiring for some place, for some street. And I go down the street, down that one, down the other, and I can never get out, I'm always in a maze. And when I wake up, I've got palpitations of the heart, I feel it, bang – bang – bang.

*   *   *

Ooh – you've no idea how we lived. Fancy – five of us in one bed. And me mother used to be trying to cover us, you know. And the night-man would come and knock on the door. Well, she would have to put some of us under the table . . . 'Don't move now, there's a man coming, I'll get summonsed', and if that man found three of us in that bed my mother was brought to Court and fined five shillings. And you would have to go out to the back-yard in the shivering cold and sit on the lavatory until he went. The good old days! There were no good old days.

*   *   *

She said to me one day, she said, 'I think the bird's egg-bound.' So I said, 'Well, have you got a book on budgies?' So she set out and bought a budgie-book, you see. So, that was last Friday. So, last Saturday she rang me up to say there was no eggs, Sunday no eggs, so I said: 'Why don't you take it to the university?' So she said: 'Oh well, in the budgie-books,' she said, 'it says you have to keep it in the one heat like and she said and if I took it out in the cold it might get pneumonia.'

Well, I felt like saying 'To hell with the budgie-book,' you know. I mean, she could have wrapped it up. So anyway, she got a vet in. So he came and he opened the cage to get the bird out, and Madge, this pal of mine, her dog had come in and the bird fluttered out of his hand on to the floor and the dog pounced on it and killed it, you see. So this doctor picked it up, this vet picked it up and he said to her 'Oh', he said, 'this bird isn't egg-bound, it's got a tumour', and he just threw it on the fire.

'Oh', she said – she nearly went mad – she said.

'Oh, my kids'll go mad, doing that!' 'Oh, cremation', he said, 'is the most hygienic thing,' he said, 'That'll be seven-and-six'. And he charged her seven-and-a-tanner!

Spring comes to Scotty Road

Spring, glorious spring.
For spring flowers I don't give a farden.
Spring, glorious spring.
In my mind I turn over me garden.

You can get peas from chip shops;
I don't want no roses;
I go to my tool-shed as soon as Bent's closes.
As the wife wields the vacuum I gently dozes.
In spring, glorious spring.

Spring, glorious spring.
I slip on a new lightweight jersey.
Spring, glorious spring.
I go for a sail on the Mersey.

By New Brighton bathing pool there's a quiet nook,
Where I can sit reading an improving book,
And can I be blamed if I take a sly look?
In spring, glorious spring.

Spring, glorious spring,
My wife has removed all her curlers.
Spring glorious spring,
I get a new whicker from Sturla's.*

I get out my bowls, to the green make my way,
And stretch on a bench for the rest of the day.
You can get too much exercise I always say.
In spring, glorious spring.

Spring, glorious spring.
The judies are playful and fickle.
Spring, glorious spring.
The slap comes long after the tickle.

In jiggers and doorways and down Penny Lane
The sap in the scouse-tree is rising again,
And our parlour sofa is feeling the strain.
It's spring, glorious spring.

The fellers are caught by the judies' fair snares,
And soon Father Dooley'll be saying the prayers
Over couples that can't wait to get up them stairs.
In spring, glorious spring.

* Shop for cheap suits (whickers), and so on, on easy payments.

Merseyside pubs' nicknames

Fat Annie's	Duck Ouse
Ugly Mug's	Muck Midden
Widow's Retreat	Bull's Tit
Sweat Rag	Dandy Pat's
Flat Iron	Doll Ouse

Street games

In a forgotten part of the south end of Liverpool, derelict with
cleared slums, can be seen three holes about two inches in diameter.
These are the Segs, Lass and Up for three holes, or Segs, Lasses

and Up – the competitive game old gaffers played till a few years ago. I found a group doing so in this district when helping with *Morning in the Streets*. Sports cartoonists in the local papers often featured the adult olley-players. If the game ever became part of the Olympic Games I am sure Liverpool could field a winning team.

You had, from a starting point, and using the knuckle of the thumb, to propel your olley in turn into each of these holes, knocking your opponent's olley out of the way if possible. First in the third hole won his opponent's olley.

We improvised holes from scooped mud and played in the gutters. And you just don't get that kind of gutter in the suburbs. In this South End district, until a few years ago, lived Bill Cogley, formerly headmaster of St Malachy's School in now demolished Beaufort (pronounced Bewfid) Street. During his retirement years he gave time to copying out in an old exercise book in fine pointy writing, notes on the games and songs and sayings of children.

Here are some of Bill's notes, God rest his soul. (In *Morning in the Streets*, Bill was photographed blowing his whistle to get his children into school; he told me later he had never had so many children in school. Half of them were from a nearby council school determined to be in the picture.)

Many observers of children at play have noted their freemasonry. It is true there is a brotherhood among gangs and a shutting out of others; a fondness for dressing up; a desire to rise, *in one's turn* in a hierarchy; a respect for ritual. All these qualities apply to many adults. When a priest puts on special robes and utters 'magic' words, is he satisfying some deep human need born in the infancy of the world? Is satisfying such need part of the process of growing up? Is it that the priest has not put off childish things? Is a gang initiation imitating freemasonry or freemasonry reverting to childhood?

Back slang and other forms of secret speech which delight children is another manifestation. Many non-masons know the 'secrets' and have read the ritual. The secrecy of secret lingos is not very difficult to penetrate. We had one which involved reversing the whole word (tinip for pint? there always has to be latitude for a little adaptation; you couldn't say *tnip*). Or putting the initial letter at the end of the word and adding ay or some other short syllable – *aray ooyay oingay otay ethay icturespay* (are you going to the pictures). Speed helped to puzzle an eavesdropper, but after a while it was no more successful as a barrier than the upper class *pas devant les enfants.* (In my social class, this was 'little pigs have big ears'.)

Anthropology is not an exact science any more than philology. There is much guessing, and some practitioners, for my money, are no better than the astrologers and British Israelites. Most of our kids' games have been going on a long long time, and are known all over the world. Accept this mystery as we accept the initial mystery of being alive at all. Play the game. Forget origins. So let us leave the study and get out into the street for some games.

Have you ever played Utney (pronounced 'ootnee', which has a suggestion of India if you must think of origins)? It was (says Liverpool teacher, writer, broadcaster and speech expert John Farrel) a sort of leap-frog in which the player who was Utney leapt from a line on to the back of a bent over player, the frog, in one go. The rest of the players did the same. On the second round Utney marked with his foot the spot where he landed after his leap and the frog moved to that place. Utney then prescribed how the rest should leap – 'one and over', 'two strides and over', etc. This continued until either a player failed and the game began again with the failure as frog, or a player, viewing the distance, weighing the conditions, challenged Utney to do it. If Utney did it, the challenger dropped out humiliated. If Utney failed then he became the frog and a new Utney was chosen.

This game, which you might think a little too energetic for a hot climate – but what about polo? – should be a good lesson for life.

Altered circumstances in urban life is one reason for the disappearance of many of the old games. For some, you can't get horse muck as easily as you once could. We could often only get a tin after a grubby search in a muck heap. A lady who played the game, as Kick the Can, in India in Victorian days said, in a letter to the *Radio Times*, that they used two pound golden syrup tins. We'd never heard of golden syrup, our syrup was thick black treacle, sold in bulk at a penny a cup, at the corner shop.

We could usually find an empty conny-onny tin. Conny-onny is condensed milk, also gear on dry bread. The tin would be the cheap Calf brand. Nestles, pronounced without the accent, was posh. Sometimes we flattened cans under cart or tram wheels and used them as a sort of quoit in Slide the Can, a totally different game, now forgotten.

Not forgotten, but no longer played, are Blowover and other games with cigarette cards because alas, there are no cigarette cards any more. Nor Buttons, or Cherrywobs, though buttons and cherries still exist. That is something to investigate. It is many years since I've seen a game of Buttons or Cherrywobs. They were games with an element of acquisition in them, a primitive Monopoly. As with Conkers (not a city game anyhow) and games with Marbles, the boy with the most – at the end of the season – was cock of the walk for the moment.

An added reason for acquiring a large number of cherry stones was the belief in a false rumour that a big store in the town was prepared to give good money for them. They were wanted, the false rumourer said, to make dolls' eyes. Similar false rumours recurred. One caused piles of ripped cigarette packages in streets and playgrounds. Inside the gummed flap of each package of a well known brand of cigarettes could be found a printer's mark which resembled, if the imagination was strong enough, the silhouettes of two sailing ships. We were told that anyone finding a third ship would get a large reward from the tobacco company. I never heard of anybody finding one.

For the same reason certain combinations of tram ticket numbers were sought and, in recent years, threepenny bits bearing the design of a sailing ship. They weren't common and were worth something – a fabulous sum of course.

For city boys, the accumulation of marbles was the desired thing. Buttons, and most games with cherry stones, are versions of games played with marbles, played to win. We call them 'ollies' which I suppose is a corruption of 'alley'. You'll recall that a glass olley had a higher value than ordinary marbles, as was the case with the delly in Buttons.

'He's got all his marbles' is general slang for 'He's smart, he has his wits about him.' I recall a Liverpool saying years ago: 'His duck's off and his olley's down the grid.' This means 'He's daft; he's a loser.' A Liverpool firm near my birthplace specialised in the unusual form of mineral water bottle which had an olley in its neck. To get the lemonade out of the bottle, one had to push the olley down the neck, so that it slipped through a hole in a glass shelf on the inside shoulder of the bottle. I don't know what there was about this bizarre sort of bottle. It's not to be seen these days, but old Scousers can get a sharp attack of nostalgia at the mention of the olley in the bottle. By a slow and tricky process, a slot could be made by the shelf large enough to slip in current coins of the realm, making a novel money box. Unlike the average money-box, the coins could not be easily slipped out after insertion, and you could only get the total sum when the bottle, being full, burst. The things people think of!

About 1915, my brother was very friendly with a neighbour's son, named Phil. Phil was, like so many of us, lightfingered and proud of it. Later he did quite well as a petty thief. One has to start in a small way, and Phil stole quite often for the fun of it. Getting employment in a toy factory, he started to nick, without being detected, ollies which he gave to the kid brother of his pal Jack. He told my mother they were throw-outs – they just weren't round enough, so it was all right for him to take them. They looked all right to me, though maybe there was some fault with the one that got stuck in the barrel of Jack's Daisy air-gun. I wildly intended to use it as a lethal weapon against the German spy I was keeping an eye on about that time, but it got me no medals, only a belt over the lugs by Jack.

Yes, we like our ollies in Liverpool. As grown women will play skipping rope outside the factory, with a large rope held across a whole street, so grown men play the ollies game Segs, Lassies and Up, the competition being keen, and successful marbles being cherished by a player as he might have his own billiard cue or set of darts or bowls, and show-off topers their individual tankards at the local. ('Old Bill been in, Flo?' 'No, you'll not see old Bill no more; he got uffy. He's took he's tankard away.')

There are a lot of the old street games which kids today don't play because they don't have streets, and there are more open spaces. When, fifty years ago, a Liverpool slum kid had his first trip to the country – Eastham Woods, on the Cheshire side of the Mersey, a rural, peaceful area now utterly built over – the teacher in charge would say, 'Now, let's have a game of cricket'. The kid would reply: 'How can we, sir; there's no lamp-posts!'

There are lamp-posts of sorts in the dreary suburbs, though they are not always placed so as to be suitable for wickets and are so tall as to cause even greater disputes than we had over the lamp-post wicket in the old neighbourhood. When a boy who had been clearly stumped or run out in street cricket (we rarely had an umpire) refused to leave the crease and his objection could not be over-ruled because of some such factor as his greater pugnacity, or his ownership of the bat, he could be made to accept a sort of trial by ordeal. He was to hold the bat perfectly still in front of the wicket while remaining quite still himself. The bowler aimed at the wicket and if he now hit it, my laddo had to go out with grace or bravado and an angry glance at the bat before throwing it down for the next batsman. As few batsmen went out with a good grace the bat was seldom handed to the next player.

As we rarely had enough on both sides to have one side field while the other waited to bat, all had to field and those who were waiting to bat would join the opposition against a team mate. It was the same lack of real team-spirit which often solved cases of conscience such as to catch or not to catch. Fielding itself demonstrated many ways in which our game differed from that at Aigburth or Old Trafford or even the Village green game sentimentalised by so many. The side which had to bowl was usually decided by a toss, as in the routine game: one side of the bat was spat upon and a neutral threw the bat in the air. Each captain had named a side. (We rarely had a penny to toss; if anyone had he wouldn't be playing cricket.)

The losing team had to bowl. Both sides hoped to bat first. It might, however, be that the owner of the bat (as rare a possession among us as a penny) and inevitably the captain of one side would arbitrarily decide that, led by him, his side would bat first. 'Me for second; me third', occupied him till he took his stance with none of the niceties of middle and leg. We usually bowled underhand, often because we had to admit girls who, for some reason, weren't much good bowling overarm. Everyone had a go at bowling; there were no 'overs'. Underhand bowling also had the effect of reducing the risk of 'sloggers' from the batsmen.

Courting

Mr Simon who, with Mr Littler, appeared for the prosecution, in opening the first case, dwelt upon the perversion in Lime Street within the last few years from a respectable street to a disorderly one, by the opening of these houses . . . The following evidence was then adduced.

Police Constable Hough: Lime Street is my district and I know the defendant's house. It is generally kept open until four or five o'clock in the morning. I have seen prostitutes and their followers outside during the night. Inside I have found prostitutes and men whose language has been obscene and disgusting and has been disorderly . . . The neighbourhood about this house is almost entirely inhabited by low people . . . Eight or nine prostitutes to forty or fifty men. Two men fought and were taken to the Bridewell . . . .

Inspector Smith: I have seen at the defendant's house convicted criminals and returned convicts, male and female, and prostitutes . . . I have found them there one, two and three in the morning. Outside, gentlemen have complained that they could not pass along the street for solicitation . . . I have never seen a respectable person in the house except perhaps an elderly gentleman . . .

Police Inspector O'Brien: The men and prostitutes walk about or sit reclining on each other . . .

Mr W. Gray (attorney): I board and lodge at the defendant's hotel and I should say it is well conducted . . . I was aware before going there that it was frequented by women of the street . . . It was very difficult to get chambers in Lime Street . . . I have been told counsel for the prosecution has been in there . . .

Recorder: Mind how you conduct yourself; it is not far from the witness-box to that dock.

Mr W. Gray: This is the only place in Liverpool where you can get a cup of coffee and a cigar in the evening as is done in foreign places. (Laughter).

(Solomon Abrahams was called but did not appear.)

Recorder: This is a case, it was clear, of a nuisance which it was desirable to stop . . .

– *Liverpool Weekly Mercury*, April 16, 1859.

Penny Lane

'A pennorth a chips an' a 'a'porth a peas, an' after you wid the vinegar, please', was the song. The chips would be wrapped in a page from a penny paper. Children were still grateful for 'the Saturday penny', though there were fewer fathers and brothers about to donate it. Hence the shout from mum as a lad dashed off to spend it on *Broncho Billy* or *The Exploits of Elaine* at the Adelphi, Christian Street, where the film matinee cost all that: 'How dare you go to the Delly when yer father's in the Dardanelles?'

At that, some unregenerates 'bunked in'. Boys knew secret entrances to all the children's cinemas, like the Lytton in Everton (The Clutching Hand), the Savoy – or 'Saveloy' – in West Derby Road, the Electric in London Road. But they could become exits through which the old – or youthful (he would hardly be of military age, though conscription had not yet come) attendant, armed with a potstick as big as a baseball bat, would project them if copped. This potstick was also used for boys who stood in the camera's ray of light to make signs on the screen – with the admonition 'Get sat down, youse!'

The chipshop song and the rather vulgar one about the cockshy stand at West Derby Road's World's Fair,

> You know me Anty Nelly?
> She 'ad a wooden belly,
> Ev'ry time you knock 'er down,
> Three shies a penny,

shows it was in Liverpool's penny age that I had arrived. A few years later, through shortages caused by the U-boat campaign and – on the home front – increased wages, it was already beginning to fade until now Penny Lane, the street the Beatles have told the world about, should be at least 10p Lane.

I first spotted the trend when my penny popular became a three ha'penny one. And Uncle Dan, Boer War veteran who could still get a glass of ale for a penny, had to pay twopence for his penny magazine.

The Penny Bazaar, in my first year as a Scouser, was crammed with bargains for young and old. It even survived the war with less varied stocks. I bought my mother a pincushion with a 'silver' base for a penny in one in 1916. You could get autograph albums, a box of crayons, giant exercise books, photograph frames (much in demand then, naturally), notepaper and envelopes in penny packets, a bundle of postcards, also in growing demand, toys galore, a bundle of 'transfers', a comb, a toothbrush, a packet of needles, hairnets, a belt for a lad's trousers, a fishing-net (to catch 'jackies' on a park lake), a yard of elastic (for the 'catty'), 'jokes' like fake teeth and itchy-koo powder, a Jew's harp and, of course, a penny whistle.

A penny stamp would take a letter to France or anywhere. Thrifty boys put one on a sheet of paper supplied by the post office; when twelve had been stuck on you handed it in at the post office to start a savings account. Maybe to draw it out the next week, for a shilling could make you the richest lad in the street. After 'mugging' a mate to the pics, you could buy for the remaining tenpence two comics (hence the old Liverpool rebuke, 'don't be soft, you talk like a ha'penny book'), a 'pennorth of fades', three small oranges, a Monster bottle of minerals, a large lucky bag, three-quarters of every kind of sweetmeat – American chewing nuts, liquorice laces, Everton toffee, nougat (pronounced nugget) stickalice, aniseed balls, a real ball, two 'wet nellas', and. . . . a penny bun. Sets for toy theatres were, of course, 'penny plain'.

A penny would buy – whisper it not – five cigarettes. And mam could buy a penn'orth of bits at the butchers, a carrot, a turnip and an onion for another penny, and two pounds of potatoes to make a nourishing threepenny stew. She could also get a cup full of rich, red jam, a tin of milk, a packet of tea, a packet of sugar – all a penny each. A tin of polish cost a penny, a lad's haircut no more – and the wise barber gave the young client a pencil as 'bunce'.

Trams gave very long rides for a penny – twopence first-class! 'Okey pokey, penny a lump', shouted the icecream man.

'Ead's a penny' was still the call of the pitcher at the game of toss. Penny brag was played in back entries.

The theatres were no longer Penny Gaffs. But as you queued to enter – folk were only just being conditioned to queue in Liverpool – a penny was quite enough to give to the singers and banjoists and acrobats who entertained us. Words and music of popular songs were sold in sheets: *The Tears of an Irish Mother*, one penny – that was fair enough.

A taxi pulled up at the 'early door' (this privilege, a piece of one-upmanship, cost threepence more) and out stepped a subaltern with his befurred judy ('Murry Mint, coinin' it on munitions, two an' t'ree pounds a week!'). A penny would be an adequate tip for the fawning commissionaire. (It was enough for the church plate on Sundays.) The girl, ahead of her times, might have bought her packet of 'poudre' or a 'lip salve' for twopence altogether. Thus empires fall.

As one mounted the stone steps to the gallery of the Hippy (or the Roundy or the Pivvy or the Blood Tub) the protectors on one's heavy boots (a penny a card) made a pleasant din; from the wired-in gas jets on the walls – gas mantles cost a penny – shone light enough to show the stern warning on a notice: 'Ladies Without Bonnets Not Admitted.'

When a lad went to shop he might be lured from comics and chewing nuts to the first of the one-armed bandits, The Clown. If you could get a metal ball into the clown's cap you doubled your money. People are still trying to do that, fifty-odd years after.

As I brood unwontedly on economics and puff a shilling cheroot – they used to be called penny stinkers – I wonder if in the year

2000 my grandson will tell his son about the brave days when you could get a haircut for ten shillings (as we called this little coin then) or a whole package of chips for fifteen. And be heard with the degree of boredom and incredulity with which I listened to Uncle Dan recalling a ha'penny pint in the canteen at Bloemfontein and a ha'porth of plug tobacco to put in his penny pipe?

Street names in Liverpool

The visitor to Liverpool would probably recognise street names one could meet with elsewhere, some of which had more character-istic names in an earlier period. Such are Islington (formerly Folly Lane) and Mount Pleasant (Nightingale Lane). Dogkennel Lane (Byron Street) was another loss. Yet we have some fine old names still, like Lad's Lane, Tithebarn Street, Hackins Hey. Who was the Lad? And who was the Captain of Captain's Lane? Coffeehouse Bridge and Limekiln Lane have also a pleasant old-time sound.

The visitor might ask if it was Chesterton's 'rolling English drunkard' who gave us Askew, Crooked and Zigzag roads though we have an Abstinence too. He would find us a loyal and royal city with thirteen Kings, a Queen, a Princess, nineteen Victorias, eleven Alexandras, five Coronations and six Jubilees.

What does the postman think of his multiplication? Of the three Long Lanes with many turnings, of seven schools – but only one Scholar – seven Vines, and one Vineyard, twenty-four Seftons, eleven Mosses, twenty-five Parks and nine Olives. There are nine-teen Brooks. One sees an older, rustic Liverpool with, perhaps, the solitary scholar in an Orchard looking for an Apple or Orange (three of them, with eight Peels).

Interesting too are the group names. There are Dickens names (Micawber, Nickleby, Winkle), Shakespeare names (Othello, Macbeth, Romeo), and poets (Roscommon, Pope, Ben Jonson). Scott is remembered with Marmion and Ivanhoe, and there are place groups for Scotland (Oban, Argyle), London (Clapham, Harrow), the Wirral area; the Lake District. There are twelve Cambridges, but only eleven Oxfords. And we get rivers recalled by Alt, Ribble, Cam, the months (July, August, September) and Cunard ships (Mauretania, Saxonia).

Further rural reminiscences are The Croft, Summer Seat, The Willows, the Poplars, Greenway. And there is a very religious note. We get 114 saints (including Tudno and Domingo) for whom there

re twenty-three Churches, thirteen Chapels, three Kirks, a Cloister
nd a Chantry. There is even a Paradise. There is a Monk, a Vicar,
Friar, a Nun and two Abbotts (with three Abbeys). In the district
alled 'The Holy Land' are David, Jacob, Isaac and Moses.
The visitor might ask if they are all holy in these places and
ealthy in Hygeia Street. Are they warm in Coal Street? Gloomy
n Hamlet Street? Orators in Canning Place? Amorous in Dido
treet? Are they free in Liberty Street? Stand-offish in Boycott
treet? Strictly scientific in Huxley Street? One may well feel chilly
n Breeze Hill. Anyhow, by hook or by crook, Abacus is first in
he book.
Many good old streets have gone and many fine sights once seen
n the streets so that the city is now little different from Manchester
r Leeds. No Bill Cox with his stuffed cats, for instance!

> We have our Castle Street but castle none;
> Redcross Street but its legend who can learn?
> Old Hall Street we have, the old hall's gone,
> Tithebarn Street but no barn,

s a Liverpool poet noted with regret. Why should we have
orrowed Cheapside, Drury Lane (though it had one of the first
heatres ever outside London), or Hatton Garden? The Goree –
vhere thirsty loafers showed credulous visitors the actual chains
o which slaves were tied – is going soon and the Cassy (Castiron
Shore) went long since and much else. Where's Troy and where's
he Maypole in the Strand?

FRANK SHAW

A Biographical Note

This biography has been adapted largely from Frank Shaw's penultimate book You Know Me Anty Nelly, *published by Wolfe Publishing Ltd in 1970.*

Frank Shaw wrote a good deal and appeared before the public a good deal and, in both capacities, was very versatile. But his work, at least in the last twenty years of his life, was usually about Liverpool in some form or other.

In everything he wrote during that time there was some reference to Liverpool, especially its unique adenoidal dialect, Scouse, which he spoke fluently.

'I've been writing since I was a schoolboy fifty years ago', Frank said. 'Don't know when I didn't write, wrote a play at ten, a hymn to the Trinity before that, had poems in print in my teens. But my first stuff in print was when I was eleven, in St Francis Xavier's College Magazine. I was writing about Scouse then, with, believe it or not, the uncle of Peter Moloney, my rival in the Scouse industry – though I was the first in it. But for twenty years I wrote about history, politics, short stories set elsewhere and never mentioned the dear old 'Pool.'

Father of four, grandfather of six, he retired from H M Customs in 1968. 'I worked full-time for them for forty years while being a part-time writer. Unkind superiors put it the other way about. Now I'm a full-time writer.'

He also performed regularly for Radio Merseyside, mad
records, and did TV work for both sides.

With Denis Mitchell he did his first broadcast with Bessi
Braddock, Arthur Askey, and other Liverpudlians for Liverpoo
Civic Week, 1951; later with Mitchell and cameraman Roy Harri
he shared the Italia Prize for the year's best documentary, th
BBC's *Morning In the Streets*, set mainly round Dingle, Everton
Scotland Road, and featuring schoolchildren at play.

His last three books, written in association with others, *Oxta*
Book of Liver Verse, *Lern Yerself Scouse* ('best title I ever created')
Gospels In Scouse (which was also recorded) carry the Liverpoo
theme this book does. But before them he wrote the standar
Court Procedure For Customs Officers (he was Publicity Office
for the Customs officials' union). From 1967-1969 he held th
annual award for the Civil Service Writer of the Year, the Matthew
Finch Silver Cup. He has written for a variety of periodicals, her
and in the USA, from *New Statesman* to the *Prescot Reporter*
Liverpool University's *Sphinx* to Billy's *Weekly Liar*. He eve
smuggled Scouse into the august pages of *Punch*, appearing fo
two years running, in the annual *Pick of Punch*. He worked for th
Central Office of Information and Canadian Broadcasting.

He also wrote the Unity Theatre play, in Scouse, *The Scab*
ran the *Pot of Scouse* review at the Everyman in 1967, has been a
local councillor, school governor, club performer, patron of War
on Want, Jesuit novice, and, at the very beginning, a little lad in
Tralee.

'A long journey, I hope to go much farther but my heart will
always be round the back streets of the 'Pool.' That is why he made
for the port's posterity, if any, with actor Jack Gordon of Unity,
the recordings of Liverpool customs and speech - now in the
City archives.

Although (he said) 'slung out of the church choir - for . . .
miming' he appeared at Fritz Spiegl's *Scouse-and-Strauss* concerts;
on the sacred podium of the Liverpool Philharmonic he smoked a
cigar and shared a bottle of stout with Stan Kelly (author of
Liverpool Lullaby, etc.) while reading the *Liverpool Echo*. With
fellow-'singer' Glyn Hughes he ran the Scouse Museum, a perfectly serious project with some unique exhibits such as the
Aintree Iron and a 'purr' of docker's boots. (What's special about
docker's boots? - 'They get sweatier!')

In 1947 Frank was a member of the British delegation to the
International Town-planning Congress at Hastings. In 1968, at

Warwick University, for a thesis proving that Shakespeare was a Scouser – and because Stan Kelly was a member of the faculty – Frank received the honorary degree of M.Sc. (Master of Scouse). He gave talks to youth clubs, townswomen's guilds, pensioners, Rotary and Noel, and the lads in the Blue Boar lounge, Huyton. He has been chairman of a youth club, a working men's club, a literary club, a bowls club. 'I have set a *New Statesman* competition, judged a Miss Liverpool contest, read the lessons in a Prodessan cherch, and I am a fully paid-up member of Michael Barsley's Left-handers' Association.' All this and a serious student of linguistics, as witness a long series in the *Lancashire Dialect Magazine* and 'Why We Speak That Way' in the Saturday Book 1967.

On his retirement, Frank finally had the time to start work on *the* book of Liverpool. He finished the manuscript only weeks before his death in August, 1971.